Reader Comments
(about the book this book is based on)

"In a pull-no-punches style, Marcus cuts to the chase in the often confusing and treacherous book publishing and book marketing game. I find his approach refreshing because so many authors I speak to as a book publicist really need someone like Marcus, who has no hidden agenda, to tell it like it is. The book is a must read for all authors whether they are first time authors or on the *New York Times* bestseller list. It's written in a serious but entertaining style with a little humor tossed in. I highly recommend it."
–R. Scott Lorenz, book publicist

"Marcus draws on his extensive experience as a self-publisher to offer chapters that include: title selection, book layout, cover art, working with printers, pricing, marketing and more. The author's writing style is readable and easy to follow, with a touch of humor thrown in. At the same time, he's not afraid to skewer inaccuracies wherever he finds them. This book is a goldmine of information, and well worth the price."
-Lawrence Rotch, author of *Gravely Dead*

"I have purchased five books on self-publishing and I wish I had gotten this one first. It has all the information I've been looking for. The author uses a self-deprecating style that doesn't overwhelm the would-be author-publisher."
-Kristina Creighton, author of *The Practical Palate Cookbook*

"Michael Marcus' book on self-publishing was detailed, complete and easy to read. It is the best I have read on the subject. It was very helpful. I do highly recommend this instructive book to anyone who wants the complete instruction guide to getting your written works out there."
-Charles Eastland, author of *The Fire Poems*

Also by Michael N. Marcus

Books:
- ◆Internet Hell (2011)
- ◆Easy E-books (2011)
- ◆555 Ways to Self-Publish Better Books (2011)
- ◆399 Valuable Self-Publishing Tips for a Penny Apiece (2011)
- ◆Independent Self-Publishing: The Complete Guide (2011)
- ◆Self-Publish Your Book Without Losing Your Shirt (2011)
- ◆A Self-Published Book Doesn't Have to be Ugly (2011)
- ◆Get the Most out of a Self-Publishing Company (2011)
- ◆Avoid the 100 Worst Self-Publishing Misteaks (co-author, 2011)
- ◆Become a <u>Real</u> Self-Publisher (2010)
- ◆Stupid, Sloppy, Sleazy (2010)
- ◆Stories I'd Tell My Children (2010)
- ◆What I Most Wanted to Get Out of School Was Me (2010)
- ◆Phone Systems & Phones for Small Business & Home (2009)
- ◆The AbleComm Guide to Phone Systems (2009)
- ◆Telecom Reference E-book (2009)
- ◆I Only Flunk My Brightest Students (2008)
- ◆What Phone System Should I Buy? (1996)
- ◆CB Bible (co-author, 1976)

Blogs:

◆**Book Making** is where Michael discusses writing, editing and publishing—and other things that interest him or bother him. www.BookMakingBlog.blogspot.com

◆**My Final Quarter-Century Above Ground** deals with dying and death—with appropriate irreverence. www.BloggingAboutDeath.blogspot.com

◆**911 Wackos.** Some folks call 911 for strange reasons. Sometimes they get into trouble after the call. Sometimes the 911 operators get into trouble. www.911Wackos.blogspot.com

◆**For The First Time (or the last time)** talks about changes in society and technology: first toilet paper, last country to get TV, etc. www.4TheFirstTime.blogspot.com

◆**Oh How Stupid** provides an occasional look at some of the stupidest things done by human beings. www.OhHowStupid.blogspot.com

◆**Letters to April Wong** is a collection of ridiculous and scam emails sent to a person who does not exist. www.LettersToAprilWong.blogspot.com

◆**Dial Zero** discusses what's silly, stupid or surprising in telecom. www.DialZero.blogspot.com

There may be more by the time you read this.

Brainy Beginner's Guide to Self-Publishing

Make the right decisions and publish a superior book

Michael N. Marcus

SILVER SANDS BOOKS
www.SilverSandsBooks.com

195 Magnolia Road
Milford CT 06460
books@ablecomm.com
203-878-8383

ISBN-13: 978-0-9830572-2-2
Printed in the USA
Version 2.13 (CS-7)
Library of Congress Control Number: 2010915421

Please use the physical or email addresses on the previous page for corrections, questions and comments.

Portions of this book were previously published online and in *Become a Real Self-Publisher* and in *Get the Most out of a Self-Publishing Company* .

This book is distributed by Ingram Book Group, Baker & Taylor and NACSCORP.

◆Editor: Sheila M. Clark
◆Front cover photo by Barbara Helgason

Notes: ①This book's purpose is to educate, inform, instruct and entertain. ②While this book should be helpful, no book can tell you everything that you might want to know or need to know about the topics it tries to cover. ③Conditions, particularly prices and website addresses, may have changed since the book was written. ④Some errors may not have been detected and corrected. ⑤Neither the author nor the publisher will be held liable or responsible for any actual or perceived loss or damage to any person or entity, caused or alleged to have been caused, directly or indirectly, by anything in this book. If you won't accept these terms, please stop reading.⑥Some material appears in multiple places in the book to aid people who don't read the entire book.

More about the author: www.MichaelMarc.us
Help & info for self-publishers: www.BookFur.com
Early book evaluation: www.RentABookReviewer.com

Create Better Books with the
Silver Sands Publishing Series
www.silversandsbooks.com/booksaboutpublishing.html

INTRODUCTION

Why "Brainy Beginner's?" There are already books about self-publishing for "dummies" and "complete idiots." Dummies and idiots can't publish books, and probably shouldn't write them. This book is for smart writers—but not necessarily geniuses—who want to learn about self-publishing.

Why is a dog on the cover? See page 10.

Why does the dog wear glasses? Eyeglasses are a common visual cliché to indicate high intelligence. Albert Einstein, Sigmund Freud, Steve Urkel and Groucho Marx wore glasses. So does the author.

Make the right choices. I'll help you decide whether to set up *your own* publishing company or use the services of a self-publishing company. If you decide to use one of those companies, I'll help you choose the right one, and choose which services to buy from the company, which to get elsewhere, and what to do yourself.

Publish an outstanding book. I'll help you decide what to write about, what to call your book, and even how much to write. I have tips and advice based on my 40-plus years writing and editing, and personal experience self-publishing more than a dozen books. I'll help you make your book good enough to compete with the hundreds of thousands of other new books published each year.

Writers are often unable or unwilling to have their books published by "traditional" publishing companies—the big guys like Random House. Many writers manage to get published anyway, and maybe even receive some praise, and maybe even make some money.

Some writers—like me—set up their own small publishing companies. Many other writers use the services of self-publishing companies. Other companies including Apple, Amazon, Barnes & Noble and Alibris are now glad to provide publishing and distribution services for self-publishing authors.

These companies allow anyone who can type to become a "published author" quickly, and to compete for the attention of the reading public. There is no longer a need to go through the years-long process of finding an agent and publisher.

The downside is that self-publishing companies publish a lot of badly written books and sometimes do a bad job of publishing and promoting them.

I've had books published by big-name traditional publishers and small specialty publishers, going back to 1976. They greatly disappointed me.

I didn't like the books and I didn't like my earnings.

In 2008, I decided to form my own publishing company to publish one book. You are now reading the fifteenth book I published in a little over two years, and more are on the way. This book will share what I learned, and my enthusiasm.

There is more than one way to skin a cat, cook an egg, have sex and publish a book. I have not tried all of them. This book tells you what I've learned (about books—not about cats, eggs or sex). I know what works for me, and the same process has worked for others. If you follow my advice, it will probably work for you.

STOP PLEASE, before you decide to write a book, find out if you're good enough.

Unfortunately, because it has become so easy to write a book and have it published, the quantity of bad books seems to be increasing.

I can't restrict who buys this book and uses the information and advice it contains. But I do have a little test that may help a bit to reduce the number of bad books.

Before you expend any money, time or effort in self-publishing, I strongly urge you to **take the crap test.**

There are three versions of the test. Choose one or more.

① Submit an article of at least 1,000 words to a newspaper or magazine. Convince an editor that it is not crap, get paid at least $200 for it and actually see it in print, or...

② Join a writers' group, actively participate, do the assigned homework and get the honest opinion of the group leader and most of the participants that what you write is not crap, or...

③ Take a college course in journalism or creative writing, do the assigned homework and get the honest opinion of the instructor or professor that your work is of professional caliber and is not crap.

If you fail the crap test, you can still go ahead and publish.

Your ego may be bruised by the criticism you'll receive, and the money you'll spend on publishing and promotion may as well go down the crapper. To test your publishing potential with minimal investment, first try blogging or an e-book.

Good luck.

MNM

CONTENTS

You can read whatever is important to you in whatever sequence you choose, and skip what you don't care about. Some chapters are mainly for customers of self-publishing companies. Some are for authors who form their own publishing companies. Most chapters are for all authors.

♦ Some chapter names below were edited to save space.
NOTE: An arrow (➜) in the text indicates that something is important. You can surmise what ➜➜ and ➜➜➜ mean.

THANKS

◆To **Rita Marcus,** my mother. Mom's an avid reader who encouraged me to be one. If you read more, you'll probably write better.

◆To **Bertram "Bud" Marcus,** my late father. Pop was one of the world's best storytellers and is a major influence on my writing.

◆To **Marilyn Marcus,** my wife, for not complaining when I'm at the computer instead of in bed at 3 a.m. Marilyn says she'd rather share me with a computer than with another woman.

◆To **Sheila M. Clark,** my eagle-eyed editor and classmate in Mrs. McGarthy's room in 1956/57. If you find any errors, I made them *after* Sheila did her work, so blame me. Or blame Mrs. McGarthy.

◆To **everyone** who buys my books.

About the dogs: **Barbara Barth** is the extremely talented author of *The Unfaithful Widow* and *Covered in Fur: Life with Dogs;* and an online buddy. We're both dog lovers. (I live with one. She lives with five.) Barbara has been trying to convince me to put a dog picture on the cover of one of my books. OK, Barbara, you win! The pooch on the cover is a golden retriever, just like my four-legged son, Hunter, shown here.

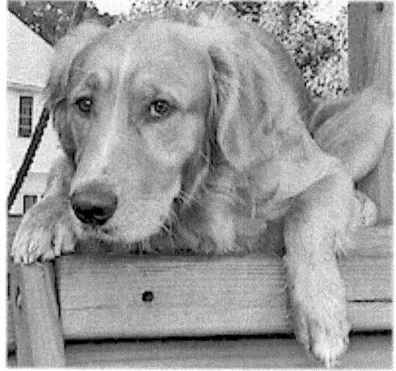

Also, most books about publishing have a writer or a reader or a book on the cover. I've already done those, so I figured it's time to try a dog.

CHAPTER 1
It can be tough to get published—or easy

Because of consolidation in the publishing business, it has become much harder for a new author to get published by a big "traditional" publishing company.

Book publishing is now dominated by a handful of giant companies which have absorbed competitors and now publish about half of the dollar volume of American books. Their books dominate the shelf space in bookstores.

During the "Great Recession," these publishers fired staff, cut back on acquisitions of new books and reduced their promotional programs which sell new books. While there are hundreds of brands ("imprints") on book covers, the majority of them belong to the "Big Six"—Random House, Penguin, HarperCollins, Simon & Schuster, Hachette and Holtzbrinck.

Book publishers seldom take risks today; they like to be fairly sure that a book will sell well, so they select books that are similar to books that sold well in the past.

There are fewer bookstores on the streets of America than there used to be. Traditional "mom-and-pop" neighborhood booksellers are disappearing as "big box" stores like Barnes & Noble and even Walmart and Costco sell a growing percentage of America's reading material. These stores concentrate on the most popular titles which sell quickly, and are less likely than small independent stores to take a chance on a new author or niche subject. Giant bookseller Borders was liquidated as this book was being completed.

But while "bricks-and-mortar" retailers are locking their doors for the last time, the online booksellers such as Amazon.com, BarnesAndNoble.com and dozens of others in dozens of countries are able to offer a limitless number of titles. Many thousands of book titles can be rapidly delivered almost anywhere, often at discount prices and with free shipping. Books that are sold on the Barnes & Noble website but are not stocked in Barnes & Noble stores can be easily ordered *inside* the stores at computerized kiosks. Target.com offers many more book titles than the physical Target stores. Amazon.com has "affiliates" which provide additional online points of entry to Amazon's huge book selection. Electronic "e-books" can be produced and distributed quickly and inexpensively.

Many writers have become publishers. Mark Twain and Virginia Woolf did it. Ben Franklin and Gertrude Stein did it. Jack Canfield, co-author of the *Chicken Soup* series, did it.

So did I. So can you.

New sales channels are developing, with unlimited cyber-shelf-space to accommodate an infinite number of book titles about any imaginable subject. At the same time, personal computers, powerful software, Print-On-Demand and e-books are making it easy for thousands of writers to publish.

This awesome new power should be used responsibly. While there is great satisfaction in seeing your name on the cover of a book, I hope you will write what other people will want to read and that they'll like what you write.

Four paths to publication:

①Traditional "trade" publishing

How it works: You write a book, try to find an agent who thinks it can make money, who tries to find a publisher who thinks it can make money. (Some small publishers accept un-agented submissions.) The publisher pays you an advance against future royalties, paid every six months.

How long to see a book after you finish writing: Six months to ten years, or it may never happen.

How much it costs: Nothing, other than possible research costs and office supplies. The agent will keep 15% of what a publisher pays you.

Advantages: High status, minimal investment, easy access to terrestrial bookstores, advance money, respect from book reviewers and other authors.

Disadvantages: Hard to get an agent and publisher. No control over appearance of book, price or even its title. You are stuck with designer, illustrator, photographers and editors chosen by publisher. Publisher may not do adequate promotion. Book may be killed after a few months. Royalties may be tiny, or zero.

②Independent self-publishing (printed book)

How it works: You write a book, set up a small publishing company, hire editor(s), designer, maybe an illustrator, maybe a photographer, maybe a publicist, maybe a book coach, get ISBN, Library of Congress number and copyright, pick a printer, conduct marketing and publicity.

How long to see a book after you finish writing: Days.

How much it costs: $30 to $1,000 or many thousands.

Advantages: Complete control, speed to market, guaranteed publication, possible high revenue, personal satisfaction, money should come in quickly.

Disadvantages: May have to learn a lot, need to find right suppliers, may have to purchase software, may be hard to get reviews, hard to get into terrestrial bookstores.

③ Independent self-publishing (simple e-book)

How it works: You write a book, and either format it or pay someone to format it as an e-book. You hire editor(s), maybe a designer, maybe an illustrator, maybe a photographer, maybe a publicist, maybe a book coach, conduct marketing and publicity, choose sales channels.

How long to see a book after you finish writing: A few minutes to a few weeks.

How much it costs: Nothing to many thousands.

Advantages: Complete control, speed to market, guaranteed publication, possible high revenue, personal satisfaction, money should come in quickly.

Disadvantages: May have to learn a lot, need to find right suppliers, may have to purchase software, may be hard to get reviews, some people don't read e-books.

④ Using a self-publishing company

How it works: You write a book and choose a company to do some, most or all of the work to produce and promote it. You pay them money before they do anything, and earn a royalty on each book sold. You can also buy books to give away or to sell independently.

How long to see a book after you finish writing: A few weeks to a year.

How much it costs: $195 to $50,000 or even more.

Advantages: Guaranteed publication, minimum work.

Disadvantages: Low status (and possible prejudice), possibility of getting a bad book, little or no control over book appearance, hard to get reviews, hard to get into terrestrial bookstores, books may be overpriced.

Since you are reading this book, I will assume you have decided to become a self-published author. That's wonderful, but you have a great many decisions ahead of you. This book will help you to select the best way for you to self-publish, and will help you produce the best book, for the best price, whichever way you choose to go.

You don't have to do it all yourself

Some homeowners go to Home Depot and order a complete custom kitchen. Some go there and buy ready-made cabinets and counters, take them home and set them up. Others buy lumber, paint, hardware and tools—and do all of the work.

Self-publishing is similar. You can still call yourself a self-publishing author even if you don't do *everything* yourself. At a minimum, you'll need an editor—because no writer should edit her own words. Even editors who write books need editors. If you think you can design the interior but not the cover, you can hire a cover designer or artist. That's how I work.

Because of the recession and cutbacks by major publishers, there are plenty of skilled professionals, including freelancers, available for every part of the process. If you are not a good writer or are too busy to write, you can hire a co-author or a ghostwriter.

Or, you can simply write your manuscript, pick a title, and pay a self-publishing company to do everything else.

Some reasons to be independent, and not use a self-publishing company

1. With a self-publishing company, you may wait up to a year after you finish writing for your books to go on sale. If you are an independent self-publisher, your books can be selling less than one week after you finish your work.
2. With a self-publishing company, you may get an ugly book, with editing errors and bad typography.
3. With a self-publishing company, you will receive a "royalty" of a small percentage of the cover price of each book. An independent self-publisher can make much more.
4. Books that are more valuable to readers can have higher cover prices, and generate more profit. Self-publishing companies may restrict you to a cover price based on page count, not the value the book has for its readers.
5. With a self-publishing company, you may wait six months after a book is sold before you see any income. Depending on the distribution channel, an independent self-publisher can get paid the same day a book is sold. You may have to wait one to three months, but not six.
6. If a self-publishing company assigns an ISBN (International Standard Book Number) to your book, it will be forever tied to that company, not to you or your company!
7. Using these companies, you may be limited to using the artists and designers the publisher chooses.
8. Using these companies, YOU PAY FOR the cover design and interior layouts, but they usually BELONG TO THE PUBLISHER. If you want to take your business elsewhere, you'll need a new cover (which may confuse buyers), and the interior will need to be designed and assembled again.
9. Some people will not be impressed.
10. Your books are unlikely to be stocked by "bricks-and-mortar" booksellers.
11. It will be harder to get book reviews than if you can get a contract from a traditional publisher.

Some reasons not to be an independent self-publisher

1. It's more work than the other types of book publishing.
2. You'll need to have—or develop, or hire people with— additional skills such as book design and publicity.
3. You'll have to make *lots* of decisions, and may have to do research before you can decide what to do. Very basic choices such as book title, length and price can have major impacts on sales. You may not be qualified to make the choices because you just don't have enough experience.
4. You have to be a manager—coordinating work needed from other people and companies.
5. You may have to tell people that their work stinks, but you may not know that it stinks.
6. It costs more money than using a traditional publisher, which pays the costs of publishing, pays you an advance and— you hope—will pay royalties when books are sold.
7. *If* you can get a contract from a traditional publisher and you have a very popular book, you may make more money and do less work than if you self-publish—but you'll wait longer for the money.
8. Even though you will have a lot of control, you can't control everything. You can't control the state of the economy, you can't force people to be interested in your topic, and you can't control which booksellers are willing to sell your book or what they'll charge for it.
9. If the book fails, based on whatever measure you choose to apply, most or all of the blame is on you.
10. Some people will not be impressed.
11. Your books are unlikely to be stocked by "bricks-and-mortar" booksellers.
12. It will be harder to get book reviews than if you can get a contract from a traditional publisher.

If you become an independent self-publisher, you can have complete control over your book's appearance and quality, and its price, marketing and sales promotion. You can earn more money, and get the money faster, than if you were the customer of a self-publishing company. You may start with just $30—and then spend over $3,000.

On the other hand, not every writer wants to be a publisher. Many writers prefer to stick to creative pursuits and not run a business. I won't argue with that. The prices to work with a self-publishing company range from just under $200 to over $50,000—and some or a lot of money may be wasted. This book will help you to minimize the waste.

CHAPTER 2
Why is self-publishing so popular now?

Years ago, all writers were publishers, applying a chunk of charcoal to cave walls, a chisel to stone or a quill to parchment. In the 21st century, once again many writers are becoming publishers.

Self-publishing has become a powerful, popular and often misleading *buzzword*. Self-publishing is buzzing and booming for several reasons.

①Advances in technology and falling costs have helped to **remove middlemen** between creative people and their audiences, and to equalize distribution. Tiny companies—even one-person companies—can have the image and impact of giant corporations.

- Musicians and singers bypass record companies by making CDs to sell at concerts and by putting recordings online for downloading by fans.
- Bloggers reach readers without needing newspapers or magazines to publish their words.
- Videographers can reach a huge audience on YouTube.

- Thousands of people, businesses and organizations publish e-zines, websites, catalogs and newsletters with little or no professional assistance.
- Politicians and business leaders can reach voters and customers with email, blogs and websites—without having to depend on reporters to interpret and distribute their news.

②Specialization and "**micro-ization**" have revolutionized many areas of commerce.

- Giant movie theaters have been divided into multiplexes which show many movies to smaller audiences.
- Department stores are disappearing as boutiques and specialty shops are opening.
- Major beer brands face increasing competition from microbreweries.
- Giant AM and FM radio stations are losing listeners to tiny Internet radio stations and satellite radio channels which "narrowcast" to a fragmented audience.
- The traditional "Big Three" TV networks are losing viewers to cable channels and webcasts.
- Many people now prefer food that's grown or produced nearby, rather than by a distant corporate giant.

③**Online booksellers**, particularly Amazon.com, make millions of books easily and economically available to millions of readers, worldwide.

④Electronic "**e-books**" are much less expensive to produce and distribute than books printed on paper.

COMBINE ① THROUGH ④ AND THE EARLY 21ST CENTURY IS A GREAT TIME TO BE A SELF-PUBLISHED AUTHOR.

CHAPTER 3
Why self-publish?

Back in the "gilded age" of the late 19th century, self-publishing was a leisure activity for rich businessmen and politicians. These men produced expensive, leather-bound, gilt-edged books for their own homes, to give to family and friends, and to donate to libraries.

Edith Wharton and other women self-published because most publishers favored men. In 1921, she became the first woman to win the Pulitzer Prize for literature. That was four years after the first man won the prize.

Mark Twain is said to have become his own publisher because he thought another publisher had cheated him.

Because of sexual content and "dirty words," British publishers refused to print D. H. Lawrence's *Lady Chatterley's Lover*. Lawrence arranged to have it printed in Italy in 1928 (allegedly, the print shop employees couldn't read English).

"Chatterley" was judged to be obscene in Japan in 1957 and in India in 1964. Copies were confiscated by the U.S. Post Office until the publisher won an obscenity trial in 1959. The book wasn't openly published in Britain until 1960.

You can get a copy of an ordinary paperback "Chatterley" for less than a buck, but copies of the original *self-published* book were offered for sale at over $30,000.

Walt Whitman's self-published *Leaves of Grass* is one of the most important collections of early American poetry. In 1855, it was printed in a Brooklyn print shop where Whitman did some typesetting himself—perhaps because he wanted more control than other publishers would have permitted him. A copy of this edition was on the market for $175,000—not bad for a do-it-yourself book.

In the early 21st century, as it becomes harder to make a deal with a traditional publisher, thousands of writers are taking advantage of economical printing processes and publicity opportunities to publish their own work.

I've had deals with three traditional book publishers.
- One cheated me.
- One tried to cheat me.
- One didn't cheat me, but the book that finally came out was so unlike what I had expected it to be, I was sorry I got involved. I also didn't make much money and had to wait a long time for the little money that I did get.
- The publisher that did cheat me did such a bad job on the book, and it was so unlike the vision I had for it, that I refused to let my name be printed on it.

There are lots of reasons why writers want to self-publish. Here are several:

More control: The author determines the title, cover design, page size, number of pages, price, marketing plan, publication date—everything. You even get to write the "about the author" section and choose the promotional *blurbs* (endorsements) that go on the cover. You are the boss and can't be fired. There is a downside to all of this control, however. If your book is ugly or filled with mistakes, you have no one to blame but yourself! Even if you hire people to help, *you* are the ultimate designer, editor, fact-checker and proofreader.

Personal attention: At a big publishing house, a new book from an unknown author may get little or no attention from a sales force which is responsible for dozens or hundreds of books. A self-publishing author can concentrate on one book. She can work as hard as she wants to in promoting the book to the public, booksellers, the media and book reviewers.

Complete freedom: Self-publishing allows authors to write about anything, without needing approval from anyone. (Self-publishing companies may refuse to publish books they consider obscene or libelous.) There's also freedom to ignore publishing traditions if the author wants to try something new.

Fun: Many people who could afford to pay for an oil change like to work on their own cars. Many people who could buy beer or wine or pizza like to experiment with their own special recipes. Lots of people who can buy food like to grow vegetables or go fishing. Do-it-yourself seems to be a common human urge, and now it is possible with publishing. My first book was published by Doubleday in 1976. I'm much prouder of the books I published myself starting in 2008—and they were a lot more fun to work on.

Niche marketing: Because of personal, professional or business connections, a writer may feel she or he is better able to market books to a specific group of potential customers than a traditional publisher could reach through traditional sellers.

Speed: With conventional publishing, it can take years to find an agent and a publisher. With independent self-publishing, a book can be on sale a week after it is written. If you use a self-publishing company, it usually takes a few months

Durability: The author determines how long a book remains on the market.

Keeping the book current: The author determines when a new edition should be published.

Regular income: With conventional "trade" publishing, royalty checks (if there are any) arrive twice a year. With self-publishing, money can come in every day, week, month, or every three or six months—depending on the sales channels.

Higher income: Book royalties from traditional publishers pay about 8% of the cover price. Self-published authors can make more money, even from books with lower prices. (You may make more money per book if you are an independent self-publisher than if you use a self-publishing company.)

Rejection: The vast majority of books submitted to traditional publishers are rejected. Major publishers are driven by "hits." They want books that are bought in the tens of thousands, but their judgment is not perfect. Most books do not become best-sellers, and in a few months they're sold on the buck-a-book tables. Aside from bad writing, there are other reasons why a book may be rejected—such as an unknown author, a subject's limited appeal, a too-controversial subject, an abundance of other books on the subject or the inappropriateness of the book for a particular publisher. But a rejection doesn't mean that a book shouldn't be published at all.

Keeping an old book in print: At some time, the sales volume of almost every book drops to the level at which its publisher decides to discontinue it. It becomes "out-of-print." If that has happened to a book you wrote, you may be able to negotiate a deal with the original publisher to return the rights to you so you can republish it yourself. When sales drop to the point where the first publisher kills the book, there may not be much demand for the self-published version. But even a *little* demand can create income for the author; and proper marketing and/or updating may be able to boost the sales.

Chance of attracting a traditional publisher: According to the *New York Times*, "Louise Burke, publisher of Pocket Books, said publishers now trawl for new material by looking at reader comments about self-published books sold online. Self-publishing, she said, is no longer a dirty word." At least one book from a self-publishing company was later re-published by a mainstream publisher and got on the *New York Times* Bestseller List. While dreaming of writing a bestseller is a pleasant diversion, and perhaps a good motivator to write a high-quality book, it should not be your prime objective. Realistically, you probably won't sell a lot of books and won't make much money, so you'll have to have other ways to define "success" and "satisfaction."

Some of the reasons above are *my* reasons. I established Silver Sands Books in the fall of 2008 to publish one book. In less than a year, I published four books, started three others, and had more on my to-do list. After two years, I had published ten books and more were "in the oven."

ADVICE & ENCOURAGEMENT

You don't have to be the smartest person in the world, or know more than everybody else, to give advice and get paid. You can make a pretty good living if you know more than 90%, 80% or even 20% of the people in the world—if you can reach them.

Self-publishing makes it easier.

I sincerely believe that every human being is born with a unique set of talents, and it is our obligation to identify our talents and find a market for them. This applies whether we are trying to be admitted to a top college, get hired for a job, win an election, start a revolution or write a book.

Self-publishing makes it easier.

Communication is one of the most fundamental human urges. Until recently, there were significant barriers that kept most people from distributing their thoughts to others.

Self-publishing makes it easier.

Albert Einstein said, "Genius consists of 1% inspiration and 99% perspiration." If you sweat a lot, you may be more successful than writers who don't sweat much.

CHAPTER 4
The changing definition and implications of "self-publishing"

In the late 20th century, the terms "vanity publisher" and "subsidy publisher" were applied to the companies that provided pay-to-publish services. Those companies and their writer-customers were derided by other publishers and writers. Writers identified as "self-publishers" were ignored or belittled.

In the 21st century, self-publishing has gained increasing respectability, and the term is now so much in vogue that companies *love* to call themselves "self-publishing companies" to attract business.

Literary agents—who often function as gatekeepers on the road to traditional publishers—typically reject 99% of the book proposals and manuscripts they receive. Self-publishing companies, since they make most of their money by selling services to writers rather than by selling books to readers, probably accept 99% (or even 100%) of their submitted manuscripts.

The **lack of selectivity** is a major cause of self-publishing's bad reputation. Even though traditional publishers make many bad guesses (they frequently reject books that become successful with other publishers and accept books that quickly be come failures), their selectivity and financial commitment provide a powerful endorsement for the writers and books they choose to accept.

Some publishers will produce books with little or no literary merit to cash in on a celebrity author or subject. Some books will never be acceptable to mainstream publishers merely because of limited appeal, regardless of their literary merit.

➔While the book publishing business is going through radical changes, there is still undeniable prejudice against self-published books. To rise above the prejudice, it is vital that your book be as good as it possibly can be. If you care about the reaction of the public and book reviewers, you *must* have a professional editor and cover designer. If you are writing just for fun—or just for family—you can skip the experts

Below are some of the words and phrases used by some pay-to-publish businesses to describe their services and to attract customers. Most of these companies provide pretty much the same services. PublishAmerica is a special case, and I have more to say about the company later in the book.

alternative publishing	joint venture publishing
assisted self-publishing	on-demand publishing
author originated publishing	personal publishing
cooperative publishing	print-on-demand publishing
co-publishing	print quantity needed
custom book publishing	provider of services to
do-it-yourself-publishing	independent authors
fee-based publishing	publish-on-demand
free self-publishing	self-help publishing
hybrid publishing company	self-publishing
independent publishing	short-run book printing
independent self-printing	short term printing
indie book publishing	subsidy publishing
indie publishing	supported self-publishing

I've rethought my position as the self-anointed and self-appointed Guardian of Language.

For two years, I expended a lot of effort and a lot of words attacking the term "self-publishing company." I criticized companies that used the label, pointing out that it MADE ABSOLUTELY NO SENSE, because no person or company can self-publish someone else—just as no one can self-educate, self-immolate or self-medicate someone else.

For better or for worse, the meanings and implications of words do change—and I can't stop the changes.

At one time, a "girl" could be a boy. Now, "bad" can mean good. "Hot" and "cool" can mean the same thing.

Many people—and media including *The Wall Street Journal* and *Writer's Digest*—use the term "self-publishing company." There's not much point in my continuing to bang my head against an unyielding concrete wall. Or to pee into the wind.

THEREFORE, I will no longer debate the semantics and illogic of "self-publishing company"—but I will continue to let people know which companies lie, produce substandard books, overcharge customers or do a bad job promoting books.

MAYBE, there's really not a heck of a lot of difference between writers who hire separate designers, editors and publicists—and writers who get all of their services in a convenient package from one source.

HOWEVER, there can be a big difference in those writers' books. For those willing to gain the knowledge and expend the effort, independent self-publishing can be extremely rewarding, and can produce better books. This book will help.

After I bought this book,
I redesigned two of my books.

Unlike years ago, when future printers worked as apprentices to expert printers, anyone can now put words on paper. A lot of those words are just dumped into a book, with little preparation, thought, knowledge or artistic ability.

Fortunately, there's a wonderful book that tells you what you should and should not do.

The Complete Manual of Typography by James Felici is both a beautiful book to look at and a complete—yet easy-to-understand—reference work which will be very valuable to any self-publishing author.

The book includes typographical history, plus secrets and tricks which used to be passed from father to son (but seldom to daughters). It will help you avoid stupid mistakes, and enable you to make your books both prettier-looking and more professional.

CHAPTER 5
What's wrong with self-publishing companies?

It's possible for a writer to get a decent book from a self-publishing company—if the writer picks the right company, buys the right services at the right prices, knows what makes a good book or a bad book, considers independent editors and designers, and demands high quality. Unfortunately, many writers are greatly disappointed by books produced by self-publishing companies. Many of the books look lousy, are poorly edited or not edited at all, and are under-promoted and overpriced. Many self-publishing companies lie.

Despite similarities, using a self-publishing company is not the same as independent self-publishing. With either independent or assisted self-publishing, writers spend their own money to get books designed, printed and marketed. But with independent self-publishing, a writer has more control and may make a better book and make more money. With independent self-publishing, writers usually do more work, and many seem to enjoy it. I know I do.

For many years there have been ads aimed at writers, with headlines like "We want to read your book," "Manuscripts wanted," and "Authors wanted." The advertisers promise to enable you to become a "published author." The ads are not from traditional publishers or from literary agents, but from self-publishing companies which use the author's money.

There is only one customer a self-publishing company is interested in selling to: the author/customer. Independent self-publishers and traditional publishers hope to make money by selling books to readers. Self-publishing companies make most of their money by selling publishing services, books and over-priced trinkets to their authors. Companies like Random House don't have to advertise to attract writers and receive manuscripts.

Ahead are some of the words and phrases used by pay-to-publish businesses to describe themselves and to attract customers—and some of their deceptions and distortions.

Schiel & Denver claims to be a **book publishing services company**, **book publisher** and **provider of services to independent authors**. The company is outrageously dishonest. It says, "You can rest assured your book will go on sale at over 160,000+ online and traditional retail stores, in over 100 countries." That's extremely deceptive. While a book may be *orderable* at thousands of stores, that's not the same thing as "on sale at" with the implication of on-the-shelf availability. S&D also lies about having its own printing facilities.

Author Solutions issued a powerful promotional brochure titled, "The Next **Indie** Revolution." They portray indie book publishing as the artistic heir to indie films like *Night of the Living Dead* and indie bands like Vampire Weekend. Actually, indie publishing existed before movies or compact discs existed, but it wasn't called indie publishing. More importantly, customers of Author Solutions are NOT indie publishers. The company claims that "Authors have two options when choosing indie book publishing:" vanity publishing and supported self-publishing. The company ignores independent (i.e., real "indie") self-publishing, where the author *is* the publisher.

Outskirts Press has called its business **on-demand publishing, custom book publishing** and **independent self-printing.** **B**rent **S**ampson is the boss of Outskirts Press. He has very appropriate initials. He lies a lot.

Brent wrote, "The majority of independently self-published authors find it nearly impossible to secure distribution through book wholesalers . . . ."

First of all, Brent has *no way of knowing* the experiences of the majority of any kind of people.

Second—and more important—it just isn't true. If a self-publishing author has books printed on demand by Lightning Source (the leading POD printer for both independents like me and companies like Brent's), it's almost impossible *not* to secure distribution through the major wholesalers. It happens automatically!

Brent says independent self-publishers "are left with thousands of unsold copies and without an effective way of getting their books into the hands of readers" and "The independently self published authors I know all have boxes of books in their garage and park their cars on the street." Apparently Brent knows the wrong people.

Brent's website warns of the "hassles of independent self-publishing, like guessing print-runs, managing inventory, and the responsibility of order fulfillment." Well, I'm an independent self-publisher, and I *never ever* think about print runs, inventory or order fulfillment. The biggest hassles I deal with are typosos. (That was deliberate.)

Brent also wrote about the high costs of setting up websites. Actually, it costs *very* little to set up a website.

The big BS-er says getting an ISBN (the unique identification number for each book) is a "headache." I ordered ten ISBNs in about five minutes. All I needed was my computer and a credit card. I never touched the Tylenol.

One of the oldest **self-publishing** companies tried to scare people considering independent self-publishing by saying, ". . . ask yourself whether you will have the time to coordinate manufacturing a book, to promote it and advertise it, and to ship, keep records, collect bills, etc." There is no denying that book promoting is a lot of work, but you can't expect *any* publisher to do all of the promotion for you. If you use a Print-On-Demand printer such as Lightning Source, there's no need to coordinate manufacturing or to ship books or collect bills. Record-keeping is minimal and advertising is optional and can be inexpensive.

GM Books uses the **co-publishing** label. They warn that self-publishing "transforms a writer into a business manager and instant publishing technician. This carries the risks of simple mistakes costing thousands of dollars." GM also says, "There will be an initial fee for reading your manuscript, whether or not we mutually decide to publish. The author provides us with a clean double-spaced manuscript on computer disk. . . ." As an experienced independent self-publisher, I find it hard to conceive of *any* mistake that could cost thousands of dollars, and I know that any publisher who charges a reading fee should be avoided. A company like this could survive on the revenue of rejected manuscripts and *never* print a single book. Also, requiring a manuscript to be submitted on a disc rather than up-loaded or emailed is *very* 20th century. Stay away!

Aachanon Publishing says it is a **self-publishing service provider**. It claims "it provides all the necessary services for authors to make their book: professional copyediting and proof reading; choice of layout and design; in-house cover design; and quality book printing." They offer no marketing or sales assistance, and no distribution other than shipping you cases of books. Aachanon authors have to set up their own distribution channels. Unlike other companies that want to work with self-publishers, Aachanon does not provide ISBN numbers or copyrights. Aachanon shows authors' books on its website, mostly with the authors' names and addresses for ordering. Strangely, some titles show Aachanon as the source for books, but the site is not set up for online ordering. The company's website has some really stupid errors in grammar and typography—even in a section touting their editing services—so they may not be your best choice for editorial assistance.

Both AuthorHouse and its sister company, Trafford Publishing, have run Google ads with **Cooperative Publishing** as the headline, so they assume there must be writers interested in a co-op deal. However, I found nothing on their websites that describes the program, perhaps because it doesn't really exist. A Trafford press release says it has led the **independent publishing** revolution since its establishment in 1995." Trafford certainly has a healthy corporate ego, but if you use Trafford, you're not independent.

Lulu.com claims to rank #1 among self-publishing websites and to provide **free self-publishing**. But Lulu's publishing is *not* free if you expect to see actual books. Lulu boss Bob Young told *Publishers Weekly* that "**We publish a huge number of really bad books.**" If Bob knows they're really bad books, he shouldn't publish them. Bob also misspelled "misspell" and confused "less" and "fewer." A publisher should know better.

Infinity Publishing says it provides **author originated book publishing** and **print-on-demand publishing** and produces higher quality books than Lightning Source. Based on a sample Infinity sent me, that's a lie. The book was terribly produced and would scare away possible customers, not win them over.

The Pegasus of publishing

Some types of publishing are like the Pegasus, Unicorn, Loch Ness monster, or Big Foot.

"**Joint venture publishing**" and "**co-publishing**" are so hard to find that they may not exist.

Beckham Publications Group says it provides joint venture publishing, where "two parties decide to invest in a project and share in the profits generated. The investing partners are the author and the publisher."

Authors pay Beckham a fee to design, edit, manufacture, and deliver a specified quantity of books for the author to re-sell. Beckham also prints copies to go to booksellers and pays a royalty on each book sold. The company can provide extra-cost promotional materials and services such as press releases.

Beckham says, "Larger houses take 12 to 18 months to pro-duce a book . . . . However, your **joint venture self-published book** can be produced in half the usual time commercial pub-lishers take." If Beckham takes six to nine months to put books on the market, it's slower than most self-publishing companies and much slower than independent self-publishing.

Beckham's fees are determined by how much work needs to be done, book size, artwork and number of books printed. The author must buy some books to sell or give away. Beck-ham gets a copyright and assigns one of its own ISBNs.

Company boss Barry Beckham said that an author who might collect $2 per book in royalties from a traditional pub-lisher could collect $9 from his company. But since the author makes a big investment, he will not get back his investment until about 500 books are sold (which may never happen).

The Beckham website says, "Our editors are prepared to correct textual matters like grammar, punctuation and spelling." They may not be adequately prepared. The website misidentifies Virginia Woolf as "Wolf" and Stephen Crane as "Stephan." Virginia with the extra "o" was a writer. Virginia with just one "o" is a sculptor. The site also says "trims size" instead of "trim size."

Following Beckham's instructions, I submitted ten sample pages of manuscript to find out if I was good enough to meet its publishing standards and how much it would charge.

After nearly four weeks I received this email: "Attached is our estimate of $4,555 that includes our services and 100 copies delivered to you." **That price is so high it seems like the investment formula for the "joint venture" is 100% for the author and 0% for Beckham.**

Beckham provides a lot of services, but the price is thousands of dollars more than what an independent self-publisher would pay. And in order to make back my investment and earn a tiny profit, I'd have to sell those 100 books for about FIFTY BUCKS EACH. How many would you like to buy?

Subsidy publishing usually has no subsidy

It's sad that the publishing business—which depends on communication—often communicates poorly.

Terminology used to describe pay-to-publish companies is imprecise, inaccurate and in flux. At one time, the companies were subjected to the pejorative terms "vanity presses" or "vanity publishers." As a reaction, some labeled themselves "subsidy publishers," and most have now metamorphosed into "self-publishing companies" or use other labels mentioned earlier in this chapter.

What's wrong with self-publishing companies?

There is no better example of bad communication than the use or misuse of the word "subsidy." The term "subsidy publishing" is almost never used properly. In other fields (e.g., subsidized housing, subsidized daycare and subsidized transportation) the "customer" pays *part* of the cost of the service. Another entity such as a government agency or employer provides a subsidy to pay for the rest.

In most subsidy publishing the author-customer pays 100% of the cost of publishing. There is *no* subsidy—unless you consider the money paid by the author to be a subsidy to the publisher. (Since the payment is 100% of the cost, it's not really a subsidy.)

Companies such as AuthorHouse and iUniverse advertise to attract mouse clicks and money from writers searching for the phrases "subsidy publishing" and "subsidy publisher." Writers who are aware of how the term "subsidy" is used in other fields might logically assume that they will have to pay only a portion of the cost of having their books published and that the publishing company will pay the rest.

But it doesn't usually work this way in subsidy publishing.

You'll pay hundreds or thousands of dollars to have your book prepared and printed. Since you're paying 100% of the cost of publication, you're really NOT getting a subsidy. You might be better off farming. Or becoming a publisher.

A legitimate "co-op" or "joint venture" publisher depends on fees paid by authors, but the publisher invests some money in each publishing project. That's a *real* subsidy. Since the publisher is risking its own money, it should be more selective in the titles it accepts. It should also be motivated to provide better editing, design and marketing services.

With a real co-op or joint venture publisher (*if you can find one*), you will have less control than if you were an independent self-publisher, but may not have to spend as much as you would with a typical self-publishing company or if you publish independently.

While *you* may know that you had to meet higher standards than if you used a regular self-publishing company, it is unlikely that the pros in the book business will be impressed. On the other hand, people who don't recognize the publisher's name on the book may think you did just fine.

Every writer is wonderful...to some publishers

Except for books that appear to be obscene or libelous, a self-publishing company will generally print anything. Some companies automatically send a letter of praise for a submitted manuscript without reading it. There have been experiments where intentionally horrible manuscripts were said to have high sales potential, and a book said to be **written by a dog** was accepted.

Literary agents—who often function as gatekeepers on the road to traditional publishers—typically reject 99% of the book proposals and manuscripts they receive. Self-publishing companies, since they make money by selling services to writers rather than by selling books to readers, probably accept 99% (or even 100%) of their submitted manuscripts.

The lack of selectivity is the prime cause of self-publishing's bad reputation. Even though traditional publishers make many bad guesses (they frequently reject books which become successful with other publishers and accept books that quickly become failures), their selectivity and financial commitment does provide a powerful endorsement for the writers and books they choose to accept.

Some books, regardless of their literary merit, will never be acceptable to mainstream publishers merely because of limited appeal. A company that wants to sell tens of thousands of copies of each title will not be interested in a family history, unless it's a very famous family like Obama or Kennedy.

While the book publishing business is going through some radical changes, there is still undeniable prejudice against self-published books. To rise above the prejudice, it is vital that your book be as good as it possibly can be. If you care about the reaction of the public and book reviewers, you *must* have a professional editor and cover designer. If you are writing just for fun—or family—you can skip the experts.

Who cares who published your book?

◆Zoe Winters is a romance writer and blogger. She says, "The average reader doesn't care how a book gets to market. If the book is good, it doesn't matter if your Chihuahua published it." ◆Author and blogger S.G. Royle wrote, "People don't buy books from publishers. They buy them from authors." ◆Edward Uhlan founded Exposition Press—an early and important pay-to-publish company—in 1936. He said, "Most people can't tell the difference between a vanity book and a trade book anyway. A book is a book." ◆On the other hand, many booksellers and reviewers *can* tell the difference and *do* care—and may reject a book solely because of its publisher.

This is a good reason to shun the tarnished brands and establish your own publishing business. Here's the logo for mine:

SILVER SANDS BOOKS

The type ("Algerian") came from MS Word.
The picture cost $3.75 at Fotolia.com.

Advertising what
can't be sold

There's no such thing as **Publish-On-Demand**, even though PublishAmerica insists that "Publish-On-Demand" is the real meaning of "POD." (Most of the world knows that it means "Print-On-Demand.")

"Publish-On-Demand" makes no sense, but companies want you to think they'll provide it. Llumina Press, BookSurge, Outskirts Press and others have advertised the meaningless phrase aimed at ignorant writers who don't know the difference between printing and publishing. **They're not the same thing! Printing is** *part* **of publishing. Printing can be done on demand. Publishing can't be done on demand.**

Publishing is a complex, multi-stage process which takes a writer's words from manuscript to books being sold. The end result of a publishing project—which may be a million books or just one book—can take weeks, months or even years.

With Print-On-Demand, books are printed one at a time or a few at a time, as orders are placed by readers through booksellers. Books are usually in the hands of readers a few days after an order is placed. That could not happen if a publishing company had to start the entire publishing sequence each time that an order for a book arrives.

Advertising what
is seldom sold

With "co-op," "cooperative" or "joint-venture" publishing, the author and the publisher should share the expenses and the profits. In reality, with the co-op publishers I've examined, the cost of publishing is so high that it looks like the author pays 100% of the cost—plus a nice profit. That's not very cooperative.

Some alleged co-ops charge much more than regular self-publishing companies. The deceptively named Author's Publishing Cooperative charges $14,800 PLUS about $3,000 for editing, $1,500 for cover design and $2,000 for typesetting. Authors pay for printing, too.

Don't get the royal shaft on royalties.

Some self-publishing companies try to impress potential customers with the prospect of earning big royalties on each book sold. If you earn a "royalty" of 50 cents or $6 per book, but you've already paid $300 or $3,000 or $13,000, you're really just getting your own money back—very slowly. Some publishers are vague or misleading about how royalties are calculated. They may offer what seems to be a very high percentage, but it's based on the wholesale price of a book, not the retail "cover price." ➔➔➔**50% of $8 is not better than 20% of $20.**

Study the contract carefully BEFORE you sign it.

If you're not happy with the work done by a publisher, you may want to move on to another company. The change could be very expensive if the next company has to start from scratch because you agreed that "Author may not utilize the formatted Work and cover with any other publisher," or if there is a huge fee to turn over the "work product" you paid to produce.

Read the next paragraph three times:

If you are not skilled, knowledgeable and attentive to details, you may end up with an ugly, error-ridden book which will embarrass you and that no one will review or buy. If you don't know what you're doing, *don't do it*. Get qualified help. In publishing—as with most things in life—you get what you pay for.

,?

Comma, or no comma

The second-smallest piece of punctuation can be confusing and complex, and subject to much disagreement. Its use is so complicated that a book could be written about it. In fact, I may write the book—even if I'm the only one who reads it.

1. "I'm going to the movies with my friend Billy" implies that I have several friends, and one is named Billy.
2. "I'm going to the movies with my friend, Billy" implies that I have just one friend, named Billy. (It could also mean that the speaker is addressing Billy, but that's another matter.)

According to the authoritative *Chicago Manual of Style,* it used to be that a lack of commas signaled restriction: that is, the meaning of "friend" in the first sentence would be restricted to Billy, implying that I have other friends as well. Commas signaled nonrestriction: that Billy is my only friend, so his actual name is ancillary, disposable information. It was a pretty good system. Commas in nonrestrictive constructions have become optional, which is fine when the likely meaning is obvious (as in "my wife Marilyn") but unhelpful in the case of a friend. Many people add commas where they aren't needed, which adds to the confusion.

CHAPTER 6
The silly little secrets of self-publishing companies

Secret #1: Most use the same printing company

A publishing company is not a printing company. A printing company is not a publishing company. Most modern book publishers do not own printing presses. The vast majority of books published by self-publishing companies are not printed by those publishing companies. Most of their books are produced and shipped by Lightning Source. It prints over a million books each month—often one at a time.

Self-publishing companies want you to think they are unique and special. Some may have better designers and editors than others, but there is no reason to believe that books published by Outskirts Press or Schiel & Denver or iUniverse will vary in physical quality. Their books may pop out of the *same printing press* seconds apart, along with books published by Random House, CreateSpace and my own little company.

Some companies lie about having their own printing facilities. Schiel & Denver says, "We ship worldwide from <u>our</u> USA printing facilities based in TN, PA and ME" and "Our book publishing company operates printing and distribution centers in the following locations . . . ." Two of the locations the company lists are cities where Lightning Source prints books.

Infinity Publishing brags that it has its own printing presses but sometimes uses Lightning Source, Infinity says, ". . . its books are not as high quality as ours . . . ." That's a lie.

Secret #2: Some apparent competitors are owned by the same parent company

In the old days of Detroit, the car companies engaged in what was called "badge engineering." There was often no difference under the hood of a Dodge and a Chrysler, or a Buick and an Oldsmobile, or a Ford and a Mercury. The main differences were in the headlights, grill, interior trim, tail lights, brand name, marketing pitch and price.

Similarly, bedding manufacturers make slight variations for competing retailers to make it hard for people to comparison shop at Macy's and Sleepy's.

In electronics, Panasonic and Quasar cordless phones came out of the same factory, but had different colors and model numbers and were sold by competing dealers.

Badge engineering now exists in the book publishing business. Author Solutions, Inc. (ASI) owns former competitors AuthorHouse, iUniverse, Trafford, Wordclay and Xlibris; and started a Spanish-language division called Palibrio. ASI also operates the self-publishing businesses for traditional publishers Harlequin, Thomas Nelson and Hay House, and for *Writer's Digest* magazine.

There is little or no difference between the books produced by these different brand names. Some are aimed at specific genres (such as chick-lit or Christian) while others will take money from just about anyone. An ASI editor, marketing person or cover designer may work on projects that will bear the brand names of multiple companies.

Each brand offers multiple "publishing packages." The packages have different names, but there is little real difference, and little reason to choose, for example, iUniverse over Xlibris or Hay House's Balboa Press.

Xlibris packages are priced from $399 to $13,999, Dellarte (Harlequin) packages range from $599 to $1599, iUniverse from $599 to $4200 and Trafford from $799 to $7199. Although these price ranges are different, what you get at each price point is very close, with little or no difference in value.

On the next page are details on three different $999 publishing packages offered by different Author Solutions brands. Some will have definite advantages to some authors. Other differences will be meaningless.

All three include copyright registration, but only Westbow includes a Library of Congress Control Number registration. Balboa and DellArte charge $90 for it. You can get one for FREE, with a few minutes' work.

Read carefully. What they offer may not be what they *seem* to offer. For example, DO NOT be falsely impressed by the inclusion of an "editorial review." It's not the same thing as real editing, and may lead to a sales pitch for expensive editing.

Dellarte says, "The Editorial Review is *not* a full manuscript edit, nor is it a replacement for the Dellarte Press full range of editorial services."

➜ Be aware that the self-publishing field is very competitive. As with cars and travel, there are abundant deals, discounts and free add-ons and upgrades. When you are offered a price, don't be afraid to ask for a better deal, an upgrade or some freebies. Some items that may have significant value to you, have little or no cost to the publisher.

BALBOA PRESS — EMBARK PACKAGE $999.00

Included Services	
ISBN Assignment	✓
Author Volume Discounts	✓
Channel Distribution to 25K Retailers	✓
Cover Design	✓
Personalized Back Cover	✓
Interior Book Design	✓
Image Insertions/Text Treatments	10
B&W Interior Color Cover	✓
E-book Formatting and Distribution	✓
Complimentary Author Copy	✓
Sold on Amazon.com, BarnesNoble.com	✓
Personalized Balboa Press Bookstore Page	✓
Included in Balboa Press Catalog	✓
U.S. Copyright Registration	✓
Free Paperback Copies	10

WESTBOW PRESS — Essential Access $999.00

Softcover Format	✓
ISBN Assignment	✓
Complimentary Author Copy	✓
Retail Channel Distribution, including Amazon.com	✓
Library of Congress Control Number	✓
U.S. Copyright Registration	✓
Image Insertion / Text Treatments	10
Book Interior and Cover Design	✓
Free Paperback Copies	10
Reps Working to Sell to Christian Book Buyers	✓

DELLARTE PRESS — ASPIRATIONS $999.00

ISBN Assignment	✓
Complimentary Author Copy	✓
Softcover Format	✓
E-Book Format, including Amazon Kindle & Sony Reader	✓
Channel Distribution to 25K Retailers including Amazon.com	✓
Free Paperback Copies	15
Author Volume Book Order Discounts	✓
Personal Assistance & Customer Support	✓
Simple Book Layout	✓
Enhanced Cover Design	✓
Google & Amazon Online Book Search	✓
Editorial Review of Manuscript	✓
Editorial Review of Manuscript	✓

CHAPTER 7
What do you get for $195, or for nothing?

Self-publishing companies sell their services in packages priced from under $200 to over $50,000. A few companies even advertise FREE publishing. It's very important to know what you need, what you'll get, and what you won't get.

Can you really get a book published for less than $200, or for free? Yes—and no.

Emerald book printing (b/w interior, color cover)

Price: $199

The Emerald printing package is the no-frills method of turning a manuscript into a perfect bound paperback for your personal use only. It does not include an ISBN nor distribution of any kind. Scroll down to Product Details for more information and be sure to review the

---

The $199 **Emerald** publishing package from **Outskirts Press** actually provides what looks like a "real" book. The package is notable not for what it *includes*, but for what it *excludes*.

Most notable is the lack of an ISBN, which means that the book can't be sold by bookstores. An Emerald book is not even available on the Outskirts online bookstore.

For $199 you are limited to one book size (5.5×8.5 inches) and a choice of two cover designs. You get exactly *one* book which you can read, give away, sell or display on your mantelpiece. You can order more books if you want to. They won't be pretty, but they *are* books.

The top package from Outskirts costs $1099. Some other publishers may charge over $50,000. Be careful. A big investment won't guarantee a great book, and may kill any chance of making a profit. Be sure of your goals and your budget, and act accordingly.

Strangely named **Aachanon Publishing** beats the $199 Outskirts Emerald deal by $4, and provides THREE "free" books—not just one. With its **Budget** package, you are limited to a maximum of ten black and white illustrations or photos in the text, the book size is 5×8 inches (a bit smaller than the Outskirts competitor), and you can have up to 300 pages. The color cover is preformatted and can include two author-provided photos or illustrations. As with the Outskirts Emerald package, there is no ISBN. You must provide distribution—booksellers won't sell the book.

Strangely named **Wasteland Press** calls itself, "the cheapest full service press on the internet." Its **Basic** package matches the Aachanon $195 price but provides FIVE books in either 5.5 ×8.5-inch or 6×9-inch size. Maximum book length is 275 pages. There is no limit to the number of photos or illustrations. The company offers faster publishing than most competitors, and its covers are "designed from scratch and are uniquely individual." The samples I saw are quite nice. Books are sold on Wasteland's website, and provide a 15% royalty. That's very low for sales on a publisher's own website..

By the time you read this, some company may offer a publishing package for $179, or $99.

What do you get for $195, or for nothing?

Some of the websites for self-publishing companies tout "free" publishing programs. What you get for free is hot air. If you want real books, you pay real money.

CreateSpace, Lulu, Wordclay, UniBook and others who advertise free publishing will not charge you to upload your book's files. They assume you will do all of the design, editing and promotional work yourself or hire others to do it.

How can they publish a book for free?

➜ They can't. They're *lying*.

Their publishing is free as long as you don't expect any books to be produced. Every book they print, or distribute as an e-book, is paid for. Their notion of publishing does not include the final product—a book.

CreateSpace is an Amazon subsidiary that lets you "**Self-Publish a Book-Free**." The only free things I saw on its website are "free tools to prepare your content for publication" and an ISBN that identifies CreateSpace (not you) as the publisher.

The company has two low-cost publishing programs. The standard program is sort of free. The $39 **Pro** program can provide so much more profit per book that you'd have to be an idiot or a pessimist not to go for the Pro.

With the "free" standard plan, apparently you don't have to pay a penny to upload your book's files into the CreateSpace computer and make it available for printing when orders are received. HOWEVER, each time a book is printed, you *do* pay a fee, and you have to order at least one book.

If you want CreateSpace to do more of the work in designing, producing, promoting and distributing your books, you can pay up to $4,999 for a publishing package.

Lulu says it is "the only publisher that offers you all that it does for free." The company has run online ads touting "**Publish Your Book—Free**," "**Free publishing**," and "**Free Self Publishing**." Its website promises, "**free book publishing**," but the publishing is free only if you don't want any books to be printed!

A 250-pager with decent paper will cost $9.50 in quantities up to 24. Shipping is additional. That doesn't seem like free.

If you want Lulu to do more of the work in producing, promoting and distributing your books, and to send you a batch of books, you can pay up to $4,499 for a package.

Wordclay says, "You can sign up and **start publishing your book for free**. There is no cost to register with our Web site and create your account. There is no cost to use our publishing wizard to turn your work into a published book . . . . We have additional goods and services that you can also purchase through our Services Store, but again, there is no obligation. The basic publishing experience of getting your manuscript into a finished book is entirely free." Here, too, the "free" publishing doesn't actually include printing any *books*.

UniBook advertises "**Free Self Publishing**." It says, "Getting your book self-published is easy. All you need to do is take a few minutes to upload your files and choose your publishing options—that's it. Your book is instantly available for purchase worldwide in the UniBook online bookstore." UniBook apparently has no mechanism for getting your books into stores or online booksellers. On a 300-page paperback selling for $18.95 you'll get a royalty of about three bucks, which must be paid to you through PayPal.

CHAPTER 8
How much do the free books cost?

The printing packages from most self-publishing companies include some "free" or "complimentary" books. They're *not* free.

Schiel & Denver claims to be a "Christ-Centered Publishing House" and employs "staff who . . . lead with high ethical and professional standards." The company brags about providing "FREE soft cover copies on publication." They are free only if you ignore the payment of as much as $19,999 for a publishing package. What would Jesus say?

With **Outskirts Press**, the charge for a publishing package can range from $199 to $1,099. You'll get as many as ten "free" books that you actually paid for as part of the package.

Wasteland Press doesn't promise free books, but it *does* promise "FREE shipping" of between 5 and 500 books, FREE ISBNs, and a FREE booksellers' return plan. However, since you'll have to pay the company from $195 to $3,100 to publish a 250-page book, the alleged freebies are being paid for with YOUR money.

Lulu says, "After publishing and once you approve the work, we will send you a complimentary copy of your finished book for you to review and enjoy." That "complimentary" copy may have cost you as much as $1,369.

Aachanon Publishing will give you three "free" books, after you've paid up to $595 for a publishing package.

Xlibris seems unusually generous with freebies. They'll give you a whopping 250 paperbacks and 25 hardbacks with their "platinum" package. Oh—by the way—they're free only if you've paid $12,999 for the package.

Pay attention to the teacher

Arlene Miller is an English teacher, and previously worked as a newspaper reporter, technical writer and book editor. She has a lot to teach people who speak and write.

Arlene's book, *The Best Little Grammar Book Ever!* may actually *be* the best little grammar book ever. Packed into a compact 120 pages, the book provides information, answers and advice which will be valuable to *every* writer. It belongs on *your* desk.

You can check it when you have a question, or just stick a finger between two random pages when you have a minute or two of spare time. I guarantee that you'll find something useful, and you may avoid looking stupid or amateurish.

Arlene taught me to use quote marks around short things like song titles, to italicize big things like book titles, and which words to capitalize in book titles. She also discusses "concrete nouns" and the "predicate nominative"—which I assumed had become extinct in the Neanderthal era.

CHAPTER 9
How to get the most from your publisher

"Most" involves two things:
①Getting the *most for your money* (not purchasing overpriced or unnecessary services and trinkets)
②Getting the *most perfect book possible*

◆Pick the right company. Don't base your decisions on the glowing recommendations on the publishers' websites. Check the web for unhappy customers. Read evaluations on such websites as **www.BookMakingBlog.blogspot.com** and **www.sfwa.org/for-authors/writer-beware**. Read the Better Business Bureau reports. Contact authors who have expressed disappointment and ask for details. Keep in mind that companies may get better—or worse—over time. Beware of self-publishing companies which do not provide proper support for *book* publishing and marketing. **Blurb** specializes in photo books. **Café Press** specializes in T-shirts, mugs and posters.

◆Don't base your decision on price alone. Quality is paramount. YOUR name will be bigger than the publisher's name on your book, and YOU will be blamed for the mistakes the publisher makes but you don't catch and correct.

♦Writing is an art. Self-publishing is a business. Like it or not, you will be running a business, and like any other business manager, you must do a cost-benefit analysis (even informally) of every product and service you buy. A $10,000 publishing package may not produce better books than a $3,000 package, and will put you much deeper "in the hole" before you sell the first book. A $5,000 promotional video may make you feel like a superstar, but it may not sell any books to the people who see it, and there is no way you can force people to see it. Xlibris charges authors $199 for 100 promotional postcards—nearly two bucks apiece and much more than you'd pay to a printer like VistaPrint. But since the Xlibris book royalty is just 10% for books sold on Amazon, **each $19.95 book will earn you just enough money to pay for a postcard. A $9.95 book earns enough to buy half of a postcard.** And, of course you still have to pay for the publishing package, and stamps.

➡♦The most expensive publishing packages—typically costing from $7,999 to $50,000 or more—are like vacation timeshares. They should *not* be purchased as investments with an expectation of making a profit. They may make you feel good, but with a $50,000 investment, there is not a snowball's chance in hell that you will sell enough books to make money.

➡♦Any self-publishing company or printer has the ability to make excellent books, but they often don't. Bad books may be the result of sloppy page formatters, unskilled cover designers, distracted or inexperienced editors, or even malfunctioning printing and binding equipment. YOU are the customer, and the general contractor. It is important that YOU establish high standards and demand that your publisher deliver a first-class product. Carefully examine (and have others examine) each generation of proof, especially before you approve the final proof for printing and distribution.

◆Don't pay for overpriced trinkets and services which you don't need, or can get for less elsewhere. Remember—most self-published books don't sell very well. When Random House sells a million books, it makes money from the books. When Outskirts Press sells 14 books, it needs to supplement the income by selling bookmarks, postcards and press releases. Outskirts will even sell you expensive customized Keds sneakers with images of your book cover for $99. If you want to be a billboard, you can show a much bigger book cover on a $12.95 Zazzle T-shirt than on a $99 pair of Keds. Zazzle, by the way, will do custom Keds for $60.

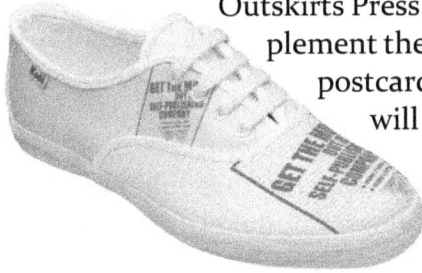

◆Don't skip copyediting, and consider more extensive editing services, particularly if you are an inexperienced writer.

◆Ask for details about services you are considering. Phrases such as "aggressive promotion to appropriate markets," "pervasive online availability," "distribution of your press release to up to 100 targeted media outlets," and "a veritable buffet of powerful publishing tools" are pretty much meaningless.

◆Don't be afraid to ask for changes in the package or contract. Everything in life is negotiable (even life itself). Self-publishing is a very competitive field and there is little difference in the end products produced by the competitors—unless you look very closely. You can ask for more "free" books or posters instead of bookmarks, or for the special July prices in October. The publishers want your business. Make them earn it.

◆Study sample books before committing to a publisher. Publishers and printers should be willing to send you several, and you can buy some, too. Surprisingly, some of the promotional books intended to show off publishers' best work are *terrible*.

◆Your contract is not lifelong and is probably not exclusive. If you're unhappy, you can try another publisher for the same book or your next book. While some self-publishing companies produce excellent books and have reasonable prices, others have done terrible work and overcharged their customers.

It is possible to get a high-class book, at a reasonable price—*if* you choose the right company, carefully check its work, perhaps do some work yourself, and consider independent editors and designers.

◆Don't be seduced by low-ball/bare-bones publishing packages—*or* by super-deluxe packages. A $199 book will probably look like junk. A $399 book probably won't look much better. A $50,000 book will never earn back its cost of publication.

◆Let the publisher do the "grunt work" which you don't want to get involved in.

◆Concentrate on the creative process to make a good-reading, good-looking book which you can be proud of and perhaps make money from.

◆Inspect your book carefully before it goes on sale. Even if a stupid mistake was caused by someone else, *your* name is on the book, and every error is ultimately *your* responsibility.

◆Don't rely only on others for marketing and publicity. *Your* book is more important to *you* than it is to anyone else. *You* must sell *your* book. Even if you pay others to promote *your* book, if people don't buy it, it's *your* fault—and *you* suffer.

Chapter 10
The worst mistakes of authors who use self-publishing companies

Even before the covers are opened, books bearing the brands of self-publishing companies are dismissed by some reviewers and booksellers. They often assume that the books are dreadful, and a writer must do everything possible to overcome the initial prejudice.

The worst mistake of self-published authors is lack of editing or inadequate editing. Because editing is an option, some writers—out of ego, ignorance or economic necessity—skip editing. This is dangerous.

No writer should be her own editor. Even professional editors who write books should hire other editors. It's not just a matter of errors in spelling or grammar. You may have words in your mind that you think are on the page, but are really not there. You may "fall in love" with a word, phrase or chapter which is really unlovable.

A fresh set of eyes with a different point of view is critical. You need someone else to make corrections and to ask questions. But, sometimes even having a "professional editor" will not lead to a professional-quality book. I received this email (slightly edited) from an author: "I have had some scathing reviews due to the errors that were left in my book after I paid a small fortune for editing with Outskirts Press . . . . Outskirts made me feel paranoid about not getting their editing service, but when I did it was as if I had no editing at all."

The second biggest mistake is the lack of professional design—especially on the cover. Many do-it-myself covers, like the one shown, are dreadful. They proclaim, "I AM AN IGNORANT AMATEUR!"

Best in
self-
ublishing

How to Get
Published
Free

& Print on Demand

Plus Marketing
Your Book on
The Internet

Amazon
Borders
Buy.com
Books A Million
Barnes & Noble

avid Risin

Skillful and attractive design is also important inside your book. One common newbie error is using *full justification* and not hyphenating words.

I purchased *U-Publish.com 5.0*, co-authored by Dan Poynter. Dan is no ignorant amateur, and is generally recognized as an authority on self-publishing—but this book is ugh-lee. It has oversized indents, no hyphens, and the type is condensed sans serif. Word spacing is atrocious. There are "rivers," and "orphans" which could have been easily fixed. Empty pages have headers and numbers—a major sin.

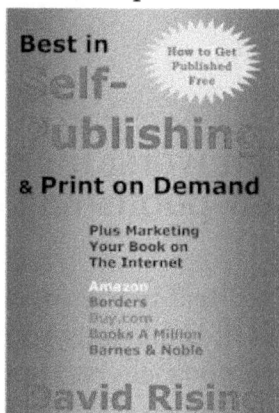

> Watch your money. Do the free and inexpensive promotion first. Use e-mail rather than envelopes and stamps; send copies to book reviewers and stage local autographings and mini seminars.

Dan boasts that he is "the father of self-publishing," "the leading authority on how to write, publish and promote books," and is "on the leading edge of book publishing." He provides useful information, but if Dan thinks crappy typography is acceptable, he's fallen off the edge and into the abyss.

CHAPTER 11
Some numbers to think about

U nless you are a superstar author, a *traditional publishing contract* will pay a royalty rate of about 6 to 10% of the suggested retail price. There may be a sliding scale based on sales volume with a higher percentage paid as sales rise. There may be a lower percentage applied to certain kinds of sales, such as to book clubs or through off-price promotional deals. For the sake of simplicity, we'll pick a flat 8% and ignore any percentage that might be paid to an agent.

Let's also assume an initial print run of 5,000 books with a cover price of $20 each. If they all get sold at full price, the bookstores collect $100,000 and maybe $40–$45,000 works its way back to the publisher through a wholesaler which collects a piece of the action.

You, the smiling person whose name is on the cover, probably got a $5,000 advance against royalties when you signed your contract. Eight percent of $100,000 is $8,000, and since you already got $5,000, you get just three grand more. That's not much to show for years of blood, sweat and tears. If you have to deduct taxes and an agent's commission, you'd probably be better off grilling burgers than writing books.

If you used a self-publishing company and somehow managed to sell 5,000 books, you might make more money than with a traditional publisher—but not as much as you could if you set up your own publishing company, did more work, and had your books printed by Lightning Source—the same printer that most self-publishing companies use—or CreateSpace.

With **Lulu**, the cost for one 5.5 by 8.5-inch paperback is $11.75, and up-front costs range from zero to $1369.

With **AuthorHouse**, the up-front charge ranges from $598 to $1198. The price includes ten "complimentary" books that you've already paid for. Your book can include up to ten graphic images without an extra charge. You'll also pay $170 for a copyright registration that you can get yourself for $35. Non-complimentary 200-page books will cost nearly $10 in 1-99 quantities.

With **Outskirts Press**, the initial charge for a publishing package ranges from $199 to $1099. You'll get up to ten "free" books that you actually paid for as part of the package.

If your book has a $19.95 cover price, you'll earn "royalties" of $1.05 to $3.05 per book shipped by the publisher to a bookseller or its customers. If you want to buy books yourself, you'll pay $6.98 to $8.98 per copy.

Outskirts says, "Unlike with other publishers, the price you pay as the author is unrelated to your retail price or to the number of copies you order." That does not seem to be true because their online pricing calculator does show a bit of a difference based on the cover price, and a bigger difference based on the price of the publishing package you choose.

Infinity Publishing will charge you at least $499 to publish a book, and more money if you want it edited, promoted or available at booksellers. If you want to buy copies of your own book you get a "discount" of 40 or 50% off the cover price. If you have them print a 250-page, 5.5×8.5-inch book, you'll pay $7.48 or $8.97 per book.

Lightning Source is the dominant on-demand printer, serving self-publishing companies, independent self publishers, and "traditional" publishing companies.

What you pay and what you keep with a 200-page $19.95-list book

	Traditional publisher	You plus Lightning Source	Lulu	Author House	Outskirts Press
Set-up fee	$0	$117*	$0** to $1369	$598 to $1198	$199 to $1099
What you keep on a book sold on Amazon	About $1.60, or less if you have an agent	About $12	About $4	About $4	$1.05 to $3.05
What you pay to buy a book	About $10	About $4	Up to $9.50	Up to $9.83***	About $7

Information may not be current. Shipping charges may be added, which can lower the profit when you order books to resell yourself. Lightning Source does not charge extra for shipping to booksellers' customers.

* Lightning's fee includes $37.50 for cover file, $37.50 for interior file, $30 for proof (delivered next day), plus $12 annual file maintenance.
**Zero-dollar figure from Lulu does not include printing any books.
***AuthorHouse book purchase price from *The Fine Print of Self-Publishing*.

IMPORTANT FACTS OF LIFE

◆Most writers love to write but few people get rich from writing (or from poker, painting or singing). Learn as much as you can about writing and publishing, and work as hard as you can to produce a fine book. But don't quit your day job and don't remortgage your house to finance your publishing.

◆Although a first book *can* be profitable, don't assume that your first *will* be profitable. Write your first book for the joy of it, or to impress your friends and family, or to change some minds, or as a learning experience or a business builder. Over months and years, as you improve your writing skills and learn more about the publishing business, the profits may come. If writing is not either fun or profitable or both—stop writing.

◆ Most books lose money—even those published by media giants with huge staffs of highly paid and experienced experts. Million-sellers are very rare in the book business. In self-publishing, thousand-sellers are very rare.

◆You'll probably see ads proclaiming "FREE PUBLISHING" and you'll also encounter publishing packages priced under $200. Here's the truth: ①No company will print and deliver a book for free. ②Unless you are prepared to spend $1,000 or more ($3,000 or more would be better), you probably won't get a high-quality book and will not be able to tell many potential readers that the book exists and convince them to buy it.

CHAPTER 12
What should you write?
What shouldn't you write?

Nonfiction generally outsells fiction in number of titles, but in most years the bestselling fiction books outsell the bestselling nonfiction books. About 44 million copies of *Harry Potter and the Deathly Hallows* have been sold. While some nonfiction such as *The Purpose Driven Life* have surpassed individual Potter titles, most nonfiction books sell in much smaller numbers. In nonfiction, pick a topic which people care about, that you can contribute something new about. If you write novels or poetry, write e-books—or write for love, not for money. It's been said that poets and novelists are interesting to talk to, but nonfiction writers have nicer homes.

◆Fiction and poetry are not *necessary* to readers. People who want to read a novel may be content to borrow a copy from a friend or the library instead of buying it—even if they have to wait a few weeks.

◆Fiction books are entertainment. That means they are options. They are *expendable* when money is tight; and they have to compete with movies, ball games, video games, music and more.

◆Novels may be read just once or twice. A nonfiction book, particularly an important reference, might be referred todozens or hundreds of times and be a vital part of a personal or business library.

◆Fiction is usually timeless. We still read the works of Dickens and Homer. Your new novel must compete with other books written centuries ago.

◆Nonfiction is usually information or instruction, and may have a limited lifespan before it becomes obsolete. Readers want the latest information. They may replace your book bought just a year or two ago with your new version—or a new competitor.

◆People will generally pay more money for information than for entertainment. The more important the information is, the more you can charge for it. However, the more people who are likely to be readers of your book, the more expensive it will be to reach them.

Obviously, if you are a self-publishing writer, you can publish anything you want to.

HOWEVER, if you want to make money rather than just fulfill a dream or impress your family or inflate your ego, it's better to think carefully about what you publish.

It's extremely difficult to sell many copies of self-published fiction or poetry—or the memoir of a non-famous person—on paper. In order to sell thousands of copies, you'll have to be either extremely lucky (not likely) or generate a huge amount of "buzz" through viral marketing, public relations and advertising (time-consuming and often expensive), or you'll have to impress one or more reviewers enough to praise you in the media (not likely). ➔It's easier for an unknown author to sell $1.99 e-books than $19.95 p-books (books printed on paper).

Another reason not to self-publish fiction (unless aimed at a narrow and easy-to-reach audience) is that most fiction is aimed at the mass market. You'll be competing with big publishing companies with much more experience, much bigger budgets and much better distribution than you have.

The world is not waiting for your novel, poetry or memoir to be published. If your book should appeal to "everyone," can you afford to let everyone know about it?

It's much easier to target a market and devise a promotional strategy for nonfiction. If you write a book for owners of small businesses, Little League coaches, obstetricians or pig farmers, it's much easier to target them with your marketing.

Novels, memoirs and poems depend on **push marketing**—you have to "push" books on a public that has no need for them.

On the other hand, if you write nonfiction about an interesting and important subject or—even better—a how-to book, you can use much simpler **pull marketing** and have a much greater chance of success.

➜ With pull marketing, you take advantage of an *existing desire* by the public to know more about a subject. Readers will "pull" the books from you.

Find a niche! People who want to know more about growing strawberries, raising an autistic child, getting a college scholarship, building a log cabin or traveling with a dog will search for that information on Google, Amazon.com, or elsewhere, and there's a good chance they'll find your book. (But finding your book doesn't necessarily mean they'll buy it.)

Timing is important. Sales of Jerome Corsi's book questioning President Obama's birthplace dropped to almost nothing because it was published shortly after Obama released his birth certificate to the public.

Pick a hot topic, and one that may stay hot, or at least warm, for a few years. Consider combining two hot topics such as "Gay weddings on a tight budget."

Pick something you know about, which you can contribute something new about, which lots of people care about, and which lots of people have not already written about. If there are other books on the same topic (and there probably are), make sure you have something important to add so your book can be better than its competition.

There's good news for self-help and Print-On-Demand ("POD"), bad news for novels.

According to book info authority Bowker, the most popular books in 2009 suggest that publishers were trying to give readers more resources for success in a bad economy.

"Changes in major publishing categories indicate that publishers expected the sluggish economy to continue its impact on consumer spending. Categories that grew tended to be in areas that could contribute to workplace knowledge and budgeting. For example, output increased in technology (+11%), science (+9%) and personal finance (+9%). The big category losers were in areas impacted by changes in discretionary spending. Cookery and language titles each declined 16% and travel continued its year-over-year decline, down 5% in 2009 (it took a 10% loss in 2008). **Fiction also saw a second year of decline**—down 15%."

"In contrast, there was another extraordinary year of growth in the number of "non-traditional" books in 2009. These books, marketed almost exclusively on the web, are largely on-demand titles produced by reprint houses specializing in public domain works and by presses catering to self-publishers and "micro-niche" publications. Bowker projects that 764,448 titles were produced that fall outside its traditional publishing and classification definitions. This number is a 181% increase over 2008—which doubled 2007's output."

Here's some potential bad news, and some advice:

- You may be fighting a losing battle, unless you are offering something unique.
- In many fields where people are looking for advice, you'll face a lot of competition, often from better-known experts with more money for promotion.
- Those who want to steal your audience and gobble up part of your lunch include other authors, magazine publishers, TV show producers, video makers and website operators.
- The Internet is usually more up-to-date than printed books. Timeliness is not a factor with all subjects, but it definitely makes some topics less suitable for books than they were in the past.
- Some of your competitors are giving away what you want to sell.
- Libraries can be competitors—not just customers.
- If you've put information online with websites and blogs that people can read for free, your book will be competing with your own free words. Make your book more complete than what you give away. Modify your online content to

plug your book and to point out that the printed book is better than the online freebie.

- It's important to investigate the competitive environment before you commit to publishing.
- If you go ahead, don't print lots of copies the first time. For test marketing, POD will give you a big advantage over a large offset print run.

And some good news and advice:

- Major retailers that sell few books or no books—such as Radio Shack, Bon-Ton and Kohl's—sell e-book readers. They expect e-books to become a big business. If you limit your books to paper, you will limit your sales. If you publish an e-book, you may have a competitive edge over a writer who publishes only on paper.
- e-books can be sold for *much* less than paper books and can make it easier for a novelist, poet or memoirist to build an audience and make some money.
- It's definitely possible to make money with self-published fiction—if you work hard. Amanda Hocking writes young-adult paranormal romances. In April 2010, she began self-publishing e-books and in less than a year reportedly sold more than one million copies! With nine books (mostly priced from 99 cents to $2.99), she earned $2,000,000. That's likely a first for a self-published writer, and impressive for *any* writer. Despite the huge income, she had enough of self-publishing, and accepted a $2,000,000, four-book contract with St. Martin's Press. Hocking said, "I do not want to spend 40 hours a week handling emails, formatting covers, finding editors, etc. Right now, being me is a full-time

corporation." Hocking says she became successful because of intensive online self-promotion, word of mouth and a popular genre—stories about vampires and trolls.

- Zoe Winters has excellent advice for fiction writers (and other writers) in her *Becoming an Indie Author: Smart Self-Publishing*. I read the Kindle e-book version—an informative bargain priced at just $3.99. The book is particularly useful for authors who want to produce e-books.

You can sell the same words more than once.

School kids know that they can modify the report on James Buchanan done in fifth grade and submit it again in sixth grade. In college, I used variations of the same term paper for courses in both American Culture and U.S. History. As a freelance writer, I often sold variations of the same article to multiple magazines with different audiences, such as *Rolling Stone* and *Country Music*, or *Esquire* and *Ingénue*.

It works the same way with books.

This book is one of three spinoffs of my *Become a Real Self-Publisher*, and includes material from that book. This book has led to additional spinoffs.

All of these books include material originally posted on my blogs, and some material written for my books eventually shows up on my blogs. Recycle, reuse, repurpose, revise, sequelize, serialize.

GIVE THE PEOPLE WHAT THEY WANT

Readers like to read different forms of books. People who prefer paper pages may want a paperback or a hardcover, or may want to give a hardcover as a gift.

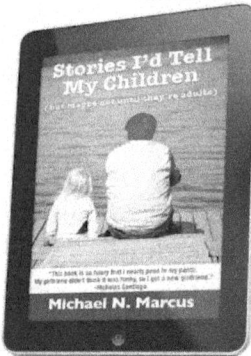

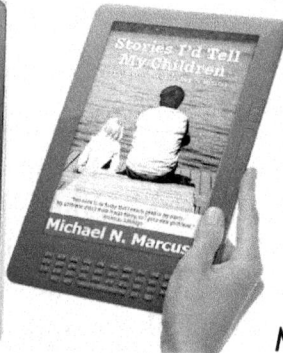

People who prefer e-books, may prefer to read on an iPad, Kindle, Nook, Sony Reader or a PC.

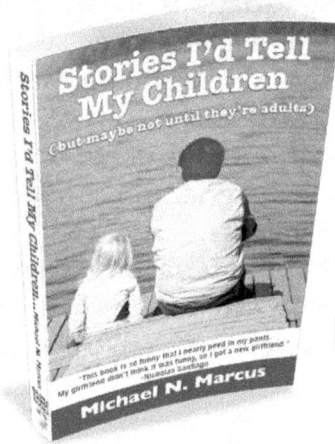

Many people like to listen to audio books, or need books with large print.

If your book is not available in multiple formats, you may lose business.

CHAPTER 13
How much should you write?

The UN's Educational, Scientific and Cultural Organization declared 49 pages to be the *minimum* length for a book. A publication with fewer pages can be a leaflet, pamphlet, booklet or brochure. Call it a book, and you risk offending nearly 200 nations. The *maximum* page number is determined by printing equipment and how much people are willing to pay, carry and read.

Despite the UNESCO decree, no book has 49 pages. Books have an even number of pages even if some pages don't have numbers on them. An individual piece of paper in a book is called a *leaf*. Each leaf has two sides, called pages. A 100-page book contains 50 leafs. Or leaves.

Publishers don't have to obey the United Nations. Outskirts Press can make "books" with as few as 18 pages. Most publishers can produce books with as many as 1,000 pages.

With nonfiction, you need to have enough pages to cover your topic adequately. Don't skimp, or pad. The book should not be so big that it will be priced a lot higher than its competitors or seem like "too much to read." It should not be so short that it seems incomplete, or doesn't offer value for its cost.

The cost of each additional page is insignificant. There is a prejudice against very thin books, so try for a minimum of about 120 pages. Thin books just don't seem like real books.

Novels can be much longer than nonfiction. Tolstoy's *War and Peace* is about 1300 pages long.

➔ Strangely, the price you pay for a publishing package does not usually vary with the number of pages in the book. However, the page count *will* affect the selling price, and your "wholesale" price.

When dealing with editors, you'll find two parallel systems for discussing book length: **page count** and **word count**. It's important to be able to make the transition back and forth.

A book's page count is not certain until it is formatted. Many factors determine how many words will fit in a book with a specific number of pages, including page size, type size, line spacing, margins, indentations, headers and footers, number and size of illustrations, front and back matter, etc.
An 8.5×11-inch page holds about twice as many words as a 6×9-inch page (the size used for this book). A 200-page manuscript can yield a 400-page book (with no graphics), and have about 100,000 words. This book has about 96,000 words and its Word file size is about 13MB.

About how many words will fit where?		
	8.5X11-inch page. 1-inch margins.	6X9-inch page. 1-inch margins.
11-pt Times New Roman	745	360
12-pt Times New Roman	630	310
11-pt Constantia	660	315
12-pt Constantia	570	275

CHAPTER 14
What should you name your baby?

Every book needs a title. Many book titles are cliché phrases which seem to be absolutely perfect for a particular book. Unfortunately, many cliché phrases are absolutely perfect for *lots* of books, and the title of a book can't be copyrighted.

Both Danielle Steel and Queen Noor of Jordan wrote books called *Leap of Faith*. At least five books are titled *Fatal Voyage*. At least four books, two songs and a movie are named *Continental Drift*. At least 24 books are titled *Unfinished Business*. You can write books with those titles, too.

If your name is Harold Gordon, you could write and publish *The Autobiography of Harold Gordon*. There is nothing to stop an unknown author—or Danielle Steel—from writing a book with the same title. Danielle could also write *The Autobiography of Barack Obama*.

If you want to call your next masterpiece *Holy Bible*, *Hamlet*, *War and Peace*, *From Russia with Love* or *The Da Vinci Code*, you can. You might get sued. You might win, but it won't be a pleasant experience. You'll probably also confuse and annoy a lot of people—so try to come up with something original.

⬆More than a dozen different books are titled *Caught in the Middle*. If you like the title, you can use it, too. You can even use it for several different books.

An identifying term in a book series *can* be trademarked. If you publish *The Complete Idiot's Guide to Harry Potter,* you'll probably be sued by *two* publishing companies, and lose twice.

If you're writing a nonfiction book, the subject will suggest the book's title. The subject has to be *in* the title to attract browsers in stores if your books are sold there. ➔The subject-in-title is also critical for online shoppers searching for keywords or key phrases in search engines or on websites.

Assuming the core of your title is something like "auto repair" or "sailing," you need just a few words to fill it out. Some typical phrases are "how to," "plan for," and "buyers guide." Try this handy **Title Generator Table** to get started. Pick one item from each column:

30 Days to Better	Gambling	Profits
Insider Secrets of	Hollywood	Sex
Save Big on	Solar-Power	Investments
World's Greatest	Auto Repair	Secrets
The Truth About	Wall Street	Fraud
Become an Expert on	Pentagon	Negotiations

Any of those titles should make it very clear what your book is about, and—except for the sex—would also be boring and forgettable. Try to inject a little bit of humor, whimsy, mystery or novelty. Find *something* that will separate your book from competitors' books without hiding its subject. ➜ Strive for a title that explains the book's benefits and the problems it solves.

Come up with about a dozen possible titles. Print them up in big type, one title per page. Hang them on the wall. Stare at them. Within a few minutes, you'll likely eliminate a third of them. When you get down to about four finalists, make mockups of book covers, actual size, with your name, a subtitle if you have one, and some kind of suitable illustration.

➜➜➜ The subtitle gives you a second chance to sell your book. It's very important online, and in stores. Pick a good one.

➜ Try multiple versions with minor differences, even just changing or dropping a word. Sometimes substituting a shorter word will mean that your title can take up two lines instead of three, so you can use bigger type or a bigger cover photo.

You can hang the mockups on the wall if you like, but I prefer to wrap them around an actual book and live with them.

Hold each one up and look at it from various angles.

Maybe try different typefaces, line breaks and subtitles.

After a while, you'll probably come down to two leading contenders. It's time to gather a "focus group."

Ask five or ten people for their opinions. They don't have to be experts in marketing, graphic design or publishing—just people who can read and whose judgment you respect. You don't have to gather them all in one place at one time. You can simply carry the mockups with you and ask people when you have a chance. Try not to accept "I just don't like it" as a response. You want to discover the *reasons* behind reactions.

Watch out for reactions that indicate that people don't understand what you are trying to say, or if they have a complete misinterpretation. Have a "clear title" before you start publicity and printing.

➔Pick words that sound good together. People like and remember alliterations. If your title uses the name of a fictional character, pick a name that will help your book. *Saving Silverman* beats *Saving Berkowitz. The Great Gatsby* beats *The Great Murphy*. Avoid awkward word combinations like "and end," "usually use" and "be because" on and in the book.

As soon as you have your title finalized, get it on your website and tell the cover designer to get to work.

Even if you have six months of writing and editing ahead of you, looking at the cover makes the book more real and should keep you focused and working toward completion.

Additionally, the cover may influence your writing; and your writing may suggest changes in your cover, or even your title. Let the inside and the outside of your book evolve simultaneously and interactively.

Book title generation trick

Look for a word that's **within** a word, like Inter**MEDIA**ry, Re**CYCLE**, Psycho**PATH**, Trans**PARENT** or **CONNECT**icut.

What should you name your baby?

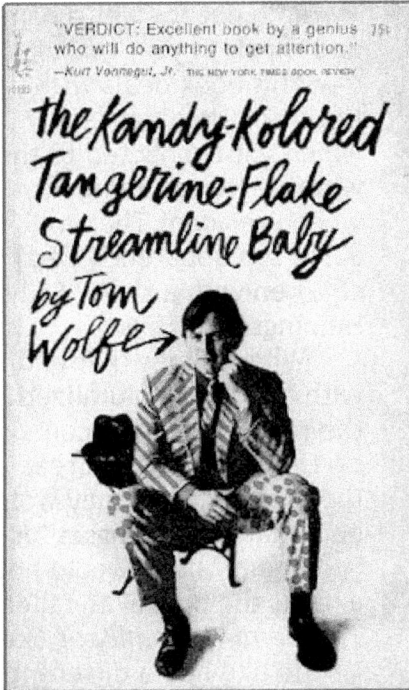

"VERDICT: Excellent book by a genius who will do anything to get attention."
—*Kurt Vonnegut, Jr.* THE NEW YORK TIMES BOOK REVIEW

the Kandy-Kolored Tangerine-Flake Streamline Baby by Tom Wolfe→

Unlike nonfiction, key-words don't matter for fiction, humor or poetry titles. You just want something distinctive and memorable.

Short is often better than long. F. Scott Fitzgerald's *The Great Gatsby* is a great short title.

←Tom Wolfe's *The Kandy-Kolored Tangerine-Flake Streamline Baby* is a great long title.

Nigel Tomm may be the long-title champ. One of his titles has 670 words.

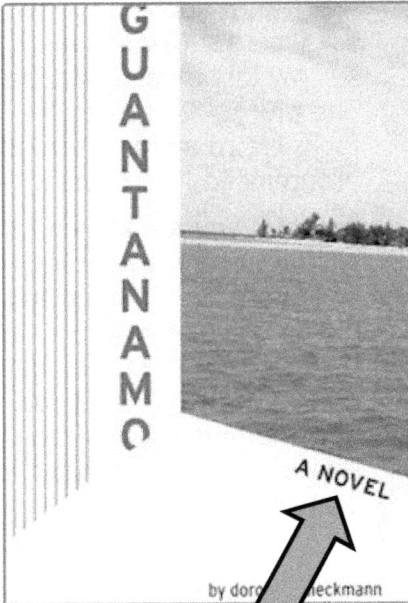

GUANTANAMO

A NOVEL

by dor...eckmann

NO!

⊘**WARNING.** If you write a novel and you put "a novel" on the cover, I may buy a copy just so I can hit you over the head with it. Dickens didn't need the label for *A Tale of Two Cities*, and Hemingway didn't need it for *The Sun Also Rises*. Find another way to let people know that your book is fiction.

THE
HEMINGSES
of
MONTICELLO

AN AMERICAN FAMILY

ANNETTE GORDON-REED

#1 BESTSELLER
STEPHEN
KING

DESPERATION

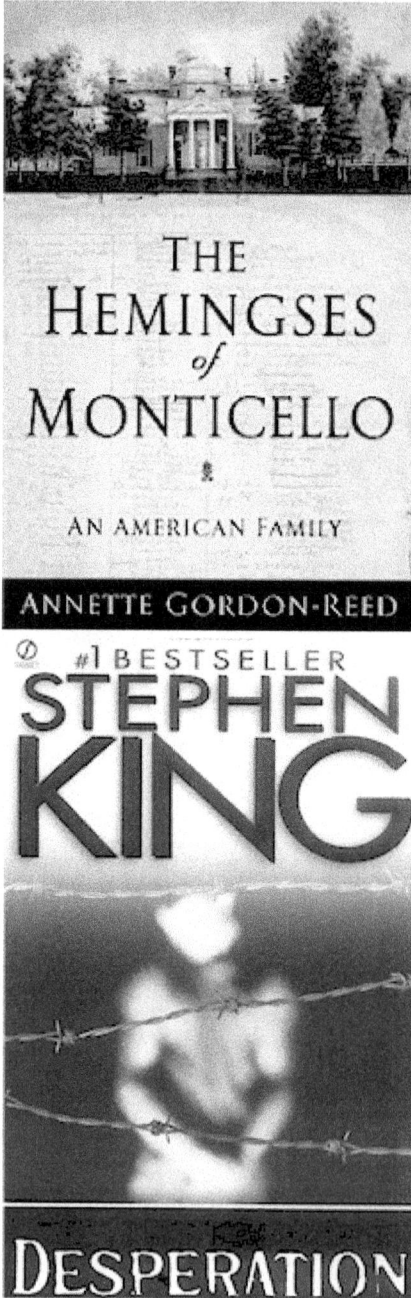

←Watch out for weird names and words in your book title.

This book deals with the black Hemings family which got connected to the white Jefferson family, when President Thomas Jefferson apparently had children with a slave, Sally Hemings.

When names that end with an "s" are pluralized, the result can be disconcerting. Until people read the subtitle, they may wonder what a "Hemingses" is.

The problem would not exist if the book was called *The Hemings Family of Monticello* and had a different subtitle. A book about "buses" would suffer similarly.

My last name is Marcus. The plural, "Marcuses," looks weird and is often mispronounced "Marcooses."

←Unless you are known for writing, conning people out of billions, or winning Olympic medals, keep your name a lot smaller than the book's title. Later on, when you become famous, you can revise the covers of your earlier books.

◀I heard a stimulating interview on NPR with Colin Ellard. He's the author of *Where Am I?: Why We Can Find Our Way to the Moon but Get Lost in the Mall.* The simple three-word title, splayed in the cross hairs of a stark urban scene, seems like the plea of someone who is distraught or deranged. In actuality, the book is a quite rational and interesting discussion of the navigational abilities of human beings and other creatures. The subtitle explains the subject much better than the title does. If your title doesn't work alone, you might need a new title. Sometimes a title and a subtitle can be switched, or a new title can combine elements of both.

◀Whoopi Goldberg is both funny and smart. Her book's title, *Book,* is only slightly funny, and not at all smart. It provides no indication of the subject ("Whoopi!" might have been a better title). A Google search for "book" shows over ONE BILLION links. Most are *not* for Whoopi's book.

Design Tip 🖰

Captions in this section use 11.5-pt type and are flush-left, instead of my normal 12-pt justified type. If you use justified type in a narrow column, you may get very ugly word spacing.

Should you announce your new book's title before it's published?

Some people think it's bad luck to tell people about a pregnancy before the baby is born. Others start blabbing and buying baby clothes on the day after conception.

There is similar disagreement about announcing a book's title long in advance. You may think that you should keep your title secret so nobody copies your idea. But the loss of advance publicity and the delay in moving up through search engine rankings is probably worse than helping a twin title.

If you think you have a hot title, try to publish fast, and maybe your book will be on sale before another one with the same title. One possibly bright note: if another book has the same title but better publicity, people searching for that book may find your book by accident and buy it.

CHAPTER 15
Marketing your books

It may seem strange to discuss marketing before I try to help you write a book. In reality, it makes sense to have a marketing plan, or at least a marketing idea, before you start to write. It's foolish to expend blood, sweat, tears, months and dollars to produce a book and later realize that there is no way to sell it; or that no one wants to buy it. You have to start thinking as a business-owner, not only as a writer. If you rely on a self-publishing company to do all of the marketing for you, you will likely be disappointed.

Years ago, if my mother said she was "going marketing," I knew she was going to come home with her car trunk filled with food, paper towels, detergent and other household supplies. To Mom, marketing was *buying*. For book publishers and authors, marketing is *selling*.

It's not the specific transaction of handing or sending someone a book after they hand you cash or a credit card or place an order online. It's really all of the steps that go *before* the transaction when a book is exchanged for money. Marketing is the process of making people aware of what you want to sell them, and then convincing them to buy it.

The first step in marketing, or in a marketing plan, is to identify your customers and your potential competitors. The more precisely you can define the customers, the more efficient your marketing will probably be. The bigger your potential audience, the bigger your potential income—and the bigger the cost of reaching readers.

Book marketing has a lot in common with the marketing of other products, but it's also very different.

◆Unlike food, books are not consumed and then replaced with identical items. ◆Unlike clothing, books are not outgrown and replaced with a larger size. ◆Unlike tires, books are not replaced because they've worn out. ◆Unlike handkerchiefs, books are not purchased in packs of a dozen identical items. ◆Unlike cars, books aren't sold to each adult in the family. ◆Unlike videogames, older books are seldom traded in for newer ones. ◆Unlike televisions, books are seldom returned after people try them and find they don't like them. ◆Unlike wrenches, the same books are not bought in different sizes.

For all of its differences, never forget that a book *is* a product. It's not bleach, pizza, or a hotel, but the fundamentals of marketing *do* apply to books.

The most fundamental fundamental is that you must develop a desirable product with an appropriate price and identifiable customers.

If you're writing a dictionary, your potential customers are all of the people in the world who can read—or are trying to learn—the language you are publishing in. Your potential market may be many millions of people, and your potential competitors probably number in the hundreds.

If your book is about your not-so-famous mother, you probably have no competitors covering the same subject, and your potential market may be eight people. Or two people.

Most books fall somewhere in between. Books intended to help fisherman, amateur mechanics and corn growers probably have potential markets in the tens or even hundreds of thousands—and dozens of competitors. Unless you are writing in a very new field, you are likely to face competition from existing books as well as books that are "in the pipeline."

In book publishing, your customers are not just potential readers. You have to court, impress and convince potential "partners." Your partners include booksellers, librarians and a wide range of influencers. Traditionally the primary influencers were book reviewers working for printed newspapers and magazines. Today, many newspapers no longer review books, and magazines are disappearing. In their place is a constantly growing group of online influencers on blogs, websites and social media such as Facebook. You have thousands of potential allies who can recommend your book—or condemn it. My own **BookMakingBlog.blogspot.com** both praises and slams books about writing and publishing.

➜ By being a self-published author you have some distinct advantages over an author who's using a traditional publisher. *You* get to decide how much to spend, when to spend, where to spend, and how long to keep spending. Many publishers spend a book's entire marketing budget in the few months before and after the publication date. You can promote as long as you want to—and can afford to.

Many of today's book buyers seldom or never enter traditional bricks-and-mortar bookstores. As with sneakers, cellphones and vacations, a growing portion of books is sold online. This means that your book must be available at the big Internet booksellers, especially Amazon and Barnes & Noble.

Fortunately, your book will be there and on dozens of other bookselling websites merely by having your books printed by Lightning Source, which prints for most self-publishing companies. If you use CreateSpace, your books have automatic entry to its parent, Amazon.com, but may not be sold by Amazon's competitors unless you choose a specific service. If you use other printers or publishers, you may have to do no work, a little work or a lot of work to get your books sold online.

Offline advertising is probably a waste of money

"Shotgun" offline ads, aimed at a huge mass-media audience are so expensive that they should be avoided unless you have a lot of money to burn. Some publishers will include your book, along with other books, in tiny ads in the *New York Times* Sunday book review section or the *New York Review of Books*. They are wasting your money.

A website (see next chapter) is vital for running most businesses in the 21st century. Self-publishing—even with one employee and zero profits—is very much a business.

Keyword-based online ads, such as Google's AdWords, are great for driving potential book buyers to your website or to sites that sell your book. Unlike a mass of shotgun pellets, they are like aiming one bullet at a single, nearby target.

Obama Biography Book
Low Prices on Obama biography book
Free 2-Day Shipping w/ Amazon Prime
www.Amazon.com/Books

Because the ads should be seen only by people who are searching for specific subjects that your book deals with, they can provide a lot of website traffic for a few cents to a few dollars per mouse click.

The bottom line is not the last word

Your publishing expenses don't end when you've paid the bills from your printer or publishing company and independent service providers. Unless you have money to market your book—to let the appropriate people know that it exists and why they should buy it—all of the time and money you already spent has probably been wasted. You should never stop marketing your book.

Technology has lowered some costs considerably. At one time, it could have cost thousands of dollars to print and mail press releases (more later). Now it's done by email. You can either do all of the work yourself or pay several hundred dollars for professional distribution. There are even some companies that will email your press releases for nothing. Their value is often equal to their cost (i.e., zero value). ➜Writers who spend nothing on press releases usually receive nothing.

If you expect your book to be reviewed (more later), you have to send out books to be reviewed. You could spend $10,000 to send out 1,000 books, or spend nothing to send out emails offering to send review copies.

A book that's been requested is more likely to be reviewed than one that just shows up. You can even mark your packages something like, "Review Copy, Per Request" to help keep them out of the Dumpster. The number of potential reviewers varies with the nature of your book, but you should probably budget for between a dozen and a hundred, or even more.

Develop a specialty and become an authority

Although I had no plans to do so, I've developed specialties in telecommunications (five books) and publishing, (over a dozen books). When you have several related books, you can promote the group, each book can help sell the others, and you can position yourself as an authority on a subject for lectures, media appearances, etc.

Your marketing timetable

If you don't start marketing until your books have been printed, you've waited much too long.

➜Start marketing as soon as you have a subject and a tentative title. On the day I approved one book for printing, it had

669 search links on Google, 66 on Bing, 79 on Yahoo, and 10 on Excite. Those links were in place, *waiting for my book to exist*.

If you write a blog or have a website in a field that's related to your book topic, show a mockup of the cover and tell a bit about the book.

As you get closer to publication date and your ideas about the book get more concrete, you can say more about it.

- You can build an email list to inform prospective customers when it's time to place orders and maybe to offer a discount for early orders or prepayments. There are services to handle your email promotional programs, such as **www.Aweber.com**. Prices start at under $200 per year for 500 subscribers.
- You can promise an autograph to the first hundred purchasers.
- You can use Facebook and Twitter to announce milestones like completion of 25%, 50%, and 75%, or the selection of the final cover or getting back the manuscript from the editor.

➜ Don't merely expect people to find your words online. Be active, not passive. Send out press releases. Send out *Advance Review Copies* to reviewers. Notify librarians, trade associations, bloggers, columnists, news editors, reporters and stores.

Once the book has been published and you start to get some reviews, let the world know what the reviewers have said. If you win an award, that's news, too. So is a new format, such as an e-book or audiobook. Any time you can come up with a reason to talk about your book, you have an opportunity to sell some copies.

Watch your book's progress

Sign-up for free Google Alerts, using your book titles and your name at **www.google.com/alerts**. Depending on your choice, you'll receive immediate, daily or weekly emails whenever your title or name is noticed by the Google bots.

This is a great way to find reviews, mentions in blogs, on-line forums and groups, and new sellers which have started offering your book.

Make your name a brand name

Any writer who expects to write more than one book, blog or article hopes that people who like one thing he or she has written will want to read more.

One good way to help people to find your work is to have a distinctive name, like actors and singers.

Jor-El, Superman's Kryptonian father's name, is unique and distinctive. So is the name of **Marlon Brando** (at left, in 1951), who played the part. Marlon Brando was his birth name.

Marion Morrison was less fortunate. He had to change his name to become **John "Duke" Wayne**.

Stephen King's name is not unique or distinctive. But, after selling perhaps 300 million books, he probably doesn't suffer from the existence of others with the same name. (Wikipedia listed about a dozen, including a Congressman, a pedophile and five athletes.)

What about a pen name?

It's not unusual for a writer to use a pen name (*nom de plume* in French). **Mark Twain** is probably the most famous fake. Twain's real name was Samuel Langhorne Clemens, but he also used **Sieur Louis de Conte**.

There are many reasons for using a pen name:

- To make the author's name more distinctive, more glamorous or more interesting
- To disguise the author's gender
- To protect the author from retribution, especially if the book is an exposé
- To avoid confusion with other authors or famous people
- To hide ethnicity or alter apparent ethnicity
- To develop different personas for different genres such as fiction and nonfiction, or chick lit and sci-fi
- To have a name more appropriate to a genre (male western writer **Zane Grey** was born Pearl Zane Gray).
- To avoid overexposure by having too many books on sale at one time
- To avoid embarrassment, such as when a professor writes porn, or to shield the author's family from revelations of an unconventional or illegal past
- To avoid confusion if your name is hard to spell, remember, pronounce or seems too "foreign" or "ethnic." Author **Irving Wallace** was born a Wallechinsky.
- To eliminate the possibility that the book could jeopardize your success in another field

Scott Lorenz, who provides marketing and PR at Westwind Communications (**www.westwindcos.com/book**), suggests some reasons for using your own name on your books:

- If you are not trying to hide from anyone
- To brand your name for speaking gigs or consulting

- So people you know can find your books
- To build trust and confidence with readers
- To use your real-life expertise to validate the contents of your books

If you have a bland name like "Arthur Williams," you might be more easily found and better remembered if you change to **Hamburger Williams** or **Xavier Nguyen Bacciagalupe** III.

English punk rocker Declan MacManus morphed into a more-memorable **Elvis Costello**.

Don Novello wrote books as **Lazlo Toth**, and appeared on TV as **Father Guido Sarducci**. Punk-rock bass player **Sid Vicious** was born John Ritchie. **Cher** was Cherilyn Sarkisian.

Sometimes just a slight change can do the job. **F. Scott Fitzgerald** is probably a better choice than Francis or Frankie Fitzgerald. Bill Smith might be better remembered as **William Harrington Smith** or **Billy D. Smith**. **Edward Jay Epstein** has written more than a dozen books, perhaps with more success than hundreds of ordinary Ed Epsteins.

For my own brand, I've chosen to include my middle initial, "N." A Google search for **Michael N. Marcus** shows over 150,000 links—and most are for me. Apparently there are just two of us. I'm the writer. He's a psychiatrist.

If you are evaluating potential alternate names or just want some fun, take a look at **www.WhitePages.com**. It ranks name popularity based on listed phone numbers.

When I checked, "Edward Epstein" was the #254,818-ranked full name, with 123 occurrences. On the other hand, **Juan Epstein**, from *Welcome Back, Kotter*, is unique, with just one listed person in the United States. It may not be a real name. Maybe Juan's real name is Xavier Nguyen Bacciagalupe III, or Sally Smith.

Welcome to Brooklyn

Inexpensive book promos: viral marketing, book cover business cards, autographs, spouses, etc.

In addition to sending press releases to media and soliciting reviews, I use "viral marketing" to build sales for my books.

Viral marketing uses social relationships to produce marketing objectives (such as sales) through viral links, like the spread of human and computer viruses. At its simplest, it can be word-of-mouth, delivered in person, and is often enhanced by the Internet, such as through "friends" on Facebook.com.

For my first self-pubbed book, I sent free copies to about 50 people (friends, relatives, business associates and people mentioned in the book) whom I thought would like the book and would likely recommend it to others. In the book was a one-page note, explaining what the book is about and asking them to recommend it to others who might enjoy it. I also asked them to post a five-star review on Amazon.com.

In addition to the note, each book contained about a dozen promotional cards that showed the book cover on the front. The back of the card shows the name of my publishing company, its web address, some complimentary blurbs, and "Order from Amazon.com."

My wife and I carry book cards to give to possible "customers." Marilyn has turned out to be an excellent salesperson. She even "sold" a book to our dentist. He asked me to autograph it when I had my teeth cleaned. My podiatrist, on the other hand, asked for an autographed *freebie*. I gave it to him.

♦**TV and radio interviews may be a big waste of time and money** because only a small percentage of listeners and viewers will be interested in your subject, and only a tiny percentage of them will remember your name or your title long enough to order it. Print and web interviews can be much more productive. However, if there is a talk show that deals with your subject, let the producer or host know that you are an expert who's available to answer questions from viewers and listeners. This can work for newspapers and magazines, too.

◆**You can place free ads on www.Craigslist.com** to direct people to your own website or to web pages that sell your books. Put the ads in appropriate sections such as pets, furniture, boats or bikes. You can also mention your books on Craigslist forums.

Autograph Advice

Autographs go on the title page; so design the page to provide "white space" for an autograph. Don't sign just your name. Try to write something personal that relates to the book, or to the person receiving it, or both. For my books about telecommunications, I often write, "I hope you never get a wrong number." When I give my funny books to doctors, I write, "Laughter is the best medicine."

◆I personally have never been an autograph collector, but I do have a few autographed books on my shelves which I got by accident. Lots of people *do* like autographs, to prove or imply that they were once in the same place as a famous person. If readers put you in the same category as Mickey Mantle, Marilyn Monroe or John Lennon, play along with it—no matter how much your wrist hurts.

If you are selling your books from your own website, competing with other booksellers that underprice you, you may be able to justify your price by including your signature and a personalized greeting.

◆**If you write books, you must be prepared to sell them.** Self-publishing is not for the bashful or meek. If you're not confident enough to talk about your book and yourself, you'll have to hire someone else to do it for you. The self-publishing companies offer various marketing programs, but your company may not do all that needs to be done and may pressure you to spend more money on marketing.

◆**Every person you encounter is a potential customer.** Even if you hire experts to toot your horn for you, you'll miss potential sales if you are too shy to toot to or talk to strangers. Don't be overbearing, abrasive or obnoxious. But there is often an opportunity to work your book into a conversation, even with the person ahead of you at the post office or next to you on a plane. If she seems interested, give her a card or two with your book cover and ordering information.

◆**You can get custom postage stamps** which show your book cover from Zazzle or others. They probably won't sell many books, but they may impress some of your relatives.

◆**Set up a Google alert** to notify you when appropriate topics show up on blogs or elsewhere. Post an impressive comment, identify yourself as "author of . . ." and include a link to your page on Amazon or another sales site.

◆**Buy or make simple counter-top displays** which can be put in friendly businesses (hair salon, paint store, restaurant etc.) Put several books on the display with your cards or bookmarks. A good source of attractive, inexpensive displays is **www.BookDisplays.com**. Tell store employees about the book and try to get them to tell customers about it. Give autographed freebies to employees.

◆ **Each book of yours can help sell the others.** In the front of this book is a list of my other books, and in the back I show some book covers and tell where the books can be ordered.

◆**Mention your book in the signature of your emails**, including a website address for ordering.

◆**Write a blog**. If you are perceived as an expert in some field, or even if you are merely entertaining, you can build a following of readers who may buy books. I like **www.blogger.com**. It's free. Create new "posts" often—at least twice a week. After a while you can rerun older posts if you lack inspiration to write something new. The blog should show your book, say something about it and provide a link for ordering it.

◆**Get a T-shirt with your book cover on the front** (from VistaPrint or Zazzle) and become a walking and talking billboard.

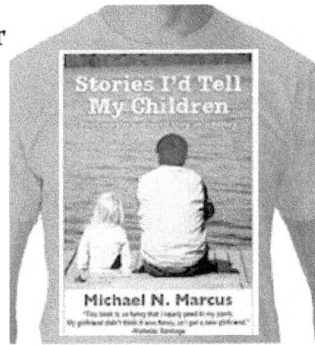

Stories I'd Tell
My Children

Michael N. Marcus

◆**If you're active on Facebook or other online communities, let your contacts know about your book**. Put the book cover on your page. Announce your 1,000th sale, your book's becoming available at a new bookseller or in a different country, a good review from someone important, etc. You can even "tweet" about your book on Twitter. Of course, none of these techniques will accomplish anything unless you can create and grow a group of followers who care about you.

◆**Have a book launch party.** Invite friends, neighbors, business associates, politicians and reporters. It can be at your home, a restaurant, a hotel, a club, a bookstore or a library. Serve refreshments, make a brief speech and read part of the book. Some authors sell books at launches. I think it's tacky to make friends feel obligated to spend money. A few years ago, a neighbor gave a book launch party. My wife felt obligated to support her and spent $25 to buy a book that neither of us will ever read. **Give books away if you can afford to.** They'll probably cost you only a few bucks each and will help create buzz. You can even make inexpensive samplers with a few chapters, blurbs, an introduction and the table of contents. Give out bookmarks or business cards, too.

◆ If you distributed pre-publication copies to gather blurbs and comments, **make sure everyone you quote in the book gets a copy** with an autographed thank-you. If non-blurbing experts or other authors are quoted, send them autographed copies, also.

◆ **Make a "preview edition" for distribution as inexpensive or free e-books.** For one of my books which sells for $15.95, I offer a sampler e-book for $1.99. It's distributed by Lulu, and can be read on a PC, Mac, e-book reader, smartphone or iPad. I selected chapters that I thought would appeal to a specific audience, and promoted the sampler to those people.

◆ **Have a powerful platform.** "Platform" is a major buzzword in current publishing. It's not the same as a political party's platform. Think of it as a metaphor for a structure that will boost you up and *make you visible* to potential readers, sources of publicity and bookstore buyers. Components in your platform include websites, blogs, business connections, social media, radio and TV appearances, quotes in media, online mentions, speeches, articles, friends, neighbors, etc. Your first book is part of your platform and should help sell your later books.

◆ **Either make your own** *sell-sheets* **or get them from your publisher.** A sell-sheet is a one-page flier, describing and promoting a new book, aimed at booksellers, libraries, distributors and the media. Use glossy paper, a color photo of the book cover and author, and include contact info.

CHAPTER 16
Your website

I t's extremely important to have a website to provide information about you and your books. It's neither difficult nor expensive to build and maintain a website. Most self-publishing companies can provide basic websites for their authors. You may pay less and even get better results if you do your own, or pay someone else to do it. If you don't have a website, you are missing a major opportunity to impress and interact with potential readers. Readers and reviewers expect authors to have websites. Don't disappoint them.

You can develop a website for zero dollars and no cents in less than an hour, and pay less than $5 per month to a "hosting company" to make the site available to the world.

Prices at 1&1 and GoDaddy can be as low as $3.99 per month. I use Network Solutions, which has plans starting at $6.64 per month, and Yahoo ($6.47 per month for the first three months, and then $9.95 per month).

Free hosting is available from dozens of companies, but they're generally not a good idea because you'll get a long, clumsy, ugly, amateur-sounding URL ("Uniform Resource Locator" or web address) like
http://billsbook.74.nrk4697.freehost123.us
instead of **www.billsbook.com**.

You may want to do a website for a specific book title, or one that covers several books, or one for you as an author, or several sites. My sites include **www.SilverSandsBooks.com, www.Self-Pub.info** and **www.MichaelMarc.us**.

The more websites you have, the more likely it is that people will find you and the more opportunities you will have to sell books. Your site or sites should have information that will be useful and interesting to potential readers, as well as to members of the media.

Many book websites include an "online press kit" that replaces the once-common cardboard portfolio. At a minimum, the kit (which is really a page or a section of a website) should include a news release ("press release") about the book, plus photos of the cover and the author and a brief author's biography.

Some book websites sell books. Mine don't. They have links to Amazon.com and Barnes & Noble, which sell my books. I want to write and promote books, not operate a warehouse and shipping department. I make money when someone follows a link and buys a book. It's easy money.

Obviously, your website should inform people what your book is about and try to convince them why it is vital that they buy it. The site is a good place to post reviews and comments from readers, reviewers and previewers, and to note awards the book has won. You can also show your table of contents and some excerpts to get people interested.

You don't need any special talent, experience or training to put a website together. Most hosting companies offer adequate and attractive templates which you can use as-is or modify if you want to. They are WYSIWYG (What You See Is What You Get) and allow you to get online in a few minutes—but you may spend the rest of your life updating and fine-tuning.

If you have stronger creative impulses, you can design a website from scratch using such software as Microsoft Front-Page (discontinued, but still useful), Adobe's DreamWeaver, and Microsoft's Expression Web and SharePoint Designer.

There are books and businesses that specialize in SEO (*search engine optimization*), the process of getting a website into a top position in Google, Bing, Excite, Yahoo and lesser search engines. The SEO experts charge for their services, but I'll gladly give you some free tips based on personal experience.

◆People search for "keywords" and it's important that your book website include all relevant keywords, used as often as possible, without seeming obvious, artificial or awkward.

Keep in mind that many potential readers don't know that your book exists, but may simply be searching for information about buying or using a product. If you have a book about bicycles or amateur beer making, you want to attract people who are shopping for bikes or hops or need advice about fixing a flat or deciding on dry vs. liquid yeast.

A keyword may actually be a phrase, not just a single word. If you think that people will be searching for "dirt bike" or "comfort bike," and those phrases are appropriate for your book, they belong in your website, too.

♦Google's legendary *algorithm* that determines a website's position has been subject to much speculation, and it's protected as carefully as the formula for making Coca-Cola.

One key ingredient in Google ranking is the number of *inbound links* to a website. Google assumes that the more sites that link to a particular site, the better that site is, and the higher it deserves to be in the Google list. Google interprets a link from Susan's website to Charlie's website as a vote by Susan in favor of Charlie.

You should create inbound links in any *legitimate* way you can. If you post a comment in an online forum, put your website address in it. If you're listed in Linkedin or active in Facebook and other social networks, promote your website there. Every email you send can list your site, and, of course, the web address belongs on your business cards and letterheads. If you have multiple websites, each one should promote the others. You can also ask the operators of other compatible but not competing websites to exchange links with you.

There are lots of schemes for getting other sites to link to yours, but some businesses do very well simply by having a good site with useful information presented in a pleasant way.

To judge your progress, you can use websites such as **www.WhoLinksToMe.com**. These are the results for one of my websites: Google PageRank: 4. Google Links: 54. Yahoo Links: 2,940. Bing Related: 309.

◆Older sites tend to rank higher than newer ones. Even if your book won't be out for a year, get a preview online right away so you can gradually make your way upward in the lists.

◆Never get a URL with a hyphen in it, unless the hyphen is part of a term like **www.self-pub.info**.

◆Short URLs are better than long ones.

◆Avoid long URLs with a high potential for misspelling, like **www.GetConstipationRelief.com.**

◆Encourage comments from site visitors.

◆Track your traffic ("hits"). If few people visit your site, maybe you don't have enough of the proper keywords or maybe you chose the wrong subject to write about.

◆Use search engines to find what people are saying about you or your book. If you find an error, try to correct it.

◆While URLs can end in a variety of ways, including the ubiquitous dot-com, as well as dot-net, dot-USA, dot-CA, dot-TV and others, it's generally best to use dot-com. If your website is DavidsBook.<u>net</u>, many people will go to DavidsBook.<u>com</u>. They may find nothing—or a competitor. An informational website can logically use a dot-info URL. I have a few of them.

◆I spelled the sample URL as <u>D</u>avids<u>B</u>ook.com. The web doesn't care about uppercase and lowercase (and neither does the email system), but by spelling your URL with uppercase letters where new words start, you make the URL easier to read, remember and type.

◆Avoid URLs with consecutive identical letters such as **www.whattoeat.com**. They can confuse potential customers and cost you business because people may think you were being cute and you chose to spell it as "whatoeat," or they'll just mistype.

◆Avoid URLs with ambiguous word breaks where it's not obvious which word a letter belongs to. These URLs can confuse potential customers and might cost you business. Whenever I see **www.releaseyourwriting.com**, I automatically pronounce it as "**releasey our writing**," not "**release your writing.**"

◆Resist the temptation to use the dot-net version of a URL that's already in use as a dot-com.

◆While it's been said that all of the good URLs have been taken, your book name should be unique, so you have a pretty good chance of getting it as a URL. If you want a URL with your personal name in it, you may face some competition.

◆Pay a few bucks so you will own similar URLs to capture bad spellers and to lock out potential competitors. Direct them to your site. On the day I typed this paragraph, I met a man who was planning to develop a website called **www.sphixus.com**. I suggested that he also register "sfixus" and some other variations. You can register several alternate "phantom" URLs at **www.NetworkSolutions.com** and have traffic forwarded.

◆Keep your *site hierarchy* relatively "flat." Each page should be just one to three clicks away from the homepage.

◆At least once a day, check to see that your website is really "on the air." There are services that will check for you, such as **www.WebsiteAvailability.com**

◆Sooner or later the *bots* (robot indexers) or *web crawlers* used by the search engines should find your website, but it can't hurt to tell them you exist. You may get emails from services that promise to *Submit Your Website to 300,000 Top Search Engines for only $299*. There are not 300,000 top search engines, or even 30. You should care about only a few. When you launch your website, notify the major search engines.

www.google.com/addurl
www.bing.com/docs/submit.aspx
www.excitedirectory.com/submit.php
http://siteexplorer.search.yahoo.com/submit

◆A *sitemap* will help both humans and bots discover all of your site's pages. A template may create it automatically.

◆In addition to search engines, there are online directories for resources in every imaginable field, from farming to diabetes. Search for them, and submit your URL. Check often, and if your site drops out, resubmit your information.

◆If you have a website that's related to your book's subject, put prominent links on it so people can order your book. My sites that sell phone equipment have links for my books about telecommunications. You can do the same thing for antique birdhouses, woodworking, baking, travel, anything.

Available from Lulu 181 pages, $5	Available from Amazon 396 pages, $19.95	Available from Amazon 216 pages, $14.95

Important website design tips

◆Avoid garish color combinations which may be fine for the bedroom walls of a 12-year-old but not for a website.

◆Avoid unreadable type and background color combos. It's tough to read navy blue words on a black background.

◆Avoid "reverse" type (light words on a dark background) except for small sections. Never do a whole page in reverse.

◆Avoid cutesy animations—out of style since 1987.

◆Avoid frames—out of style and a PITA.

◆Avoid designs that require scrolling to the side.

◆Keep your important information visible without scrolling down. (It would be "above the fold" in a newspaper.)

◆Avoid centered text except for headlines and subheads.

◆Don't use more than two or three typefaces.

◆Serif faces, such as the ubiquitous Times New Roman, are hard to read in small sizes.

◆Italics are often hard to read in small sizes.

◆Test to make sure your site looks right with multiple web browsers on different size monitors with different screen resolutions. Check it on an iPad and cellphones, too.

◆Make sure people can easily find contact information, especially your email address.

◆Have a link to the homepage from every page.

◆If your website does not allow people to order books, include links to your books on bookselling sites. Don't just mention that the book is "available at Amazon.com."

◆Have at least two people proofread the website.

◆Include important keywords as often as possible without seeming artificial.

◆Don't try to scam the search engines by using white type on a white background, black on black, etc.

◆Update often with new material, or even a new look.

◆Sound effects may be more annoying than productive.

How to increase traffic at your website

◆Become an active participant in online forums, discussion groups (on Yahoo Groups and elsewhere), and email lists. Every time you write something, include your website address and, if necessary, a brief description of its contents.

◆Submit brief articles to *ezines* which use lots of content. Every time you write something, include your web address and, if necessary, a brief description of its contents.

◆Contribute to the growing number of "free content" websites that provide material for other websites. Just Google "free content" to find them. Every time you write something, include your website address and, if necessary, a brief description of its contents.

◆Use pages on Facebook, MySpace, LinkedIn, MyLife and other social network websites to promote your books and your website.

◆Use Twitter to tell the world about your book and website (if you think anyone will care).

◆Exchange links with other compatible but not competitive websites.

◆Purchase small ads based on keyword searches from Google ("AdWords") and other search engines.

◆Write a blog which promotes you, your books and your website.

◆Include your website address on business cards and letterheads—and in your books.

◆Get listed in directories of people in your field.

◆Make sure any membership lists, especially online, include your website address if possible.

◆Get your site linked from school and association websites.

◆Use Google Alerts to be notified of mentions of your book or website or yourself to judge your progress.

◆Include your website address in your magazine articles.

Market research trick

Once you know what you want to write about, the Internet will make it much easier to do market research than before the world was online.

With a little bit of typing, clicking and reading you can find out what potential readers are interested in, and you can construct your book to address their concerns.

Use search engines to find terms like those I've listed below. Simply replace "golden retriever" with "super hero" or "Argentina" or whatever you want to write about.

"golden retriever forum"
"golden retriever message board"
"golden retriever bulletin board"
"golden retriever club"
"golden retriever association"
"golden retriever community"
"golden retriever organization"
"golden retriever news"
"golden retriever newsgroup"

...and sales trick

After your book is published, go back to visit the groups. Answer the questions you can answer, and tell people that more information is in your book, the name of your book, and where they can buy it.

CHAPTER 17
Understanding Print-On-Demand (POD)

The term pretty much explains itself. With POD, potential reading material is stored as digital files in computers, not as slices of dead trees on a shelf. The files are printed out as books when there is demand for them. Physical books don't exist until someone causes an order to reach the printing company. Books cost more to print this way compared to conventional *offset* printing, but there are few or no unwanted books to be stored, shipped or disposed of.

Traditional "trade" publishing requires some major decisions about major expenditures based on hunches. The hunches are usually based on experience, knowledge and research; but sometimes a hunch is just a hunch.

An agent has to decide if a book has enough appeal to be submitted to a publisher. After submission, the publisher has to decide if the book has enough appeal to be published.

If the book passes the first two tests, the publisher then has to estimate how many books are likely to be sold so the appropriate quantity can be printed. The sales estimate influences the advance against future royalties paid to the author.

Offset presses are generally used for print runs of hundreds or thousands of books. It was not economical to print just one or a few books at a time until the recent development of high-speed laser printers which print and bind hundreds of pages in a minute.

Agents and publishers are generally risk-averse. They tend to support books that are similar to successful books. They usually support authors who have attracted a loyal following of readers who automatically buy the authors' new books.

Despite the experience and caution, the experts are usually *wrong*. Most books *fail*. Most books *don't* sell in sufficient quantities to earn back advances. Most books go out of print within six months of publication, and existing inventory is then "remaindered" and sold on the buck-a-book tables.⬇

Barnes & Noble in Milford, Connecticut

Print-On-Demand removes much of the risk from book publishing. Because POD'd books don't exist until demand has been demonstrated, there is no danger of spending money to print books that will not be sold.

A book manuscript that is going to be offset-printed requires fairly complex preparation including the production of printing *plates*. Offset presses use ink that can be printed on a wide variety of paper types. Digital printers use *toner* that bonds to pages with heat and will adhere to fewer types of paper. Early POD books were inferior to offset-printed books, but quality has improved continuously. Today the best POD books look as good as offset books, with the possible exception of photograph reproduction—but it's good enough and getting better all the time. Lulu prints photos particularly well.

Preparation for POD is much simpler than for offset, but per-book cost is higher; and there is not much saving as the quantity increases. With offset, preparation cost can be amortized over varying quantities of books, so the per-book cost goes down as quantity goes up.

A 300-page paperback printed by offset could cost $1.84 each for 1,000 copies or $1.17 each for 10,000, or even less for 100,000. With POD, one copy could cost $5.40. There's usually a 5% discount for 50 or more and higher discounts for larger quantities—but POD prices *never* match offset prices.

Soft or Hard or both?

POD can also be used for hardcover books. The additional production cost is typically $5–$7 more than for each paperback. The difference at retail can be $10 or more—sometimes much more. WestBow Press published *Mustardseed Thoughts* by Ron Edmondson. The 376-page paperback version is priced at (gulp) $24.95. The hardcover version is priced at (BIG GULP) $39.95. It's extremely unlikely that readers will think that the stiffer covers are worth $15 more.

In traditional publishing, the first version of a book is often a hardcover. If the book sells well, about a year later the book is released as a less-expensive paperback with a new marketing campaign to attract readers.

Self-publishing packages often include both versions of the book. Sometimes the deluxe hardcovers are used as gifts by the authors and not sold to readers. Think carefully before you spend extra to produce hardcovers. It may be hard to sell them if less-expensive paperbacks are available.

Years ago there was some prejudice against paperbacks, particularly 35-cent "mass market" paperbacks printed on rough pulpy paper. Modern "trade paperbacks" are first-quality products which are unlikely to be rejected by readers. However, if you are writing a particularly large or expensive book, or one aimed at libraries or the gift market, consider a hardcover.

Because POD books generally cost more to produce than offset books, in order for them to have competitive retail prices, they generally do not offer the large markup (called a *discount* in the book biz) that bricks-and-mortar booksellers expect and demand.

Another factor limiting sales from physical stores is the lack of *returnability*—an archaic practice of the book industry seldom encountered with other retail products. Returnability costs and risks can be high. Some self-publishing companies offer returnability for a hefty extra fee, but that cost cuts into the author's profits, and bookstores generally don't want to stock self-published books anyway. Returnability is a major cost even for traditional publishers, and the industry may eliminate or minimize returns sometime in the future.

CHAPTER 18

What does a self-publishing author have to do?

1. Have at least one book idea.
2. Decide whether you will form your own publishing company, or use the services of a self-publishing company.
3. If you want the name of your own publishing company to appear on your books, pick a company that allows this option. It could be a printer such as Lightning Source, or a self-publishing company like CreateSpace. Think of several acceptable names and select one that's not already being used by another company in publishing or a related field.
4. If you choose to use your business name, register the name in the local government office that registers names—often the town clerk's office. You will get an "assumed name" certificate, "fictitious name" certificate or a DBA (Doing Business As) certificate. There may be a one-time fee or an annual fee or both. You may be required to advertise the new name in a local newspaper.
5. If you (not another bookseller) will be selling to customers in your state, and your state has a sales tax, you will have to register to collect and remit sales tax.
6. If you choose to use your business name, get whatever licenses or permits that your state or municipality requires.

7. If you choose to use your business name, open a business checking account under the business name.
8. Get business cards.
9. Set up a website.
10. Set up a businesslike email address, not a free account.
11. Write the first book.
12. Have the book copyedited and, if necessary, get more extensive editing.
13. Have the book read by laypeople and, if it's in a specialized or technical field, by one or more experts in the subject.
14. Make the suggested changes.
15. Gather the necessary photos, graphs and illustrations, or have custom artwork made.
16. Either format the interior yourself to make it book-like, or hire a designer to do it, or let your publisher do it.
17. You or your designer will insert the artwork in the proper positions, unless you're using a publisher that wants the artwork separate.
18. Either design the covers and spine yourself (probably not a good idea), or hire a pro to do it, or let your publisher do it.
19. Show several cover alternatives to people whose judgment you respect. Strive to stimulate thought and dialog—not merely "I like it," "I hate it," "OK," "wow," or "hmmm."
20. Read, read, read, and have others read, read, read—on the screen in multiple formats and on printed papers.
21. Promote, promote, promote. Let the world—or at least lots of potential readers—know that your book exists and convince them to buy it. Promotion includes news releases, book reviews, comments on blogs and websites, email signatures, your own websites, distributing business cards, mailing out letters and postcards, signing autographs at bookstore sessions, and whatever else you can think of.

CHAPTER 19
Building your "self" publishing team

Although it doesn't take a village to publish a book, it will be tough to become an author without help. If you use a self-publishing company, all of the help can be supplied by that company. You can also hire others. Here's the cast of characters:

The **writer** is probably—but not necessarily—you. It's possible that you have a great story to tell or important information or a valuable new insight to deliver to the world, but you're just not a good writer. Maybe you just don't have the time to write. In these cases, you'll need a co-author or a ghostwriter. The cost of hiring a ghostwriter will depend on the length of the book, the complexity of your topic, research and other preparation, and the ability and experience of the ghost. You could pay a ghost $5,000, or ten times that amount—or more.

Design Tip ⭐
Text Wrapping makes words follow the irregular edge of the photograph. It's attractive and saves space.

You'll probably have to pay this even if you sell just a few copies of your book, so consider hiring a ghost writer *very* carefully. Most self-publishing companies can supply ghosts. Ask to see some sample books before you select your spooky supporter.

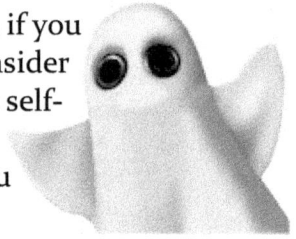

The **editor** could be—but shouldn't be—you. Obviously it's important that you read, re-read and re-read some more to polish your text to near perfection. However, it's a fundamental fact of writing life that the creator of the work will never catch all of the errors and lapses of judgment. Maybe some words, sentences, paragraphs or whole chapters should be shifted, chopped or even completely eliminated. These are choices best left to someone other than the creator.

There are several kinds of editing which can be done by one or more people:

◆**Copyediting** (or "copy editing" or "copy-editing") is looking for and fixing all of the tiny errors that infect every written work. A skilled copyeditor has good vision to spot typographical errors, is an excellent speller and a perfect grammarian. She should have an excellent memory to notice inconsistencies, such as "3 a.m." on one page and "5PM" 100 pages later.

Copyeditors generally follow specific semi-official "styles" for writing, promulgated in such books as *The New York Times Manual of Style and Usage*, *The Associated Press Stylebook*, and *The Chicago Manual of Style.* The books dictate such things as spelling, capitalization, abbreviation and hyphenation. Sometimes they agree with each other. Sometimes they don't. You can establish your *own* style, and perhaps get help from your copyeditor who may have more sense than you do.

DON'T EVEN DREAM of relying on your spell-checker to do the work of a copyeditor.

Copyediting fees can be based on the size of the work, the time involved, or may just be a negotiated flat fee. If your book is technical and requires specialized knowledge or familiarity with the subject, expect to pay more.

A typical range is $200 to $1,000. This is not a job for a neighbor or a relative. If you need to save money, see if you can hire an editor from a local newspaper, or even a good college paper, rather than a full-time professional copyeditor. Check references, and read some examples of her or his work.

Copyeditors don't need to be familiar with your subject and may not even need to understand what you are writing about. They work on the micro—not the macro—level.

A word of warning: **no copyeditor is perfect**. None will catch every error, and some may actually insert errors where there were none before. Read. Read. Read.

◆**Hard editing** (a.k.a. **content editing and substantive editing**) is an effort to actually improve what you've written, not to just correct little errors.

After working as a writer and editor for over 40 years, I don't bother paying someone to hard-edit my work. However, after seeing my finished books, I sometimes wished that I had someone looking over my shoulder to ask, "Are you *sure* you want to include that?" or "Is that what you *really* mean to say?"

A copyeditor can work on just a sentence or a paragraph or a chapter, but a hard editor should get to know the entire book before actually editing.

While the hard editor probably won't contribute more than a few words, and is not a co-author, she or he may suggest major changes in structure, particularly rearranging sequences, changing viewpoints (from first-person to third, for example), emphasizing or playing down characters or events, killing or adding material, etc.

A hard editor may be paid by the word, page, hour or project. Typical fees are $25 to $50 per hour, $1,000 per book, or two cents per word. You may save money if your hard editor is also your copyeditor—but be careful. The hard editing process may cause errors that copyediting should remove.

◆**Line editing or stylistic editing** concentrates on clarity, expression and other aspects that make reading pleasurable— or miserable. Line editor Audrey Owen says that people like her can "make your work beautiful and powerful."

An editor is not necessarily an expert

No editor knows everything about anything, and certainly not everything about everything. Authors should not assume that editors are experts. And vice versa. (If necessary, read those sentences again.)

Sometimes an editor will assume that the author *must* know what's right and does not correct an author's error. Sometimes an editor assumes the author was wrong, and then changes right into wrong. The author may not notice the change, or might assume that the editor was right.

In *Orange County Choppers: the Tale of the Teutuls*, there are several silly mistakes which were missed by *five* co-authors *and* the editors at Warner Books.

"Paul Senior" said his childhood home in Yonkers, New York was within walking distance of Yankee Stadium, in the Bronx. The stadium is about 8½ miles south. The 17-mile round trip is *not* walking distance for most people.

Paul mentioned his house in "Muncie," New York. Muncie is in Indiana. The Teutuls lived in MONSEY (pronounced "Muncie"). Someone besides me should have noticed.

In *Release Your Writing: Book Publishing, Your Way!*, Helen Gallagher says that POD printer Lightning Source is owned by Amazon. It's not. Maybe Helen's editor assumed that Helen knows her subject better than she really does.

◆**Technical editing** is major-league fact checking and is not necessary for all books. If your book deals with solar energy, Renaissance art or the Cold War, you'd better hire someone who is highly familiar with photovoltaic efficiency, Michelangelo or the Warsaw Pact—and knows the reliable reference works in the field.

Technical editors don't work only on technical books. They might get involved in cookbooks or historical novels—any book that could be tainted by incorrect information. You can pay a few bucks per page, or hundreds or even thousands of dollars per book.

◆**Proofreading** is not the same as editing, but it's related. At one time, a proofreader would simultaneously view the author's original manuscript and a near-final "proof" provided by the printer. He or she would constantly look from the original to the copy and back to try to spot errors and mark them.

Today, there is little chance of a printer's introducing an error, especially when the author provides a Word file or PDF file. Modern proofreading is usually just a close "final inspection" before the printer starts turning out books to be sold.

It's a good idea to have at least one additional set of eyes to look over your proofs. Good, inexpensive proofreading can usually be provided for $10 per hour by English majors or journalism majors from a local college.

You and your proofreaders must do your best, but don't expect to catch every error. It's extremely unusual for a published book to be error-free. If you strive for absolute perfection, your books will never reach the market. ➜ Each time you make a change—even a correction—you may create a new error which must be discovered and corrected. Be careful!

The **interior designer** could be either you or a professional. Someone has to devise (or copy) a standard for the way your pages will look. Before you commit to a designer (or to your own design), look through a lot of books and try to understand what makes them appealing or unappealing.

> ## What to expect from a first-class designer
>
> According to Michele DeFilippo of 1106 Design, "It's possible to hire someone who applies a template that has been used hundreds of times before, or who rushes through the job to quickly format paragraphs. A quality job involves looking at each paragraph and adjusting it for the best possible look, carefully balancing page bottoms, and following all the other rules of quality page composition. Hiring a designer who pays attention to these important details and who is willing to spend as much time as needed, is more expensive, but you'll wind up with a better-looking book." See **www.1106Design.com**

Sometimes a bad decision can kill the reading experience. I own a book called *Semantic Antics: How and Why Words Change Meaning.* I love reading about words and thought I would get a lot of pleasure from this book. Unfortunately, my prime emotions were frustration and outrage.

Some unnamed book designer chose to use a smaller-than-normal page size and, in order to squeeze all of author Sol Steinmetz's text into a reasonable number of small pages, she or he chose a tiny typeface which looks like what gets printed on the back of a credit card. When I was in advertising, this mini-printing was scorned as "fly poop" (actually, we used the "s-word"). It has no place in a mass-market book.

Consider your market when your book is designed. There are special editions of large-type books for people with visual impairments, but the simple act of aging can make bigger letters more appealing. My first self-published book was aimed at my fellow baby-boomers. The oldest of us were born in 1946. I chose to use 13-point type instead of the smaller and more common 12-point size used in this book.

The **cover designer** determines what the exterior package of your books will look like. Book cover design is a very specific endeavor, best left to those who have done it, and done it well, in the past. Expect to pay from $200 to $2,000, or even more. IMPORTANT WARNING: Don't forget to have the copyeditor and proofreader *closely* examine the cover. Errors can hide anywhere—even on billboards with huge type.

A **photographer** could be you or another amateur, or a professional. She or he will provide any specific photos you need for the interior or front or back cover. A pro will probably want from $250 to $3,000. Renting props and hiring models will add to your cost. For the front cover, it's *really* important that the photo be first-class.

An **illustrator** will provide any paintings, drawings, graphs, etc. needed for page decorations or to help you explain concepts in your text, or perhaps to provide the main graphic image for your front cover. You could pay anywhere from $50 to several thousand dollars for original artwork. **Stock photos** are an alternative to just-for-you photos and illustrations. They cost much less, but are not exclusively yours.

You can buy publishing services à la carte

Several years ago I got friendly with the owner of a self-publishing company and I suggested that he offer some of his book preparation services to people who were not buying complete publishing packages. He wasn't impressed with the idea, but now some of his competitors are. AuthorHive is part of giant Author Solutions, Inc. It began offering à la carte marketing assistance in early 2010. Outskirts Press soon followed, selling both marketing and editorial services.

Space Filler-Upper 📂

Many people have trouble with "which" and "that." They are not interchangeable.

Law schools teach future attorneys to use *that* to introduce restrictive clauses and *which* for nonrestrictive clauses, so legal documents are not misunderstood. It's important to be just as careful in all writing.

A restrictive clause (also called an *essential clause*) is necessary to maintain the meaning of a sentence. Example: "Cars that have electric motors are nearly silent."

A non-restrictive (non-essential) clause can be removed without changing the meaning of the remaining sentence. Example: There was a hurricane in Florida, which was bad for the tourism business.

→Sometimes "that" just sounds better than "which"—even if it's technically the wrong word.

CHAPTER 20
The split-personality self-publishing companies

Lulu and CreateSpace are similar to each other, and unlike other self-publishing companies. They can provide complete publishing and distribution—or just print.

Despite charging more for printing than its competitors, Lulu has been losing money since it was founded, and a recent plan to sell stock was canceled. The company seems to be in *constant turmoil*, with frequent revisions of its website and product offerings.

In addition to basic printing, Lulu offers "publishing packages" priced from $369 to $1369 and more deluxe "All-Inclusive Publishing Packs" priced up to $4499. The expensive packages include phone support, editing, fancier formatting and 125 books—both hardcovers and paperbacks. Optional services include ghostwriting, e-book conversion and promotion.

The price of a Lulu book is often higher than books printed by others. To make an adequate profit you'll probably set a higher retail price than you otherwise would.

➔Lulu does have two useful and fairly priced services: ①Printing one or a few books, when you're not in a hurry, can cost about half as much as using a local copy shop. Lulu charged me $13.12 to print a copy of a 400-page book, plus $6.53 to mail it. The mailing charge was higher than it should have been, but the total was reasonable because there was no setup fee. ②Distribution of "PDF" e-books has no setup charge, and you can keep 80% ($4 on a $5 book).

Lulu's Retail Listing Options:

◆"MarketReach" lists your work on Amazon.com as a marketplace listing (not the normal Amazon listing). Price: $25.

◆"ExtendedReach" lists your title and ISBN in major bibliographic databases and makes your work available on Amazon.com. If you use your own ISBN (i.e., you use the name of your own publishing business) you *will not* be eligible for ExtendedReach Distribution. ExtendedReach is free.

◆"GlobalReach" lists your title in major bibliographic databases and makes your title available to online retailers such as Amazon.com and Barnes & Noble, plus bricks-and-mortar bookstores and the Espresso Book Machine. This is the only option available if you use your own ISBN or purchase an ISBN from Lulu. Price is $75.

createspace

CreateSpace is owned by Amazon and you can use it for either basic printing or extensive services or something in between.

CreateSpace offers three families of publishing services

◆"Standard Value Solutions" are for authors who do most of the work themselves. The least expensive "Author's Express," priced at $299, requires the author to create PDF files for the

The split-personality self-publishing companies

interior and covers, but provides a little bit of hand-holding. The $499 "Author's Advantage" provides interior and cover templates you can adapt for your book, which may be better than your own designs.

◆Services in "Total Design Freedom Solutions" include copy-editing, custom cover and interior designs, press releases and a video trailer. Package prices range from $758 to $4,999.

◆In another program, CreateSpace says it lets you "Self-Publish a Book—Free." There is no charge to upload a file or use a cover template. You also get a free ISBN that identifies CreateSpace (not you) as the publisher. The standard program is sort of free. The $39 "Pro" program can provide so much more profit per book that you'd have to be an idiot or a pessimist not to go for the Pro. I self-published a 138-page book with the Pro program, I can buy books for $2.50 each. The book lists for $10.95, but is discounted to $7.38. I get paid a royalty of just over four bucks per book, which is quite good.

➜If you use the CreateSpace Pro plan, you can participate in the "Expanded Distribution Channel" which offers you the potential to distribute your book to a larger audience through more outlets including bookstores, libraries, academic institutions, wholesalers and distributors.

➜As an experiment, I used CreateSpace and Lulu to print some books, instead of Lightning Source, which I normally use. CreateSpace is extremely concerned about potential copyright violation, and demanded that I show proof that I had permission to use *every* photograph in the book. I've never encountered this, or heard of this, with other publishers or printers, and it delayed publication of the book.

Strange arithmetic

Some alleged publishing *co-ops* charge much more than regular self-publishing companies. The deceptively named Author's Publishing Cooperative charges $14,800 PLUS about $3,000 for editing, $1,500 for cover design and $2,000 for typesetting. Authors pay for printing, too. Where's the cooperation?

CHAPTER 21
Starting and running the business

Even if you think of yourself as an artist, and are using the services of a self-publishing company, you are still operating a business. To make a profit, you have to do more than just send a file to a publisher and wait for books to appear and for checks to come in. In the self-publishing business—as in any business—there are no guarantees. There is simply no way to eliminate all the risks associated with starting a small business. Failure—however you define it—will probably do more damage to your ego than to your bank balance.

You can improve your chances of success with good planning, preparation and insight. Start by evaluating your strengths and weaknesses as a potential owner and manager of a small business. Carefully consider the following questions:

◆Are you a self-starter? It will be entirely *up to you* to develop projects, organize your time and follow through on details.

◆How well do you get along with different personalities? Business owners need to deal with customers, vendors, staff, bankers, and professionals such as lawyers, accountants and consultants. Can you deal with someone who is temperamental, unreliable or cranky if your business depends on it?

◆Do you have the physical and emotional stamina to run a business? Business ownership can be exciting, but it's also a lot of work. Most self-publishing authors have full-time jobs or other businesses to run. Can you handle six or seven 12-hour workdays every week?

◆How good are you at making decisions? Small-business owners need to make decisions constantly—often quickly, independently and under pressure. A delayed decision can mean lost income. So can a wrong decision.

◆How well do you plan and organize? Poor planning is responsible for many business failures.

◆Is your drive strong enough? Running a business can wear you down emotionally. Some business owners burn out quickly from having to carry on their own shoulders all the responsibility for the success of their business. Strong motivation will help you survive slowdowns and periods of burnout.

◆How will the business affect your family? The first few years of business can be difficult for the family. It's important for family members to know what to expect and for you to be able to know that they will support you during this time. There may be financial difficulties until your publishing business becomes profitable, which could take months or years or *may never happen*. Some writers spend a small fortune on publishing and promotion, and have to adjust to a lower standard of living or put family assets at risk—not a good idea.

Chances are that you've spent many hours writing your book. You may have to spend even more time—including time away from home—to promote your book.

Why small businesses fail

The definitions of failure and success depend on your goals. Do you want to enhance your image, spread a message, change the world, entertain the world, make money—or all of the above?

Starting a small business is always risky, and the chance of success is slim. Roughly half of small businesses fail within the first five years.

Although most books—even from major publishers—do not make money, it's definitely possible to make money from writing and self-publishing. If you're not making money, you may be doing something wrong, or there may be factors you just can't control. In his book, *Small Business Management*, Michael Ames gives several reasons for small business failure:

◆Lack of experience

◆Insufficient capital (with self-publishing, more for promotion than for anything else)

◆Poor location (probably doesn't matter for publishing)

◆Poor inventory management (should not be an issue with Print-On-Demand)

◆Overinvestment in fixed assets (don't buy a $3,000 desk)

◆Poor credit arrangements (don't pay exorbitant interest)

◆Personal use of business funds (you'll probably start with personal money, but keep records, have separate accounts and let your business pay back the personal start-up funds)

◆Unexpected growth (you should be so lucky)

Some causes of failure specific to publishing

◆Your book stinks.

◆You have too many competitors and probably should not have published the book.

◆Your market is too narrow—not enough people care about the subject.

◆You didn't work hard enough at promoting it. Not enough potential purchasers know it exists.

◆Your book is hard to find. It's not available where people expect to buy it.

◆You paid too much money for a publishing package and add-ons. Your publishing company made the money that you could have made. Do you really need $2 postcards?

◆Your price is wrong. If the book's price is too low, there's not enough money left for you, and the low price hurts the book's credibility. If the price is too high, you may scare readers or lose sales to your competitors.

◆Your timing is wrong. The book came out too soon or too late. You missed the peak of popularity. The fad either never became big enough or went out of fashion before the book was published.

Some things to think about

◆Don't get the royal shaft on royalties. Some self-publishing companies try to impress potential customers with the prospect of earning big royalties on each book sold. If you earn a "royalty" of 50 cents or $6 per book, but you've already paid $300 or $3,000 or $13,000, you're really just getting your own

money back—very slowly. Some publishers are vague or misleading about how royalties are calculated. They may offer what seems to be a very high percentage, but it's based on the wholesale price of a book, not the retail "cover price."
➔➔➔**50% of $8 is not better than 20% of $20.**

◆Like eating Lay's potato chips, it's hard to stop after writing and publishing just one book. It's likely that your method of doing business will change over the years, both as you learn more and as you write different kinds of books. For some books, you'll do most of the work yourself; for others, you'll farm out a lot. You may find that the illustrator, designer or editor who seemed just perfect on your first book isn't right on the third. You may find that one 200-page book should sell for $14.95 and another one is worth $24.95 or $49.95.

◆There are many reasons *not* to start your own business. But, for the right person, the advantages of business ownership far outweigh the risks. In self-publishing, the financial risks are much less than with most other businesses. **Even if you lose money, you'll probably still have fun writing.**

◆You might find that other people start coming to you for advice and even ask you to publish their books.

◆You might find that you like marketing books better than you like writing them. You may find that you hate marketing.

◆When you have your own business, you'll probably work hard and work long hours for an uncertain return. But you wouldn't write unless you liked doing it. Your efforts can directly benefit you—not only an employer or your publisher.

◆When you have your own business, you're almost never too sick or too tired to go to work. You'll work on weekends and vacations and late at night—and you'll *love* it.

◆Be decisive! A wrong decision is better than no decision, because you'll soon know that it's the wrong decision and can then try something else.

◆Here are some of the important characteristics of being an entrepreneur: Persistence, Desire for immediate feedback, Inquisitiveness, Strong drive to achieve, Lots of energy, Little need for sleep, Eagerness to start the next day's work, Willingness to sacrifice family time for business time. You must be: Goal-oriented, Independent, Demanding (high standards for yourself and others), Creative, Innovative, Committed, Organized, Frugal, Reliable, Honest, Competitive, Tolerant of short-term failure, Flexible, Open, Willing to break tradition, Driven to succeed, driven to succeed, driven to succeed, driven to succeed and driven to succeed.

How do you finance your publishing?

Most self-published authors are also self-financers, usually paying suppliers with their own credit cards. Since you can start with under $1,000, it's seldom necessary to borrow money.

However, to achieve big sales, you need big visibility, which can be achieved through public relations, advertising or both. A public relations campaign will cost between zero and $2,000 if you do all of the work yourself. If you hire a pro, you could spend $1,000 per month or more.

Advertising a new book by an unknown author is not usually effective, except for pay-per-click ads on the web for nonfiction.

Don't advertise a novel, poetry book or memoir unless you are *super*-rich.

Writers with an insufficient credit line usually try to borrow money from family and friends. This can ruin a relationship and cause endless gossiping, so I don't recommend it.

You can try to get a small business loan from a local bank or savings & loan association, preferably one with which you already have a good relationship, perhaps based on paying off a personal loan or a mortgage. If the lender is unwilling to approve your loan, you can request that the lender submit your application to the U.S. Small Business Administration.

➜ Keep in mind that a new publishing business is definitely a gamble, and the odds against you may be greater than if you simply bet on black or red in roulette. Don't be surprised if the bank and the SBA turn you down, unless you can show that the business has been successful and will continue to succeed.

How do you get a business license?

If you plan to use a self-publishing company, you probably won't need a license. If you want to use you own business name, you may need a license or permit merely to *be* in business. It probably won't be complicated or expensive.

Licensing is generally handled through your state or local government. Check your municipality's website or look in your local telephone directory in the government section for an office that issues the necessary license or permit.

Do you need a business plan?

A business plan is usually necessary for getting a loan or attracting investors, and is also a useful tool for self-discipline, to keep you focused. Go to **www.sba.gov** and select "Writing a Business Plan" under "Small Business Planner."

Don't forget business insurance!

Casino owner Steve Wynn sued Barricade Books for defamation and won an award of over $3 million. Barricade went out of business.

➜ Remember that anyone can sue anyone for anything. A suit doesn't need legal merit to cost a defendant a lot of time and money. Some people start nuisance suits as harassment, or with the assumption that the defendant would rather settle for $1,000 instead of paying a lawyer $2,000 to defend the case.

You can be sued for defamation, libel, copyright violation, inaccurate statistics, bad breath, a missed appointment—anything. A plaintiff doesn't even need a lawyer to sue you.

Your homeowner's and personal liability insurance may not be adequate for your publishing. Ask about business liability insurance.

Some companies specialize in insurance for writers and publishers. One is **www.publiability.com.**

Lots of people have inexpensive, million-dollar, blanket liability coverage. Make sure your liability coverage will handle a lawsuit for defamation, libel or an error in your book.

Talk to your agent about business property insurance, too. It's probably not worthwhile to insure a $500 PC and a $200 printer, but if you store a thousand copies of your book, they should be insured against fire, flood and theft.

Where can you get help?

There's plenty of online help for self-publishing authors, even on the websites of the companies you won't be using.

Many writers, agents and publishers are also bloggers who dispense information every day. (I do it, too, at **www.BookMakingBlog.blogspot.com.**) For more, just do a search for "self-publish," "POD," etc.

Yahoo hosts three excellent groups:
http://finance.groups.yahoo.com/group/Print-On-Demand
http://finance.groups.yahoo.com/group/pod_publishers
http://finance.groups.yahoo.com/group/Self-Publishing
There is some overlap, but join all three. Membership is free.

The *Midwest Book Review* has a huge amount of useful and well-organized information for writers and self-published authors. See **www.midwestbookreview.com**.

Book designer Joel Friedlander offers information, discussions and valuable advice on a wide range of topics of interest to self-published authors at **www.thebookdesigner.com**

There are many other valuable online resources. See:

www.selfpublishingreview.blogspot.com
www.shewrites.com
www.invirtuo.cc/prededitors
www.fonerbooks.com/selfpublishing
www.fonerbooks.com/thepath.htm
www.newselfpublishing.com
www.mickrooney.blogspot.com
www.aeonix.com
www.self-pub.info
www.createspace.com/en/community/index.jspa

There are 12,400 Service Corps of Retired Executives (SCORE) chapters and approximately 1,000 Small Business Development Centers (SBDCs) in the United States. SCORE advisors provide free advice on many aspects of business, based on their firsthand experience. SBDCs provide a variety of assistance services to small businesses and potential entrepreneurs. You may not find a mentor with specific experience in publishing, but the members' general knowledge and desire to help are impressive. They can assist you by critiquing your business plan, your business ideas and sales pitch. To find a SCORE advisor, go to **www.score.org/index.html.** You can locate a SBDC center by selecting "Local Resources" at **www.sba.gov**.

Don't be afraid to ask experts for help. If someone writes a book, teaches a course or develops legislation in the field you're writing about, go ahead and send paper mail or email. Experts are often busy, so be patient and don't expect an immediate response.

Almost every field of human endeavor has trade associations and online groups where experts hang out. You can ask questions there, too.

➔ I respond to email questions from readers at **books@ablecomm.com.**

(Some material in this chapter was provided by the Small Business Administration. Thanks.)

Take a break. Read this to feel better

Newsweek said that a traditional publishing contract pays the author just 8 to 9% royalties, but with self-publishing, authors keep 70 to 80% of the profit. The magazine quoted thriller writer J. A. Konrath, who said, "It's an even playing field for the first time. The gatekeepers have become who they should have been in the first place: the readers."

Konrath began self-publishing e-books in 2009 and made as much money on a single $2.99 ebook as he would on a $25 hardcover. He said, "I started to be able to pay my mortgage on e-book money, then pay my bills on e-book money. I'm going to make over $100,000 this year, and a lot of the money is from the books that New York publishers rejected." He planned to release all his future novels as self-published Kindle books.

CHAPTER 22
How long does it take?
How much does it cost?

These numbers are based on my experience and research. Your mileage may vary.

Time to write and edit a book: between a week and a lifetime. The first version of this book took about nine months to make, just like a human baby.

Time to read and correct a page of text with about 300 words: two minutes

Time to copyedit a book: a few days to a few weeks

Time for major editing: a few weeks to a month

Time to design a cover: a few hours to a few weeks

Time for ghostwriting: one to three months

Time to receive a proof from CreateSpace: 3 to 5 days

Time to receive a proof from Lulu with expedited service: 3 days

Time to receive a proof from Lulu with standard service: 7-10 days

Time for a book to be on sale after submitting it to a self-publishing company: a few weeks to a year. Morris Publishing says your order ships in 20 business day, and 12-business-day rush service is also available. 48HrBooks says it can produce books in (guess what?) 48 hours. Wasteland Press says two to four weeks. Some companies will speed things up for an extra fee.

Time for a book to be listed on Amazon.com after a proof is approved: one to three days

Time to be listed on Barnes & Noble and other booksellers' websites after a proof is approved: two to ten days

Time for a book to change from being *drop-shipped* by Lightning Source to being stocked by Amazon: a few days to a few weeks, or it may never happen

Time for a book to be discounted by Amazon: a few days to a few months, or it may never happen

Time for Lightning Source to process your files and ship out a proof: three business days

Time for Lightning Source to print and ship a case of 20 books: two business days

Time to receive a proof after shipping by Lightning Source: one business day

Number of printed proofs you'll correct before you decide your book is good enough to print: three to ten (my least was four, my most was thirteen, and this book took nine).

Cost of MS Word 2010: $140

Cost of MS Office 2010 (which includes Word!): $130

Cost of Adobe Acrobat: $49.99-$1198

Cost of Adobe Photoshop Elements 9: $80

How long does it take? How much does it cost?

Cost to design a cover: $200 to $1,000 or more

Cost to copyedit: $200 to $500 or more

Cost for major editing: $500 to $1,000 or more

Cost for ghostwriting: $5,000 or more (maybe a lot more)

Cost of least expensive self-publishing package: $195 (Aacha-non Publishing and Wasteland Press)

Cost of most expensive self-publishing package: $50,000 (Arbor Books). Options can add $35,000 more!

Minimum markup percentage ("discount") Amazon will work on: 20% (or 10% if they give a discount to readers).

Cost to ship a 300-page book by Priority Mail: $4.95

Cost for Lightning Source to ship one 300-page book the least expensive way: $3.80

Cost for Lightning Source to ship one 300-page book with tracking: $5.52

More expensive shipping service options for Lightning Source to ship one 300-page book faster: $7.27 - $36.40

Average number of errors in a professionally-produced 300-page book from a major publisher: six

FREE*

I may open a **free Lamborghini car dealership** and use Lulu, Wordclay, UniBook and CreateSpace as my business models.

The normal price for a fantastic Lamborghini Gallardo LP560-4 is over $200,000. With our new technology, I'll be able to GIVE you a Gallardo for FREE. You'll be able to look at the car online any time you want to *without paying a penny*.

*However, if you actually want a physical vehicle titled in your name that you can touch and drive and keep in your own garage, you will have to pay $210,194 plus taxes, delivery charge and the registration and title fees.

It seems to me that until e-books or mental telepathy become widespread, printing will be an intrinsic part of publishing books. Therefore, "Self-Publish for Free" is baloney.

CHAPTER 23
Prices, discounts, markups

Every book, like every other item that is sold, needs a price. A book is unlike cars and food. A book *is* like other artistic expressions like paintings—its price does not have to be related to its cost of production. Many self-publishing companies don't seem to understand this.

There's a long-standing price guideline in traditional (not POD) publishing. The *cover price* printed on the book is about eight to ten times the cost of manufacturing.

There are multiple paths that a book may take between the printing press and the reader.

A publisher usually sells books through one or even two levels of wholesale middlemen before books reach a retail store. The store expects to have a markup of about 40%, and the wholesaler receives about 15%. Combine the two figures and you get the common 55% *trade discount*.

A book that costs $1.50 to manufacture could be sold to a wholesaler for $7.18, sold to the store for $9.57, and sold to a reader for $15.95. (See chart ahead.)

Some books are sold directly from publisher to bookseller, or even directly to readers. Some books, particularly those promoting religious or political views or a business, are sold below cost or even given away if the message is more important than money.

The bookselling sales path is complex, costly and filled with waste. Traditional publishers—and therefore readers—pay for the cost of warehousing, handling, shipping books to stores and sometimes returning them if they're not sold.

Basic arithmetic for a $15.95 book

(NOTES: Approximate numbers. 300 pages. No discount at retail. It's possible that a book with a $1.50 printing cost would have a cover price less or more than $15.95. Some booksellers pay lower prices because of quantity discounts.)

	Offset printing for physical store, with traditional publisher	POD for Amazon, with self-pub. co.
Cost to print	$1.50	$5.40
Wholesaler pays publisher	$7.18	(no wholesaler)
Bookseller pays wholesaler	$9.57	$12.76 (to publisher)
Reader pays bookseller	$15.95	$15.95
Bookseller keeps	$6.38	$3.19
Publisher keeps	$5.68	$7.36
Writer keeps	About $1.28, before agent's commission	About $1.60 to $2.40

◆The spread between the $1.50 printing cost and $7.18 price to a wholesaler for a traditional publisher (or between the $5.40 printing cost and $12.76 price to a bookseller for a self-publishing company) is "gross profit." It covers the costs of being in business, including author's royalty, salaries, advertising, rent, shipping, warehousing, insurance, taxes, etc. A traditional publisher needs to retain money from bestsellers to offset the losses on flops, and hopes to keep some profit.

◆With online sales, Print-On-Demand and self-publishing, the sales path is much simpler. There are no middlemen to keep their pieces of the selling price. A book can be sent directly from the printer to the reader. Amazon gets a piece of the action but it has to cover only administrative expenses and profit, not warehousing, order picking or returns.

The obvious conclusion is that a self-published author can price a book lower than a big publisher can—but obvious is not accurate. A 300-page book sold by a mainstream publisher may cost $1.50 to print, so it can support a $15.95 list price (or less).The same-sized book produced with POD could cost $5.40 to print. With the "8×" formula, it would be priced at $42.95—and might be so costly that no one would buy it.

But if you choose to ignore physical bookstores (except for special orders), you can be much more flexible in your pricing. Online booksellers will accept a discount as low as 20%. The book that costs $5.40 to print and has a $15.95 cover price can be sold to Amazon for $12.76. You and the publisher divvy up the difference between $5.40 and $12.76—a markup of 57.7%. If you *are* the publisher, you don't divvy up anything.

Up or down

It's generally best to keep your price in line with its competitors. You can go lower if you are trying to establish your "brand" and think a low price will attract buyers—and are willing to sacrifice income. However, if your price is *too* low, your book may seem insignificant.

If it's vitally necessary for students, business or government, a book that costs $5.40 to print with POD could bring in $29.95 or even $75. If people believe that your reference work or new theory will save them or make them many times the investment, there is almost no limit to the price.

➔Beware of self-publishing companies that dictate book prices based solely on the page count and binding type. That's not a good way to do business.

Making cents

Most cover prices end with 95 cents. This comes from the common technique of pricing other retail products and even real estate. The long-held assumption is that if someone reads "$15.95," she or he will concentrate on the "15" and will ignore the fact that the price is indeed very close to 16 bucks.

I doubt that anyone is fooled by this silly subterfuge, but it's been going on for so long that it has become the accepted way of doing business. It's like gasoline prices which always end with nine tenths of a cent.

It can't hurt to stick with the system. There's probably nothing to gain by having a price of $12.29, $16.50, or $19.99.

Some publishers reject the 95-cent scam and use whole numbers. There's nothing wrong with it, so try it if you like.

There may be some apparent glamour in pricing in whole dollars. If I was publishing a very expensive book and wanted it to have a classy and confident image that dismisses the need to discount, I'd probably mark it $50 or $100, not $49.95 or $99.99.

Xlibris likes weirdo Walmart-style prices like $17.84, $19.54 and $24.64. Interestingly, Walmart now uses lots of whole-dollar numbers—with no odd cents. Walmart said its customers prefer simple prices. Maybe Xlibris should ask book buyers.

Two important warnings

①To price your book, you have to contemplate its *perceived value*. You may think your masterpiece is worth $19.95. But if most of the competitive titles sell for $9.95–$12.95, you'd better be very sure you can justify a higher price and that potential shoppers will understand the difference *and* can afford the extra dollars.

②Self-publishing companies may be inflexible in the discounts they offer to booksellers—insisting on offering 50% or more, even if you are interested only in the online sellers which will accept 20%. The high discounts mean LESS money for you! Mill City Press provides discounts up to 55%, and WestBow Press up to 50%. Cindy, a Westbow rep, told me that no publisher could operate with 20%. She's wrong. Dog Ear Publishing can do it. So can my company.

Wholesaler vs. Distributor vs. you

With food or clothing, "wholesaler," "distributor" or even "wholesale distributor" are different names for the same type of business. It's a middleman company which buys products from a manufacturer and sells them to a retailer. In the book business, they may not mean the same thing.

Traditionally, a book *wholesaler* passively takes orders and ships books, while a *distributor* is active, with salespeople visiting and calling booksellers, and probably charging more for its services than a wholesaler does. Some books go through both a wholesaler and a distributor.

Most self-publishing companies have multiple paths to get books to readers, and the path (*channel*) determines how much royalty you will receive.

On books sold from the publisher's website, you could get a 50% royalty. This is the highest royalty percentage, but because of limited website traffic, your sales and income will probably be minimal.

On books sold through online sellers such as Amazon.com, you could get 10%, or possibly a bit more.

On books sold through terrestrial booksellers which pass through a distributor or wholesaler or both, your royalty may be just 10%.

If you buy books from the self-publishing company and can sell them yourself, you may make a profit of 50%, and may even get a royalty, too.

➜ Self-publishing companies may calculate royalties based on either the retail "cover price" or the wholesale price. Be sure you know what to expect.

A reference book you can read for fun

The Associated Press Stylebook is considered to be the "Bible of the Newspaper Industry," but it's useful for *all* writers who want to avoid silly errors and improve their craft.

It helps with spelling, grammar, abbreviations, capitalizations and more; and is also a dictionary, a textbook and an encyclopedia.

Besides accuracy, this book will help you achieve *consistency* to avoid having "homemade" on one page and "home-made" on another.

Don't consider the AP book as something to be kept on a shelf until you need to check on a specific word. Spend a day or a week or a weekend with it. Read it cover-to-cover, flip through it or just stick your finger between two random pages. I promise you'll be enlightened, and maybe even be entertained.

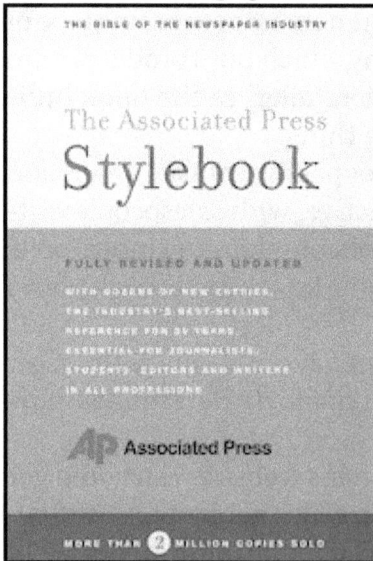

CHAPTER 24
Get real. How many can you sell?

Any writer should be able to sell between a few dozen and a few hundred copies of a book, but if you want to sell thousands or tens of thousands, you'll have to work very hard, and get lucky, and maybe even make your own good luck. Despite a few notable success stories—mostly involving selling a self-published title to a traditional publisher— apparently most self-published books sell fewer than 200 copies, and many of them are sold to people the author knows.

You probably won't get rich by self-publishing. You may feel good and receive some compliments, and maybe even advance your career. But, unless you pick the right topic, produce an excellent book, work your ass off promoting it, and are very lucky, don't quit your day job.

Don't let advertising blind you to reality. Self-publishing companies brag about the sales of their few superstars. Outskirts Press likes to tout Gang Chen, who "earned over $100,000 in author royalties in six short months."

Chen's experience is *extremely atypical* and no one should expect to emulate him. His book is a *highly specialized $69.95* study guide needed for professional advancement by a very small audience for whom the book price is not significant. Because of the small audience, it's highly unlikely that the sales volume and royalty payments will stay at the high level.

Vantage Press has some honest advice: "Please be realistic. Most books by new authors do not sell well, and most authors do not recoup the publishing fee."

Sales information for self-published books is hard to get because authors seldom reveal the numbers. David Maturo, former Finance VP of Xlibris, said that some of its authors sell as few as one or two books, and some have sold over 10,000. Maturo revealed that the average number of books sold per author is 150. He said 64% are bought by the author. That leaves just 54 books out of 150 to be sold to *real* customers.

> My own Stories *I'd Tell My Childen (but maybe not until they're adults)* sold over 300 copies in two months. That's pretty amazing. My name is not Sarah Palin. Why are hundreds of people buying a memoir by someone they've never heard of? Because they heard it's a good book.

According to Maturo, the average author expenditure at Xlibris was $1,400. The math is depressing. Authors spent about $26 to produce each of the books which were sold to the public—typically priced from $8.50 to $19.99.

A group of once-independent competing companies are now owned by Author Solutions. Its CEO, Kevin Weiss, told the *New York Times* that the average sale per title from any of the company's brands is around 150. VP Susan Driscoll told the *Times* that "most writers using iUniverse [now part of Author Solutions] sell fewer than 200 books" and 40 percent are sold directly to authors.

The *Times* said, "If a title sells more than 500 copies its first year, [iUniverse] may invest in marketing the book and invite the author to become a "Star." But of iUniverse's 17,000 published titles, the authors of only 84 have been chosen as Stars, and only a half-dozen have made it to Barnes & Noble store shelves."

Lulu founder Bob Young said, "A publishing house dreams of having ten authors selling a million books each. Lulu wants a million authors selling 100 books each."

➡️According to *Publishers Weekly,* in a recent year only 2% of book titles sold more than 5,000 copies and the average book from a mainstream publisher sold about 500 copies.

Some numbers to make you work harder

First print runs, as reported by *Publishers Weekly*:
- *The Lost Symbol* by Dan Brown: 5 million
- *Private Latitudes* by Michael Crichton: 2 million
- *Have a Little Faith* by Mitch Albom: 2 million
- *True Compass* by Ted Kennedy: 1.5 million
- *True Blue* by David Baldacci: 1.5 million
- *Under the Dome* by Stephen King: 1.5 million
- *Theodore Boone, Kid Lawyer* by John Grisham: 1 million
- *The Search* by Norah Roberts: 800,000

Some numbers to keep your ego in check

- Xlibris paid about $111 in royalties to each author from 1997 to 2003.
- Xlibris's average book sales were 33 per title from 1997 through 2004.
- Through 3/25/04, 3.4% of Xlibris titles sold more than 500 copies, 14.3% sold more than 200 copies, and the average sale number of an Xlibris book was about 130 copies.
- As of 6/04. iUniverse's sales averaged about 75 copies per title. Only 84 have sold more than 500 copies.
- Authorhouse sales were about 108 books per title.

(info collected and published by ParaPublishing)

Eating and drinking at bookstores

Seattle's Best Coffee is a subsidiary of Starbucks Corporation. Starbucks provides Starbucks coffee at cafés inside Barnes & Noble stores, and did provide Seattle's Best Coffee at cafés inside Borders stores. Starbucks started in Seattle. So, if "Seattle's Best Coffee" is really <u>Seattle's best coffee</u>, does that mean it's better than Starbucks coffee? I don't know. I have never tasted coffee and I don't plan to. ❑The cafés at both book chains serve coffee and other drinks, plus sandwiches and baked items. ❑I once had a soda and a nice chicken salad sandwich at B&N. I have never eaten in a Borders café, but I might buy a hot chocolate or a bottle of water if I'm thirsty while in the store. ❑On the other hand, my non-coffee-drinking wife and I frequently go to *On the Border* for Mexican food. Their fajitas, burritos, chimichangas, tortilla chips and salsa are **bueno.** They don't sell books, so take your own. ❑I realize that this page doesn't seem to have anything to do with publishing, but I had space to fill, and I like writing about food. ❑When you publish your own book, you can fill surplus space any way you want to. That's one of the advantages of self-publishing. Random House probably wouldn't let me insert a page about snacks in a book about books, or set the type flush-right/ragged-left like this page, and use a ❑ to indicate a new paragraph, but *I* am the boss of my book. So, this page really *does* relate to publishing.

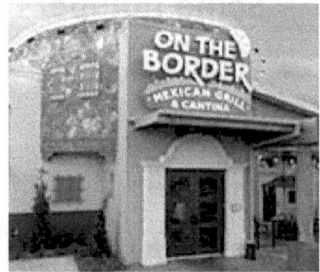

CHAPTER 25
You don't really need bookstores, but you might want to try to use them

For readers, a bookstore can be wonderful. It's a great place to spend a few minutes or an afternoon, finding exactly what you are looking for or making serendipitous discoveries. For big-name authors, bookstores are the venue for expanding riches and fame. For self-published authors, stores can be a frustrating waste of time—but they have an often-irresistible allure.

The little, local, mom-and-pop bookstores that would take a chance on a new author or a strange subject are disappearing, being replaced by big-box book retailers ranging from Costco to Barnes & Noble. They buy hundreds or thousands of titles published by scores of publishers and sold by a handful of wholesalers. These stores can't afford the time to get involved with a self-published author who has one or two titles.

Over time, if bookstores still exist, they may become more open to POD self-published authors. But now, the "business model" of traditional bookstores, with big discounts off the cover price, returnability of unsold books, and sales-promotion materials and advertising funds, are anathema to most self-published authors.

Despite all this, if you really want to see your own words and your own face on the shelves of bookstores on the streets and in the malls of America, I'll give you some tips. Read and **UNDERSTAND** the next paragraph.

In order to have your books stocked in bricks-and-mortar bookstores, you'll probably have to offer a bigger discount than if you care about online sales, only. You have to weigh the decreased revenue per book against the *possibility* of selling more books, and ego gratification.

Discuss discount options with potential publishers. You may have choices which they don't want to publicize.

When you first start out, you can ignore the big chains. Begin with a niche market, defined either by subject or geography. If your book is about New England hiking trails or old Spanish missions in California, target bookstores that sell to travelers and tourists, particularly in the relevant areas. If you live in, or were born in or wrote about Ohio, target stores in that state. In the 1970s I often visited a bookstore in Manhattan that specialized in books about cars and planes. I don't know if it still exists, but there are similar niche stores in other cities. There are specialists for many topics, and most now sell online.

If you can demonstrate success in a niche and have good reviews, you stand a better chance of later convincing the bosses at the big stores.

Independent booksellers have a promotional alliance called **IndieBound** to help them compete with superstores. The program is designed to appeal to readers who care about their local bookstores. Perhaps there is a natural bond between indie book publishers and indie booksellers. You can find out, either by joining the **Publisher Partner Program**—or just trying to sell through some stores.

You don't really need bookstores

Local mom-and-pop stores *may* be more willing to try a few books without the normal return privilege which can kill self-published authors, and store owners *may* put more effort into selling books they have paid for, rather than books they know they can return. Be persuasive—or beg—but be prepared to give in.

If you are a regular customer of a local bookstore (and most writers are fervent readers), talk to the owner, manager or buyer. Let her know that you are writing a book, and find out how the company makes buying decisions and how you can work together. You may even get advice on your book's title and cover which can help you avoid a disaster later on.

If you are talking to the branch manager of a chain store, you may be told that all orders are placed by headquarters. Some managers have the discretion to place small orders, particularly for books with local appeal.

Polish your sales promotion package and your sales pitch. Your materials and your spiel have to be as good as the promotional efforts from publishers that sell billions of dollars' worth of books. If you plan to make an in-person pitch and you've never sold before, hold a few practice sessions. Maybe you can get help from a businessperson you know even outside the book business who can be a sales coach for a half hour.

If you can't meet with the bookstore's buyer, identify the people who make the buying decisions at headquarters. Large chains often have specific buyers for different types of books. Send a sales package with a copy of your book, a convincing sales letter and other powerful and appropriate materials such as review reprints and sales data. Send it via a special courier service, like FedEx, so it's more likely to be noticed and not junked without opening. After a week or so, call the buyer to confirm receipt, and offer to answer any questions. Make it low-key, not high-pressure.

Don't take "no" for an answer.

One basic rule for selling is never to ask a question that can be answered with "no." That's why new department store employees are taught to approach a customer with "I'm Charlie. *How* may I help you?" instead of just "*May* I help you?" Don't invite a negative response.

Another rule is always to ask for the order.

Combine the two rules by asking, "Would you like to start with five books or ten?"

If you make a sale and the books have to be ordered for future delivery, leave behind one or two autographed copies. Try to get the store staff to read them and to get enthusiastic about them so they'll be able to build demand and sell the books when they are in stock.

A store's decision on whether or not to attempt to sell your book is not based on your book's literary merit. It's based on sales potential. The store's buyer will want to know what *you* will be doing to create demand, so make sure your sales package or in-person presentation includes promotional plans.

You don't need to send a big package—probably somewhere between two and six pages plus the book will be sufficient. Here are some things you should include:

- The reason for the contact—you have published a book which you think the company should order
- A short summary of the book
- Who the potential readers are and why they would want to read it
- (For nonfiction) your background that qualifies you to write on the subject
- Marketing plans
- Previous sales, if any

- Suggested retail price, dealer cost, payment terms, returns policy, names of wholesalers and distributors

Even if you are not able to make a sale the first time, keep the communication channels open. If it's a local store, say "hello" to the manager or buyer when you are making a purchase, and mention how well your book is selling elsewhere, or tell her about some rave reviews or new publicity. If you've been in contact with someone by email or postal mail, after six weeks or so you can send another message with a progress report on sales, reviews and promotion, and add a subtle hint that it's not too late to place an order. Don't forget to say "thank you."

Get your company and your books listed in the handbook (directory) of the American Booksellers Association, at
www.bookweb.org/resources/bbh/questionaire.html

The American Booksellers Association has a great online locator for independent bookstores. It's at
www.indiebound.org/indie-store-finder

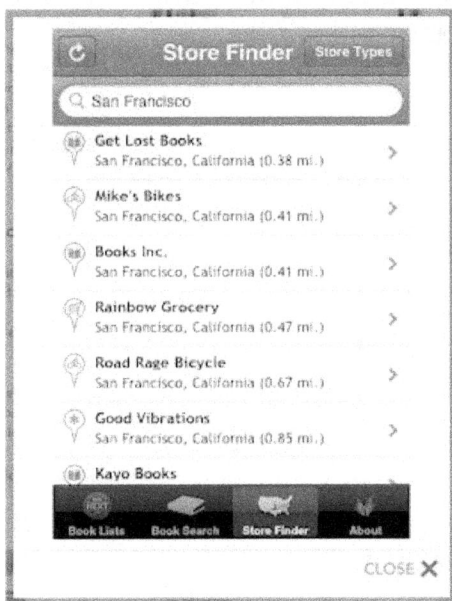

Shoppers just type in a Zip Code and distance and get an instant list, with addresses, store profiles and websites.

The Association even offers a free app for iPads, iPhones and the iPod Touch, called *IndieBound*. It helps shoppers to find independent bookstores near home or anywhere in the USA. The app also provides book information and allows online shopping.

You can support independent bookstores by becoming an affiliate. Instead of having links only to Amazon and B&N, you can also have a link that sends potential customers to indie booksellers in their area—and you can earn a commission on what they order. See **www.indiebound.org/affiliate.**

➔Local bookstores can be your allies even if they don't stock your book. Get to know the manager and salespeople. While buying something, let them know you are an author as well as a customer. Give them some free copies and a sell-sheet and tell them how to special-order the book for customers. Ask them to display a copy with a sign saying it can be ordered.

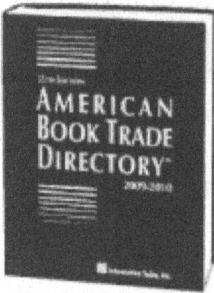

Published for over 50 years, the *American Book Trade Directory* has information on over 20,000 booksellers in the U.S. and Canada. The 1700-page book is expensive for a new self-published author (about $300 plus $25 for shipping), but it may turn out to be a worthwhile investment. For info and ordering, see **http://infotoday.stores.yahoo.net/ambooktraddi.html**

➔WARNING: Despite such promising phrases as "**aggressively promoted to appropriate markets**" (Outskirts Press) and "**unparalleled reach . . . to Christian bookstores across America and internationally**" (Schiel & Denver), don't expect a salesperson to be visiting bookstores on your behalf—unless *you* are the salesperson.

➔WARNING: Some "indie" bookstores will stock, display and promote self-published books if the author is willing to *pay a fee.* One store charges from $25 to $225 for its services. They make money even if no books are sold, If you pay $225, and sell two dozen books, you'll probably lose money.

CHAPTER 26
Selling out to a traditional publisher

Years ago, I was a copywriter at a major advertising agency in New York City. It had an excellent reputation and the writers and artists were well-paid and happy to work there. One day the owners announced that the agency was going to be sold to a much larger competitor. Some employees were concerned that their creative freedom would suffer under the bureaucracy they assumed would be imposed. One of the founders reassured us: "We're just cashing in, not selling out." If you get an offer to have a book taken over by a traditional publisher, think hard about the implications. You may or may not make more money, but you'll definitely lose the independence of self-publishing.

Some self-publishing companies play up the big-dollar deals that a few authors made when their books were taken over by traditional publishers. Those deals are extremely rare, and may not be worth pursuing—or even dreaming about.

◆A self-published author can make a nice living from sales that would bankrupt a major publisher. If you are content with your self-publishing income, there is probably no reason to sell out.

◆One possibly valid reason to make a deal with one of the big guys is to get improved distribution, particularly in bookstores that are hard for a self-published author to reach.

◆In the 21ˢᵗ century, you can't assume that a big publisher will do much promotion for you, so your ongoing work will not decrease by making a deal. And the future benefits of your previous hard work will now be shared with your new boss.

> The big reasons **nonfiction** writers self-publish are to have more control and make more money. If a big-name company takes over your book, you "sell" control for a few thousand dollars up front and the *possibility* of royalties later on. You may never get the royalties and your new boss may make big changes in your book and then kill it after a few months.
>
> The big reason **fiction** writers self-publish is because they could not interest any traditional publishers in their books. The sales prospects for self-published printed fiction (and poetry) are dismal. If you get an offer from one of the biggees, TAKE IT, but try to negotiate a contract that does not require selling your soul.

Novelist-actress-scientist Lisa Genova is a frequently touted example of a successful sellout. In 2007 Lisa paid iUniverse to publish *Still Alice*, and it was sold online. Ten months later, an agent made a deal with Pocket Books, which published it in 2009. Barnes & Noble sold more copies in the first two days than were previously sold in ten months. In its first week, it debuted at #5 on the *New York Times* bestseller list. It was featured in Target stores, which sold about a third of the copies. It's not realistic to expect to emulate Lisa's success, but it's nice to have something to dream about.

CHAPTER 27
À la carte overcharging

Self-publishing companies make most of their money by selling services to authors, not by selling books to readers. READ THAT SENTENCE AGAIN. The companies often sell high-profit add-ons at higher prices than authors would pay if they bought directly from the sources. You can even get—for FREE—some items that publishers charge for. Many options are really necessities. Some inexpensive publishing deals have low prices because they leave out a lot. Watch out for hidden expenses, and overcharges, and see what you can get on your own.

The *New York Times* said, "Xlibris charges nothing for its basic service, but because of the fees it charges writers for things like galleys and copyediting, its chief executive, John Feldcamp, says the company will be profitable even if it never sells a book." I believe him, because his company's publishing packages can cost as much as $13,999!

➜ The Xlibris profit on add-ons would make a loan shark jealous. If you want a CD-ROM of your **book files**, Xlibris will charge you $99 for a 25-cent blank disk and the time it takes to do a few mouse clicks. The Library of Congress charges ZERO for a **Control Number** and it's easy to get one. Xlibris will do the five minutes' work for you for $99. CrossBooks is a relative bargain, at $90.

Self-publishing companies apparently want you to think **copyright registration** is difficult. Wheatmark will do it for you for $199. Xlibris charges $249. Schiel & Denver charges $250. AuthorHouse charges $170. Outskirts Press charges $99. You can do it yourself for $35! It's not difficult. One company says, "We make all arrangements to take out the copyright in your name, and at our expense." That's a bit misleading. They may be sending $35 to the Feds, but that comes *after* they've received a much bigger payment from you.

I promote my books with **color business cards** which show the front covers. Look at the high prices for cards from some self-publishing companies:

◆Xlibris: 150 cards for $79 (53 cents each)

◆Outskirts Press: 500 cards for $199 (40 cents each)

◆CrossBooks: 5,000 cards for $780 (about 16 cents each)

◆Wheatmark or AuthorHouse: 1,000 cards for $250 (25 cents each)

➔You can get 1,500 cards for about $73 (five cents each) from VistaPrint. The quality and speed are as impressive as the price.

Promotional **postcards** can be useful *if* you have a good mailing list. Wheatmark will provide 1,000 4×6-inch cards for $349. AuthorHouse will do 1,000 4×6-inch cards for $500. CrossBooks charges its authors $600 for 1,000 4×6 cards. Xlibris wants you to pay $199 for 100 cards—NEARLY TWO BUCKS FOR A FRIGGIN' POSTCARD. While it is extremely unlikely

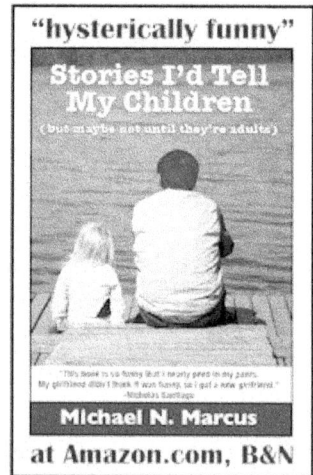

that any author would benefit from mailing out 1,000 cards, Vista-Print had a more reasonable price of about $90 for 1,000 cards

AuthorHouse will set up a **website** for $399 and host it for $29 per month. Lulu charges a whopping $600 to design a tiny, three-page site and does not offer hosting. Outskirts Press charges $299 for design and $29 per month for hosting. If you use iUniverse, you'll pay $399 for setup and $29 per month for hosting. I design my own websites for FREE with easy-to-use templates, and pay $6.64 per month for hosting by Network Solutions. Other hosting companies charge less, but $6.64 is low enough for me and I'm happy with Network Solutions—so I'm not shopping around.

Wheatmark will provide an **online press kit** for $449, plus $50 annual maintenance after the first year. It's similar to an author's website. The sample is well done, and probably worth the money—but you could design your own for free if you have the time, ability and desire. Wheatmark's per-year price is fair, and the service lets you make modifications whenever you want to, at no additional cost.

Like most of the self-publishing companies, Wheatmark will try to sell your book from its own website. For $99 per year, they'll arrange for a **web address** (like JoansBook.com) to "point to" your page on their site. You can get similar services for less than half that price from Network Solutions and other companies.

Lulu charges $100 to **write a press release**. If you can research and write a book, you can write your own release. For help, read *The Complete Guide to Book Marketing* by David Cole and *The Savvy Author's Guide to Book Publicity* by Lissa Warren. Both books cover much more than just writing a release, and belong on every self-publishing author's bookshelf.

For up to $1,799, Xlibris will **write and distribute a press release** to announce your book. CrossBooks charges $360, $720 or $900. AuthorHouse will distribute your press release using PR Newswire for $750. Balboa Press charges $900.

You can pay $680 if you go direct to PR Newswire, or just $399 with eReleases.com, which offers a discounted path to PR Newswire.

➔ The free PR services often used by self-publishing companies get minimal "pickup" from media, and may even carry ads for competing books and publishers. If your publisher is going to provide publicity, learn the details *before* you sign up.

Outskirts Press will submit your book to the Independent Book Publishers' **Benjamin Franklin Awards** for $299. You can do it yourself for $180, plus the cost of a few books.

For $164, Outskirts will be glad to sell you 120 **U.S. postage stamps** bearing the image of your book cover—that's $1.37 for each 44 cents worth of postage. But, if you go right to **www.Zazzle.com** you can order as few as 20 stamps for $17.95. The stamps are fun, but probably won't sell books.

You can get a "**Complete Internet Marketing package**" from iUniverse for $9,999. It includes "Author Website Set-Up," "Social Media Set-Up," "Google and Amazon Search Program," Barnes & Noble "See Inside the Book," and an email campaign to *ten million recipients*. iUniverse says that you'll save thousands of dollars with this package. If you do the important parts yourself, you can probably save $9,000 or more of the $9,999. If you don't buy the package, you can avoid causing ten million spam recipients to *hate your guts* and shun your wonderful new book.

iUniverse will also gladly accept your payment of $799 for their "**Social Media Marketing Setup Service**," that sets you up for a blog, and puts you on Facebook, MySpace, Flickr, Feedburner and some other online communities that I've never heard of. The ones that I have heard of are FREE.

If you want to dress up your book with **stock images** (generic drawings or photographs), AuthorHouse will charge you

$12 per image. I use Fotolia.com, and generally pay between $2 and $4 each—and can choose from over five million illustrations at prices as low as 14 cents each.

WingSpan Press will set up your book for **Amazon's Search InsideThe Book** feature for $75. CreateSpace does not charge for it, and you can do it yourself for free.

Some of the companies offer "**expedited services**" to get your book on the market extra fast. For example, the normal time to publication for Xlibris is three to four months. If you'll pay $349, they'll get your book out in less than two months. AuthorHouse will speed things up and get a book out in 30 days or less for an extra $500.

Lulu will sell you a package of **search engine clicks** on Google, Yahoo or Bing for $89, $199 or $369. Lulu says its program has "pricing that's as much as 75% cheaper than other services" and will "generate a guaranteed number of clicks to your content." For this system to work, someone must actually search for specific keywords that are related to your ad and your book, and they must be motivated by your little ad. The Click Through Ratio (CTR) is usually below 5%, but could be lower than 1% or higher than 25%.

Some keywords such as your name may be so obscure that NO ONE will search for them. On the other hand, some keywords, such as "sex" or "investment," are so popular that your tiny ad may be competing with dozens or hundreds of other ads. If the people paying for those ads are willing to pay more than you are, their ads will be put higher up on the page than yours is, and may be clicked on before or instead of yours.

Lulu's prices may not be bargains. On one of my popular websites, my average cost per click (CPC) is 55 cents. With Lulu's top plan, I'd pay $369 for 500 clicks, or 74 cents each.

"Bait and Switch" is common in self-publishing. Companies lure customers with illusory low prices and offer options that are really necessities.

Infinity Publishing says it "charges one low price of $499 to cover all aspects of publishing your book." They also say, "The only extras are marketing packages, copyediting [really a necessity and costing $0.013 per word], our extended distribution package with Ingram Book Group [costing $149 and really a necessity if you want your books to be sold by anyone other than Infinity and yourself], and photo scanning."

I could give you even more examples, but if you have not yet figured out the point of this chapter, you deserve to be taken advantage of. Either P. T. Barnum (shown), David Hannum, Michael Cassius McDonald, or Mark Twain said, **"There's a sucker born every minute."** Don't be one of them. Spend your money wisely.

So, which companies do I like?

◆For fast unbound proofs: **UPS Store** ◆For inexpensive bound proofs: **Lulu** or **CreateSpace** ◆For printing only, where you do all of the prep work: **Lightning Source** or **CreateSpace** ◆For the least expensive book publishing package with a custom cover: **Wasteland Press** ◆For refreshing honesty, flexibility and author control: **Dog Ear Publishing** ◆For various degrees of service and assistance: **CreateSpace** ◆For deluxe full-service publishing and promotion and first-class books: **Vantage Press**

Which companies don't I like?

PublishAmerica, Outskirts Press, Schiel & Denver, Xlibris, iUniverse, Infinity, Beckham, Westbow. Reasons include low quality, high price, unresponsiveness and sleaziness.

CHAPTER 28
Buying copies of your own book

Every author needs copies of his or her own book, to distribute to potential reviewers, to give to family and friends, to keep around the house or maybe even to sell. This is one area where you can really get soaked, so investigate and negotiate *before* you sign a contract.

Xlibris says that one of its founding principles "is that authors should have control over their work." Unfortunately, the company's authors can't control the prices of their books unless they pay $249 for price control. Xlibris has an **absolutely insane formula** for setting the cover prices of books, which in turn establishes authors' prices. The cover price for a 106-page book is $15.99. If you need 108 pages, however, the cover price jumps to $19.99—even though the difference in the manufacturing cost is about three cents and can't possibly justify a $4.00 difference in cover price. Strangely, the price for a book with 398 pages is also $19.99! But, at 400 pages the retail price jumps to $23.99, and that price holds all the way to 800 pages. Authors' discounts range from 30% to 60%, depending on the quantity ordered. The cost for a book with 108 pages can be $2.80

more than a book with 106 pages; but the costs for books with 108 pages and with 398 pages are the SAME.

Wheatmark says, "You may purchase additional books at 40% off the retail price."

IUniverse offers its author/customers book discounts ranging from 20% to 65% off the retail price. The discounts depend on the quantity ordered and the company offers an extra discount to authors for special events such as book signings at a "recognized venue," whatever that is.

Outskirts Press has a strange system of pricing authors' copies. For a 300-page, $14.95 book, the discounts range from 34% to 48% off the cover price. You get a bigger discount with the "diamond" package than with the "sapphire" package. However, since you'll pay $300 more for the Outskirts diamond deal, **if you want to pay less, you'll have to pay more**.

These pricing systems demonstrate incompetence, idiocy and ignorance.

➔ The retail price of a book—unlike a boat or a hammer—is often unrelated to its production cost. One fundamental point that many self-publishing companies seem to ignore is that the retail price of a book is a marketing decision and may have little or nothing to do with its printing cost.

➔ It does not cost any more to print a book with a $29.95 price printed on it than a book with $9.95 printed on it. The self-publishing companies apply author discounts to the WRONG numbers. Even if these publishers don't want to reveal their production costs, they could come up with authors' prices properly based on page count and page size, not cover price.

If my printer charges $5 to print and ship a 300-page book, and I am the publisher, I pay $5 whether the cover price is one penny, one dollar, $8.95, $10.95, $14.95, $24.95, or $150.

CHAPTER 29
Should you allow returns?

Unlike other retail products like clothing or computers, books are usually sold "on consignment." Booksellers don't have to care if they order slow-sellers or outright flops because almost all unsold books can be returned to the publisher, or even be destroyed, and still generate a refund or credit from the publisher. This adds to the cost of publishing (increasing the prices of books) and wastes natural resources.

If you use Print-On-Demand, there shouldn't be any unsold books, except for those that you choose to order for personal distribution.

To help writers who want their books to be on the shelves of physical bookstores, some self-publishing companies offer returnability. Sometimes, it's an optional, expensive paid-for service. Sometimes it's "free." Of course, nothing in publishing is ever really free. The cost of operating a system to accept book returns is paid for through the fees paid by the companies' author/customers, and by readers who buy their books.

Book returnability is an artifact of the Great Depression.

Sales of books, like sales of most non-necessities, had fallen off greatly. In an effort to get stores to take in new books, publishers offered guaranteed sales. Stores received the books on consignment, and, after several months, the money for the books that had been sold would be paid to the publishers. Unsold books would go back. This arrangement kept inventory on the bookstore shelves and helped create exposure for books on obscure topics or by unknown authors, but the logistics and waste added substantially to the cost of publishing.

The system was great for the bookstores and, although the Great Depression ended around 1939, returnability still exists a great many decades later. Bricks-and-mortar bookstores will expect returnability if they are going to stock you books. If you decide to play along, you should not be using POD because of the higher per-copy cost, and you should be prepared for a potential bankrupting shock when heavy cartons of unsold and tattered books come back.

➜For most self-publishing authors, it makes much more sense to forget about returns, forget about physical bookstores, and concentrate on sales through the online booksellers.

Some of the self-publishing companies tout their returnability programs to entice writers to do business with them, assuming that accepting returns will automatically mean that their books will soon be on the shelves at Barnes & Noble .

It may not happen. Booksellers are very wary of new books by unknown authors from a suspect publishing house; and the prospect of returning unsold books is unlikely to close the deal. If you sign up for the program, you will probably pay $500 or more per year and maybe accept a sub-normal royalty, and you still won't sell many books.

If you have a book with strong local appeal, you might be able to negotiate a sale through local bookstores, newsstands, gift stores, sporting goods stores, or whatever retail venues are appropriate. You can assume that they will want to buy on consignment. You don't have much to lose, so you can agree to a trial with an initial supply of a dozen books or so.

CHAPTER 30
Building your book

The main parts of a book are the **spine**, **front cover**, **front matter**, **body matter**, **back matter** and **back cover**.

The front matter may seem utilitarian and as boring as a real estate lease, but it can be very important. Potential buyers, both in bookstores and online, often read or skim the front pages as part of their buying decision. Pay attention to these pages. They can help sell your book.

The first pages in the front matter usually have no page numbers on them (*blind folios*), and the next pages have Roman numerals, and then there are common Arabic numbers. I avoid Roman numerals. When you publish your book, you're free to do what you prefer—but have good reasons when you break traditions.

There is no standardization for the location of the first printed Arabic number. I've seen it on the first page of the table of contents, the first or second page of the introduction, and the first, second, third or fourth page of the first chapter. I like to start showing numbers on the first contents page so readers will know where they are and how much is ahead.

What follows is a typical sequence for front matter. ➜ Items and sections are sometimes skipped, combined or shifted.

The **half title** (*bastard title*) page is the first right-hand (*recto*) page. It usually has nothing other than the title of the book in a very simple typeface, but may also have a small publisher's logo. Half titles may be planned, or added to create an additional page with something on it instead of a blank page when the printer has to add extra paper to a book. The half title page is not necessary, is somewhat archaic and its use seems to be declining—particularly in less-formal books. Why the heck should anyone have to read your title THREE TIMES (four if you count the spine) before starting to read the book? If you have a half title page, the back of it (the first left-hand, or *verso*, page) is usually blank.

Sometimes, the first recto page will have **comments** from readers or reviewers to help sell the book. Some books have several pages of comments. I think one is enough. Three pages of glowing and gushing endorsements may help to make a sale if someone is browsing in a physical store, but they are wasted on a reader who has bought the book online and wants to skip the "commercials" and start reading. One page may help reassure customers that they made a good choice, but don't waste any more trees.

Sometimes, the first verso page will have a **list of the author's other books, blogs, articles, etc.**

The **title page** may be the second recto page if you have a half title before it, or it may be the first recto page. It may be farther back if you have a comments page. It has the title, subtitle, author's name and publisher's name. It may also have names of other people involved in the production of the book, such as a co-author, editor or illustrator. The address of the publisher can go either on this page or the next page. The book name on the title page may be styled like the front cover, or have entirely different typography.

The back of the title page is usually called the **copyright page**. It has the copyright notice, the ISBN to identify your book, Library of Congress catalog information, and the printing history or revision or version. It may also contain disclaimers or legal notices and contact information.

The next recto page is often a **dedication**, where you get to thank or kiss the butts of some important people in your life, whether or not they were involved in making the book possible. I often push this page a bit farther back, after the table of contents, because it's probably less interesting to potential purchasers. Often, the page will not say "dedicated to," but just "to" or "for." Thank your parents.

The **table of contents** can be an important sales medium, so make it complete, clear, informative and well-written. If chapter titles don't explain what the chapters are about, put in some explanation. If you are a masochistic dreamer who's self-publishing a fiction book on paper, you can skip the table of contents unless your book is a collection of stories. ➡The sequence of chapters and the numbers of their starting pages will frequently change as a book evolves, so *make sure* the final table of contents is accurate. Many books leave out "table of" and call it simply "contents."

If you have **charts, tables or illustrations**, you can put a list of them and their pages after the table of contents. If you don't think people will look for specific items, it's probably a waste of paper. As with the table of contents, *make sure* the page numbers are accurate.

The **foreword** (not "forward") is an introduction, but it's not written by the author. It's often written by someone who knows the author or—even better—by someone famous. If the writer of the foreword is famous enough to increase sales, the name can go on the book's cover and title page. The foreword generally includes a reference to some interaction between the writer of the foreword and the author of the book such as, "The first time I met Pete, I was arresting him for smoking crack. I had no idea he'd become a brilliant business consultant." The foreword should explain why the book is important and well-written.

Unlike the foreword, the **preface** (pronounced "preffis") is written by the author. It's an introduction to the book (but some books contain both a preface and an introduction). This is your first opportunity to talk to your readers. You can say a bit about yourself, why you wrote the book, what you went through to write it, and what you hope it will accomplish. The preface is usually signed by the author and may include the date the book was completed and the city (but not the state) where it was written.

Sometimes, the preface is followed by an **introduction** if the book needs more explanation of what follows.

The **acknowledgment** is the section where you thank the people who helped you to research, write and complete the book. You can have just a list of names, but it's more common to have at least a sentence to explain what each person did. I sometimes combine the dedication, thank-you and acknowledgement into one section. I even thank the people who buy my books. This is a good place to flatter your seventh-grade English teacher if she was not listed earlier on the dedication page—especially if you think she'll show off the book and help to sell more copies.

The **prologue** is almost always used in a fiction book, which I hope you will not try to self-publish only on paper. It usually introduces a character, event or back-story that's important for understanding the book. Prologues are a bit old-fashioned, and often what is put into a prologue could function as your first chapter.

Now, at last, the front matter is finished and you get to the part of the book that matters most—the **body matter**, or just "body." It's usually divided into chapters, but is sometimes divided into sections (or parts) containing the chapters. The body typically takes up 90% or more of the book.

Next comes the **back matter**, often starting with the **epilogue** in a serious literary work (not a book about motorcycles). It may relate the fates of characters after the end of the main story, tie up some loose ends, or even prepare readers for a sequel. The tone of writing is usually the same as the body of the book.

An alternative or additional way of wrapping up is an **afterword**. This is a section where, as in the introduction, the author addresses the readers.

An **addendum** seldom appears in a self-published Print-On-Demand book, or an e-book. It's a section where the author can provide additional material, explanations or corrections that could not be in the body of the book because those pages were already printed. It may be an actual printed page bound into the book, or a separate piece of paper, a CD-ROM, or even an online file or blog.

Endnotes are pretty much like footnotes, but they're gathered together at the back of the book. Endnotes may be numbered to correspond to reference numbers in the text, or just refer to specific pages. They can offer information or explanations or cite the sources for statements in the text.

The **glossary** is an alphabetical listing of terms used in the book or related to the subject of the book, with definitions. Don't bother to include common words.

The **bibliography** is a list of books and other reference sources consulted while writing the book. It may also suggest further reading, even if the author didn't consult the recommended books.

The **index** is an alphabetical list of words and phrases used in the book, with the pages they are found on. Indexes can be constructed automatically by a PC, or manually by the author or a professional indexer. ➜If you make any changes that could cause words to shift from one page to another, you'll have to update the index.

The term "**colophon**" comes from a Greek word for "finishing," and usually explains why the book looks the way it does. It may include a list of typefaces used, and indicate who designed and printed the book, and possibly include some technical details of the printing. A colophon is neither mandatory nor common.

It's common for a book to have a paragraph or a page or two "**about the author**." It should be written in the third person, even if you write it yourself. Make it interesting and entertaining and convince potential readers to trust you.

If you have graphic images in your book, you should have a **list of photographs and drawings**, with the names of the photographers and artists who produced them.

Finally, after all of the *printed* pages, most books have one or more **blank pages**. Books are printed on large sheets of paper called *signatures*, which are cut to provide the needed quantities of pages. It's unusual for a book to be designed with a number of printed pages which perfectly matches the number of pages provided by the signatures. Consult with your publisher or printer to find out the possible number of pages you can have. By slightly stretching or cutting your book, you can minimize the blanks at the back. It looks really stupid—and wastes paper and money—if you have a bunch of blanks. Keep in mind that you may have to reserve the last verso page for a bar code, an identification number and "Printed in the USA," which are inserted by the printer.

CLXXX?

Traditionally, the first few pages of a book have no numbers printed on them, and then Roman numerals appear, maybe starting around VII on the contents page. Finally normal "Arabic" numbers start on an early page of the body matter.

I don't like pages without numbers. In several of my early books I bucked tradition and had "1" printed on the first page. In this book, I've compromised. I put unnumbered pages up front, and started Arabic numbering on the contents page. I didn't use any Roman numerals.

The History of the Decline and Fall of the Roman Empire is a six-volume set written by English historian Edward Gibbons. It was published in the late 1700s and covers the period from 180 to 1590. Gibbons said that the Empire was victim to barbarian invasions because Romans became weak, lazy, effeminate, pacifistic, corrupt and were both disinterested in civic duties *and* abusive of power. Gibbons wrote that Christianity created a belief that a better life existed after death, which fostered an indifference to life on earth, thus sapping the Romans' desire to work hard for the Empire.

Despite my Roman-sounding last name that comes from Mars, Rome's god of war, I have no personal experience with the decline of Rome. I would bet a few bucks (or even a denarius or two) that the dumb Roman numbering system sure didn't help the Romans to fight the Barbarians at the gates.

Here's a hyphen: ‐

Here's a minus sign: −

Here's a figure dash: ‒

Here's an en dash: –

Here's an em dash: —

Besides hyphenating, use the hyphen for "minus," (unless you are such a stickler that you want to use the REAL minus sign) and as part of a phone number or other numerical sequence if a *figure dash* is unavailable. (YES, I know that the figure dash looks like the en dash. There is a theoretical difference that's understood by a few guys on top of a mountain in Nepal, or maybe in a Burger King in Palo Alto.)

Use the en dash for ranges, such as June–August, 5:00–7:00 p.m., Ages 3–6.

Use the en dash to show contrasts or relationships: The Yankees beat the Mets, 24–6.

Use a pair of em dashes for a parenthetical remark—like this—when you want something more dramatic than parentheses or commas will provide.

An em dash can be used at the end of an interrupted quotation: Then Bill said to the robber, "I sure hope you're not going to—"

The em dash can also function as a "soft colon" in informal writing: This is the deal— if you won't wash the dishes, I won't cook. (In a case like this, I think a single dash should be attached to the preceding word with no added space, but there should be a space *after* the dash, as with a colon.)

CHAPTER 31
Writing & editing tips

Sometimes it can be very tough to type the first word. "Writer's block" affects most people who have to write—professionals as well as school kids. It can be caused by a lack of creative inspiration, by fear of writing the wrong thing, by hatred of the subject matter, by depression or even by an uncomfortable chair or a keyboard at the wrong height. The blockage can last for minutes, hours, days or decades. Henry Roth paused for 45 years after *Call It Sleep*.

For a student, writer's block might mean an "F" on a term paper. For a professional writer, the effects can be much worse. I was fired from my first job as assistant editor of a magazine when I had a two-week dry spell. Since I don't want that to happen to you, I'm glad to offer a simple and proven trick that should help you avoid either flunking or firing.

The opening word or phrase is undeniably important, but the importance can cause impotence. Fear of writing the wrong words can be like sexual performance anxiety or stage fright. The longer you stare at a blank sheet of paper or PC monitor, the more anxiety-inducing writing will become.

The need (or desire) to create something monumental like "It was the best of times, it was the worst of times," or "In the beginning, God created the heavens and the earth," or even "It was a dark and stormy night" can immobilize a writer.

Here's a simple cure for writer's block: if you can't write the first word or first sentence, JUST SKIP IT. Start farther down where you're more comfortable, and just *write*. Often, a book's beginning is an introduction. Once you've finished writing everything else, it will be much easier to write the introduction because you'll know what you're introducing.

◆It's hard to make a good index. Even good books have bad indexes. If you are sure you need to have an index, be prepared to invest a lot of time in it (when you might rather be doing something else) or maybe invest a lot of money to have someone else do it.

◆At the end of each day or after a major revision, save your book with a new file name. I like to use number sequences like software: 1.01, 1.02, etc.

◆Save your book onto your PC's hard drive *and* also onto portable media such as a USB thumb drive. Keep backup files outside of your primary workplace. Thumb drives are very inexpensive. You can afford to stash backups in *two* places. Or three.

◆You can often spot errors if you *look* at pages, but don't actually read what you are seeing.

◆Don't hyphenate words in chapter titles. Move the word down to the next line.

◆Make sure your PC has a functioning backup battery (*Uninterruptable Power Supply*, or *UPS.*) I've had good luck with UPSes from Minuteman, Tripp Lite, APC and Belkin.

◆Watch out for unintentional changes. Word can be independent, and nutso. It's not uncommon for line spacing to change or type to be dark gray instead of real black. It's easier to spot aberrations if you magnify the page up to 150 or 200% of normal size. The magnification also makes it easy to spot errors that were imported when you copied and pasted from other sources, especially straight quote marks and apostrophes that were supposed to have been changed to curlies. Word loves to put in horizontal lines (*rules*) where they don't belong and it can be extremely difficult to remove them.

◆Although Word can make numbered lists automatically, the lists may be inconsistent and unstable. It's sometimes better to insert numbers manually from the Symbol section, like ③.

◆Many people have trouble with "less" and "fewer."
    "Fewer" applies to things that are counted (e.g., apples). "Less" applies to things that are measured (e.g., apple sauce), or to concepts (e.g., freedom). You can have less wine, but fewer bottles and fewer drinks. You can have less time to travel, but fewer days for your trip. The express checkout lanes in supermarkets should be for buying *10 Items or Fewer*, not *10 Items or Less*.

◆ (From Emma Ruff, English teacher in my sophomore year in high school): "You **lie** sometimes or someplace, but you **lay** something or someone." I've remembered that since 1961

◆Traditionally, *who* is used for people, and *that* is used for non-humans. Dog owners, cat owners and the Associated Press recognize that a pet (probably above the level of fish) can be part of the family. Dogs, cats, and maybe even mice or turtles, get better treatment than inanimate objects. For an unknown animal, say, "Firemen rescued a cat *that* was stuck in a tree." If the animal has a known name, use *who*, plus *his/him/her/hers*. "Firemen rescued Fluffy, *who* was stuck in a tree."

◆"Unique" means one of a kind. It's an absolute—it can't be modified. All unique things are equally unique. Nothing can be "more unique" or "less unique" than any other thing. "Most unique" and "very unique" reveal ignorance about the English language. "Most unusual" and "very unusual" are OK, but never put a modifier before "unique."

◆Put your book away for a few weeks or—even better—a few months. When you return to it, you will discover errors you missed before and will probably have gained new insights during your absence. You'll likely realize that words and chapters that once seemed brilliant now seem insipid, silly, immature, superfluous, inadequate, out-of-date or otherwise inappropriate. However, you will probably have thought of new bits of brilliance which you can now insert to elevate the level of contemporary literature.

◆No matter how many times you read and reread, you will find mistakes in anything you've written. It's best to find them before the book is printed.

A while ago, just minutes before I had planned to send a book to the printer, I decided to check my table of contents. I had a feeling that, as I changed the length of some chapters, a page number might have changed. I actually found three wrong pages, and two chapters were missing from the table of contents. Don't let it happen to you.

◆The combination of changing paragraph spacing, changing type size and eliminating or substituting words gives authors who format their own books a lot more control compared to being subject to the whims of other editors and typographers.

◆I once decided to change a real name to a fake name in a book I was writing, to avoid embarrassing someone who might not want to be written about. I used Word's **Find and Replace** feature, which quickly made about a dozen substitutions.

But when I read through the chapter I was surprised to find a few instances of the old name which had escaped the **Find** function. ➔ It's important to do a manual verification, because Word might not notice hyphenated words or words with apostrophes or in their plural form as targets for replacement. Don't risk a lawsuit by leaving in a wrong name or word.

◆After days, weeks or years of staring at pages, it's easy to miss major goofs and little gremlins. Important work deserves a professional editor, or maybe even two.

But before it goes to the pros, let anyone who happens to be willing and handy read it—maybe even out loud—and see if he stumbles or notices anything weird that you didn't pick up.

You should listen closely, too. When words are verbalized, you absorb them much more slowly than when you scan a page with your eyes; and you're much more likely to notice errors, or awkwardness such as repetition of words or inappropriate alliterations. Fortunately for you, it's human nature to want to find fault, so there's a good chance that even an inexperienced, unofficial and untrained editor will spot some mistakes.

A book or magazine article that will sit around for a long time with your name on it deserves special care. For something with a tight deadline or that's less important—such as a blog or a website item which you can easily change—you can skip the professional editing and use a convenient unpaid amateur.

I write several blogs. I start around 3:30 in the morning. My wife would be *really* pissed off if I woke her up to read.

Even during normal business hours she's often pissed off when she reads what I've written, so I just have to trust my own editing ability (for blogs, not books).

◆An ellipsis (plural is "ellipses") is a series of three dots which can have several purposes, be governed by several standards, and appear in several forms. I use three dots with no spacing (...) to indicate a pause, or a trailing-off into another phrase. I use three dots with spaces to indicate an omission. If the omission is at the end of a sentence, I use four, like . . . .

◆There are several standards for printing numbers (*figures*) in a book. One calls for spelling out one through nine, another says you should spell out numbers through ten. In "serious" literary books you may even see "ninety-three" or "four thousand." Select a system and *stick to it*. One book in the *For Dummies* series has "10" and "ten" in the same paragraph!

EXCEPTIONS:
①Never start a sentence with a figure. Write: "Fourteen mayors are up for re-election," not "14 Mayors." You may need to rewrite to avoid awkwardness. You can say, "In 1982, the divorce rate rose to . . ." to avoid "Nineteen-Eighty-Two was the first year that the divorce rate reached . . . ."
②Use the *same style* when numbers are nearby: "eight to twelve" or "8 to 12"—not "eight to 12."
③Don't spell out numbers in addresses or prices, except for low numbers like "One Main Street" or "five bucks."

CHAPTER 32
How good is good enough?

When I was a writer on my college newspaper, I became the copyeditor *and* got a job as a proofreader at the printer's so I could have complete control of my words, and no one else could mess them up. This also meant that no one else could correct the mistakes I missed. That's not a good way to work.

When I was freelancing for *Rolling Stone* magazine, I was always rewriting until the last possible minute. This was in the pre-fax, pre-email era, and I'd drive to the airport and *pay* to have my column air-freighted from New York to California. There wasn't much profit left.

Words are almost toys for me, like a child's building blocks, Lincoln Logs, Legos or an Erector Set. Rewriting and editing—especially with a computer—is fun. I love to play with words, to rearrange them and try alternatives.

When I worked as an advertising copywriter, I was notorious for not "releasing" an ad until the last possible moment.

Someone older and wiser taught me a valuable lesson: **A perfectionist never finishes anything. Sometimes "good enough" really is good enough.** I learned to let go.

Now as a self-publisher who has to be a businessman as well as an artist, I realize that no money will come in if I don't approve a proof and let a book start selling.

However, I never stop editing.

With POD I can make improvements whenever I want to.

While this means that a person who buys version 2.23 gets a better book than the person who bought 1.28, at least I know that each version was "good enough." ➔ Every book is a "work in progress." Keep making your books better and better.

Get virtual books, for free.

It's good to have a realistic "three-dimensional" picture of a book before it exists. It will help with publicity, seeking orders, and evaluating titles and cover designs with more impact than a flat printout or monitor viewing can provide.

If you have a cover image, it can be magically attached to a picture of a realistic book or even a stack of books at **www.myecovermaker.com.**

You can choose from a huge selection of book types, and even CD-ROMs, loose-leaf notebooks, iPads, Kindles and multimedia packages.

Some styles are free. Some styles are paid for with an in-expensive monthly or annual membership fee.

The service is very easy to use, and an image takes less than a minute to produce and download to your computer.

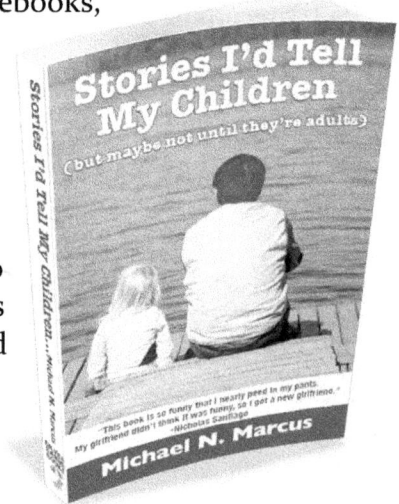

CHAPTER 33
Designing your book's covers

In the traditional aphorism, we are advised that we can't judge (or "tell") a book by its cover. That means we can't, or shouldn't, form a judgment about things or people solely by considering their exterior appearance.

In human terms, this may mean that a very ugly person could be very nice and maybe even become a perfect spouse or employee.

With books, however, it's a different story.

Even though the material packaged inside a poorly designed cover may be worthwhile, interesting, important and entertaining, if you have an ugly cover, there's a good chance that no one will ever read what you've written. In physical bookstores and also online, ugly covers are ignored or shunned in favor of more attractive and inviting competition.

In theory, anyone can design a book cover. But everyone should *not* do it. Book design requires artistic ability, taste, judgment, experience, training, understanding of the book's purpose and audience, and knowledge of the specifics of cover design and the software used to produce it.

This book tells you how to do a lot of things, but it does not provide step-by-step instructions for designing a book cover.

Your cover is too important to be left to an amateur—so I'll give you tips, but *not* instructions.

Just because someone is good at painting portraits or designing homes, DO NOT assume that person is qualified to design a book cover. It's not much more difficult to get a good cover than a mediocre cover, but there are tricks of the trade which are specific to the *online sales channel*—a channel which is crucial for most self-published authors.

➜A beautiful illustration that would be a powerful eye-grabber under the spotlight in a book store may become a tiny incomprehensible blob when displayed on a website. Subtle color combinations that win awards in art school may not have adequate contrast to allow potential customers to separate the text from the background on computer monitors.

Spend a lot of time cruising the aisles of local bookstores. If you live out in the boondocks, this is a good reason to visit the big city. Pay attention to books that are displayed face-out, as well as those that show only their spines. After a while, you should have a good idea of what works and what doesn't, and what you like and don't like.

If there are books that you really love and want to emulate, *buy* them. While you're helping other authors make a few bucks, you should get a tax deduction. You may even be able to deduct the cost of your research trip. Now spend some time inspecting the online booksellers. Pay particular attention to how books look when reduced to the size of a postage stamp (called *thumbnails* in the graphics arts business).

Also see the award-winning covers at **www.aiga.org.** It's the website of the oldest and largest professional organization for graphic designers. The site also has a good sample contract.

If you are using a self-publishing company, you may have the choice of submitting your own complete cover, or paying for the services of a designer who works for the publisher. It's possible to get a good cover—or a bad cover—either way.

Designing your book's covers

If you've hired a freelance designer, presumably you've seen and liked previous work she's done, you two get along, and you've agreed on an approximate price for the work. It could be based either on hours or a flat fee for the project. A designer who charges less than $50 an hour may not be good enough to do the job. A designer who charges more than $1,000 for the project is probably too expensive.

It's good to have a written contract or even an informal memorandum of understanding, or a proposal. Almost anything on paper which describes the work, prices and timetable will minimize misunderstandings and hard feelings later.

If you have an idea about what the cover should look like, make a sketch and show it to the designer, or send email links to covers you like. Be prepared for the possibility that your designer may actually know more about books than you do. She may tell you that your idea sucks (or something more polite). You have the right to tell a designer that her idea sucks, and request a different design—or a different designer.

The designer should provide three to six *roughs* (informal sketches) to consider. It's OK to combine elements of several and it's OK to reject them all.

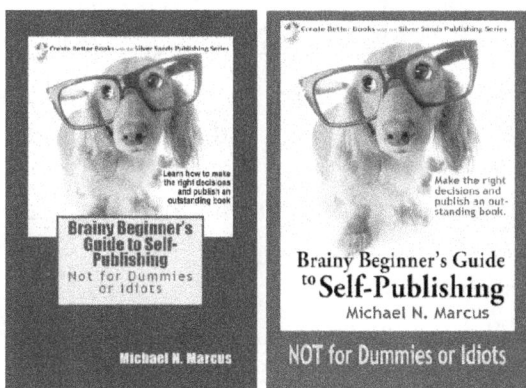

Here are early and late versions of this book's cover, both made by me with CreateSpace templates. I am definitely not a professional designer, but I like designing and am getting better at it.

Cover Design Tips

◆Make sure your book looks good in the size in which Amazon will show it. It's possible for people to click on the thumbnail image and see almost a full-size cover, but try for a design that works well in postage-stamp-size. Excellent artists have designed very attractive stamps.

◆Also consider how your book will look when converted to grayscale (black and white). It may show up in a book like this one or a catalog or newspaper that doesn't have color pages.

◆Choose the appropriate binding for your topic, audience and price. Most how-to books, like this one, are *perfect-bound* paperbacks (*soft covers*). If your book's price is $24.95 or higher, many people will expect a *hardcover* book, probably with a *dust jacket*. Hardcovers cost more to manufacture than

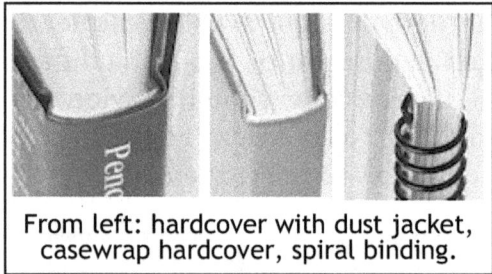

From left: hardcover with dust jacket, casewrap hardcover, spiral binding.

soft covers. A *casewrap* is a less-expensive hardcover binding without a dust jacket. Instruction manuals and cookbooks are more useful if they can lie flat when open and are often constructed with a *comb* or *spiral* binding. Unfortunately, these two binding methods are fragile and pages may become detached if the book is used frequently.

◆If you have a photo or illustration on the cover, make sure it does not overpower or conflict with the title. It should reinforce the title. Don't use a photo so big that it necessitates a small title that will be hard to read.

◆If the photo or illustration is important, make sure the title or subtitle doesn't mask it.

◆Make sure you have adequate contrast between your type and the background. Red-on-orange may work for a day-glow concert poster, but it makes a book cover hard to read.

◆Make sure the mood of the artwork complements the title and the purpose of the book. A pastoral scene with cows grazing near a brook is probably not right for a "get up and take charge" business book—even if those cows are really bulls.

⬇If you are supplying the cover design, your publisher or printer can provide an "empty" template with lines showing where you should put words and pictures, and where you should not.

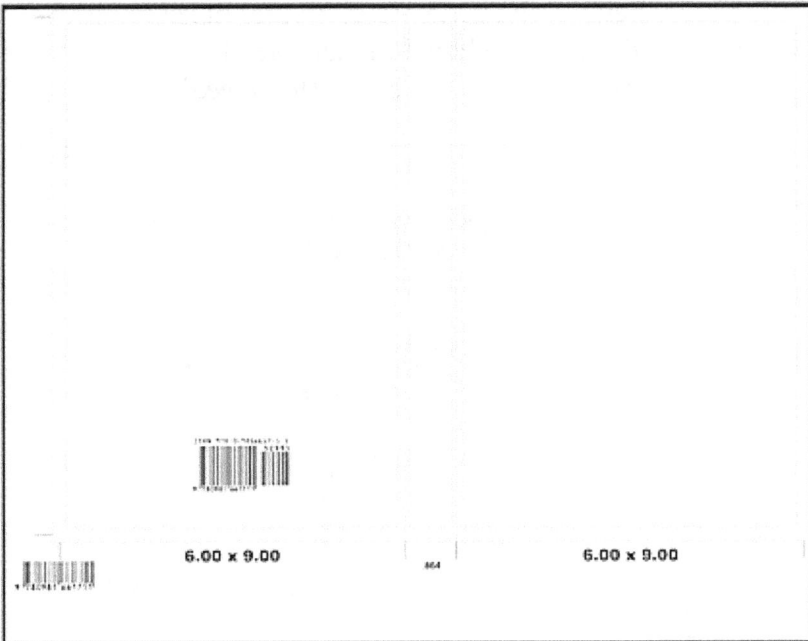

6.00 x 9.00   6.00 x 9.00

◆Book covers are very different from other "documents" in one important way: If you're writing a term paper or a letter, you wouldn't dream of letting your words go all the way to the edge of a page. Book covers (and magazine covers, ads, posters and packages) often have graphic images that go all the way to the edges. It's just not possible to predict exactly where the printer's trimming blades will chop your paper, so the cover is designed with art that "bleeds" outside the normal borders.

The typical bleed is ¼ of an inch. Keep important text and images out of the bleed space so they are not lost. A typical 6-inch-wide book cover has a *safety zone* that stops ¼ inch away from the theoretical trimmed edge. Beyond that safety zone is the *danger zone* that should not contain anything important. The danger zone and the area beyond the trim are considered to be the bleed area.

Without a bleed, your cover may have an unintended white border beyond the edge of a color graphic element. Your cover may be designed to bleed in just one direction, or it can bleed on two, three, or all four edges (*full bleed*).

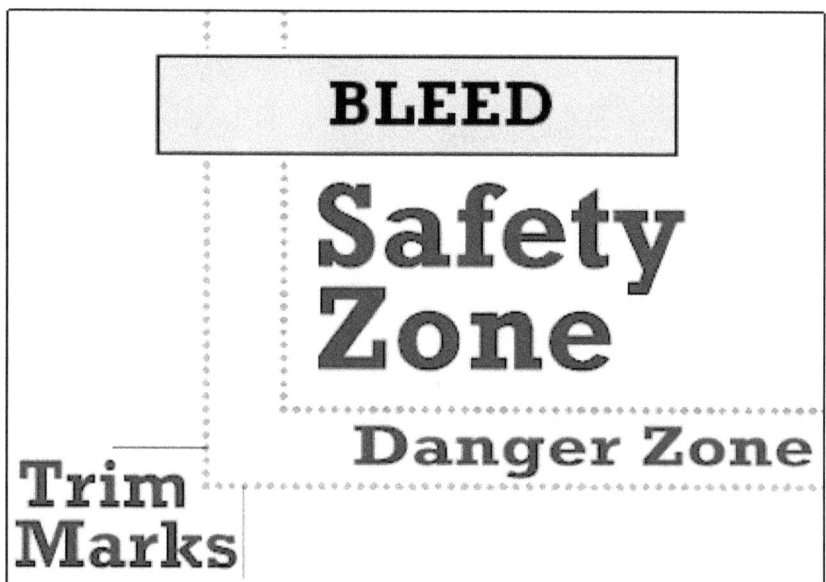

BLEED

Safety Zone

Danger Zone

Trim Marks

Diagram shows the lower left corner of a cover design template.

Designing your book's covers

Cover alignment is not precise. Don't be surprised if part of your front cover or back cover ends up on the spine. For this reason, I caution against bleeds that might accidentally wrap around. On the other hand, if your book has horizontal color bands or a large illustration that deliberately wraps around three surfaces of the cover, the design can be very dramatic with little danger.

◆Unless you have a tiny budget, do not use a pre-made cover design from a self-publishing company, where you just pick a title, a color and a typeface. It's much better to pay for professional help to get something original and interesting. If you do use a template, check out the available variations.

◆There are online "budget book design" services that can provide a cover design for about $300. I have not tried any of them, but I've heard good things about some of them. Take a look at the online samples and customers' comments. ➔Some self-published authors are very pleased with low-priced cover designs produced by freelance artists all over the world through **www.elance.com**. For $10 you can post a project description, and then sort out the proposals and references.

◆A simple design is better than a complex design. You have only a second or two to capture a shopper's attention.

◆Check the final design very carefully. It's easy to miss errors in unexpected places, like the price, a URL or a Zip Code. Have your copyeditor check the cover.

➔◆Watch out for *conflicts and inconsistencies*. Sometimes a number ("10 years in preparation") might be inside the book, but the cover says something else ("11 years"). I know of one book with different titles on the front cover and spine, and another with the wrong title on the back cover. BE CAREFUL.

Designing a cover for online selling

⬇The covers shown are about one third larger than Amazon's thumbnails. The size you see when you view the website depends on your monitor and its settings.

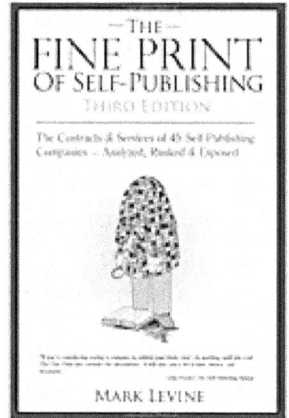

The classic book for writers, Strunk & White's *The Elements of Style*, was first published in 1959. It shows up quite well in the small thumbnail size. It's readable and powerful. On a computer monitor, you'd see the book cover in color.

It's very difficult to read the cover on my first self-published book, *I Only Flunk My Brightest Students: stories from school and real life* when Amazon shows it as a thumbnail. The lack of a border makes it fade into the white space.

Only two words of the title of *The Fine Print of Self-Publishing* are easy to read in thumbnail size, and the subtitle is completely gone. However, the dark border defines the shape and size of the book much better than my pure white books.

◆ I like the crisp and clean look of a white cover, and that's what I used for my first three books. Unfortunately, they blend into the white pages of booksellers' websites. A color background or a dark border would be better for online sales.

Some publishing authorities suggest evaluating cover designs by looking at them from three or four feet away, to determine if they are readable by the average shopper wandering down the aisles in a bookstore. It's a nice test, but it may be utterly unimportant for a book that's sold mostly online.

Some other authorities completely dismiss the value of having an attractive cover for online sales.

I disagree. I think people prefer to own attractive things. Also, a better-looking book is more likely to be noticed and picked up by visitors to one of your customers' homes or offices. Each of your books can help sell additional copies—and you don't have to pay a salesman's commission.

(This is more an issue for bookstores than for online selling, where people search by topic.) Don't deceive browsers just to attract their attention. Bikini babes don't belong on the cover of a book about gardening or contract negotiation.

Ugly cover, ugly book, terrible title, absurd price

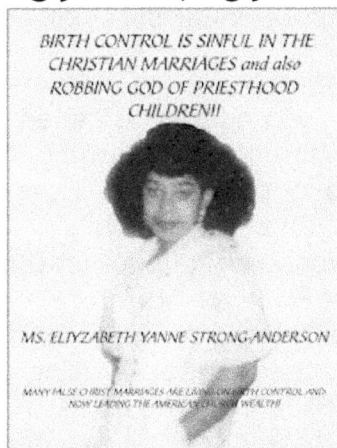

BIRTH CONTROL IS SINFUL IN THE CHRISTIAN MARRIAGES and also ROBBING GOD OF PRIESTHOOD CHILDREN!!

MS. ELIYZABETH YANNE STRONG-ANDERSON

MANY FALSE CHRIST MARRIAGES ARE USING ON BIRTH CONTROL AND NOW LEADING THE AMERICA CHURCH WEALTHE

This overpriced, ugly and weird book was recently ranked #10,255,344 by Amazon.com. It may be the absolute worst-seller on Amazon. Based on its title, cover, formatting and writing, it may also be the absolute worst book ever published.

The title is *Birth Control is Sinful in the Christian Marriages and also Robbing God of Priesthood Children!!*

It has 648 huge 8.5 x 11-inch pages and a $150 cover price! EVERY LETTER INSIDE THE BOOK IS IN UPPERCASE.

Your claim to fame

Every part of your cover is an advertisement which should help to sell books. If you are an unknown author, your name on the cover can be accompanied by a one-line bio, such as "Professor of Nuclear Medicine at Harvard University." If you have no such claim to fame, use the space for a blurb from someone to establish your credibility, either through her own fame or by what she says. If all you can say about yourself is that you wrote an unknown book in another field, don't say it. Find *someone* to say something positive about you or your book.

The front cover of Chaim Potok's *In The Beginning* identifies Potok as the author of *The Chosen*. The earlier book received rave reviews and was a finalist for the National Book Award. Potok's name in huge type implies that he is well-known, but the reference to the other book at the bottom of this book provides an additional bit of credibility, just in case someone knows his work but does not know his name.

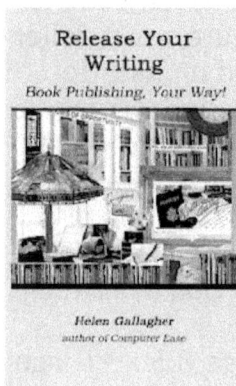

Helen Gallagher's second book is called *Release Your Writing: Book Publishing, Your Way!* The cover proclaims that she is "author of *Computer Ease*." While that first book may be a fine book, it did not win the Nobel Prize for literature and is in a field unrelated to the second book. If the likely reaction to a writing credit is "BFD," "WTF?," "Who cares?" or "So what?" find something else to put in the space that may help to sell books.

Your back cover

Every book that has a front cover also has a back cover (unless someone tore it off). In a physical bookstore, the back cover is an important selling piece. **Your back cover is an advertisement! Make the most of it.** It gives you an excellent opportunity to convince a prospective customer to purchase the book he or she has plucked from a shelf or display.

It's very different when you are selling online. Amazon does not automatically show your back cover. If you want potential customers to see it and read it, you have to upload the image yourself by clicking on **Share your own customer images**.

If you want your book to be sold by booksellers, your back cover must show an ISBN (see next chapter) and its associated bar code, which usually go at the bottom of the cover.

It's customary to indicate the book's classification, such as "humor" or "gardening," so bookstore people know where to put it. There's no rule against listing two classifications such as "history" and "geography" if they both apply. Find out how competitive books are classified, and check the huge book subject list at the Book Industry Study Group:
www.bisg.org/standards/bisac_subject/index.html

Here's what else you should include:

◆What the book is about and why people should buy it
◆Comments ("blurbs") from readers and reviewers if available
◆Your brief biography, to establish yourself as an authority in the field you are writing about
◆Your photo—a studio portrait, *not* an amateur snapshot
◆Name of publishing company, with city, state and web URL
◆List price for United States and possibly other countries, particularly Canada

What goes on the spine?

Even if all of your sales are online and you don't care about being noticed on a bookstore shelf, a legible spine title will make it easier for your customers to pluck your book from their own bookshelves.

On a crowded shelf in a bricks-and-mortar bookstore, often the only sign of your life will be a narrow spine squeezed in among dozens of competitors.

Because of the limited space available (the spine on a 200-page book is only about a half inch wide) you have to consider the trade-offs between visibility and contents.

The more you try to squeeze onto the spine, the smaller each word will be. It's important to be as big and bold as possible. In thin books, you probably won't have room for a subtitle, and maybe not enough room for even your own name.

This is where an experienced designer can make a big difference. By using a narrow typeface, your spine can have more words in the same space. Lettering should strongly contrast with the background color. It may be necessary to omit your name or use just your last name.

It's common to put the publishing company's logo on the spine, even in small size. If your book is published by a self-publishing company, its logo may hurt, not help.

The spine size is determined by the thickness of the book, which is determined by the number of pages and the thickness of the paper—so you can have only a rough layout of the spine until the number of pages is finalized.

It's possible that the spine text won't be centered between the front and back covers, so leave some extra white space (or whatever color you are using for your background) around the text. Your publisher or printer can advise you how much clearance is required between your text and the edges (the *safety zone*). A sixteenth of an inch is typical.

➔Make sure the spine text faces the right way. Every so often—even from major publishing companies—books are printed with inverted spines. The error is usually caught before books are shipped to stores. CD and DVD packages are printed improperly more frequently than book covers are.

◆When your book is standing up with its front cover facing to the right, the spine text should read from top to bottom. When the book is lying down with its front cover facing upward and the spine towards you, the spine text should read normally, from left to right.

◆Some books have vertical type stacked up on their spines. It often looks ugly because of the variation in letter width. I usually don't like it, but I can't stop you from doing it.

◆If you have a really thick book, of course, your spine text can be horizontal even when the book is vertical. If you have an incredibly thick book, maybe it should be two books.

Show some originality, *please*.

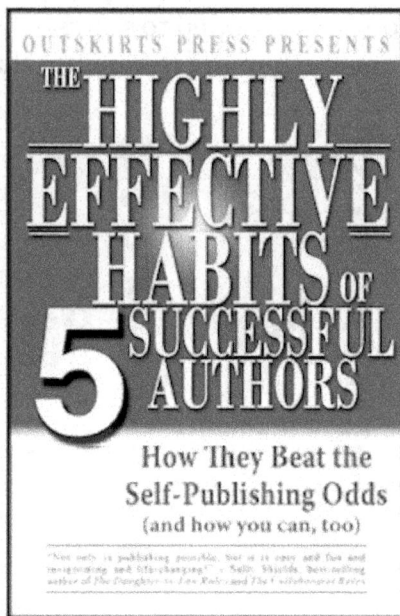

It's smart to study other books and to seek inspiration from successful authors and designers—but don't be a copycat.

The book on the left has sold millions of copies since 2004. It provides guidance for solving personal and professional problems.

The book on the right, which copied the cover design, typefaces and title style of the bestseller, is a promotional piece from Outskirts Press.

I saw four five-star reviews for the Outskirts book on Amazon.com. Two were written by Outskirts authors featured in the book, and one was written by an Outskirts employees. That seems a bit sleazy—just like the cover.

CHAPTER 34
What's an ISBN and do you need one?

ISBN stands for **International Standard Book Number**. It's a 13-digit number which identifies one version of one book.

If you plan to sell your book from the back of a lecture hall or the trunk of your car or a table on the sidewalk—or just want to give it away—you don't need an ISBN. But, if you have an intention or dream of selling through bookstores either on Earth or online—you *need* an ISBN.

An ISBN aids marketing and cataloging of products by printers, publishers, booksellers, libraries and distributors.

ISBNs are generally accompanied by a bar code—much like the UPC (Universal Product Code)—found on everything from ketchup bottles to bicycles.

The bar code you see on the back of a book is derived from its ISBN, but the two are not the same thing.

An ISBN is only a number. The bars provide data for optical scanning, most often by a cashier in a bookstore, so customers will pay the right price. The record of the sale can enable store management to track inventory levels and know when to re-order, or perhaps to decide to stop selling a particular book.

Each recent ISBN consists of 13 digits and, when printed, it is preceded by the letters "ISBN." The 13-digit number is divided into five parts of varying lengths. When printed above the bar code, the parts are sometimes separated by hyphens to make the code easier to read.

ISBN 978-0-9816617-0-4

51995

9 780981 661704

The numbers in the second row are not part of the ISBN but are commonly printed with it. They indicate the cover price (suggested retail price). The first digit (5 in the sample) indicates that the price is in U.S. dollars. The next digits show the price is $19.95. Some books are printed without prices.

What's an ISBN and do you need one?

R. R. Bowker (**www.bowker.com**), the ISBN agency for the United States, assigns ISBNs upon the request of publishers, audio and video producers, software producers and museums and associations that publish.

Bowker says you should allow 15 days for processing from the time an application is received. The first time I tried it, it took just a few days to receive my ISBNs. The second time, it took a few minutes.

Bowker assigns ISBNs to publishers in blocks of 10, 100, and 1,000 numbers—but you can get just one at a time if that's all you need. Each block is configured so that seven digits are the same. These digits, called the "prefix," identify a publishing company.

The fee for one ISBN is $125. The fee for a block of ten is just $250. If you think you'll do two books, you may as well get ten ISBNs, because publishing is addictive. ISBN fees are not refundable and you can't transfer ISBNs to others, so be reasonably sure you really will publish before you pay for ISBNs.

➔ Each binding or format (such as hardcover, paperback, video, e-book and audio book) usually has a separate ISBN. NOTE: depending on the distribution channel, e-books may not need ISBNs. Ask the distributor or bookseller. Lulu, for example, does not require ISBNs for e-books.

A new ISBN is required for a revised edition if it's a major revision, such as the addition of a chapter.

Once assigned, an ISBN can never be reused.

The ISBN is printed on the bottom of the back cover of a book above the bar code, and on the copyright page.

If you are a self-publishing author with your own brand name, you decide which of your ISBNs go with which books. If you are going to publish multiple books, keep a list of your ISBNs to make sure you don't assign the same ISBN to several books. It's common to assign the ISBN well in advance of publishing.

Once you've assigned an ISBN, you should register it with *Books in Print* at **www.bowkerlink.com** so booksellers and librarians will be able to find it for ordering.

Self-publishing companies and ISBNs

If you use a company to print your book and it provides the ISBN, your book title is tied to that company. That company is the official "publisher of record."

If you become unhappy and want to use another publisher, you will have to get a new ISBN. You can use the same title again, but you risk confusion and lost business if people search for your name or the book's title and order from the wrong publisher.

Some self-publishing companies will allow you to use your own ISBN (and company name and logo), but some will not. Some who do allow it charge you for the service. CreateSpace does not charge.

Some self-publishing companies offer inexpensive publishing packages with no ISBN. If you want your books to be sold by normal booksellers, this is NO GOOD.

Some ISBN rules (from Bowker)

Bowker is the only company authorized to assign ISBNs to publishers using an address in the United States.

You may get offers from other sources to purchase single ISBNs at special prices. Be wary. There are *unauthorized resellers* of ISBNs and this activity is a violation of the ISBN rules and of industry practice. If you use a reassigned ISBN, you will not be identified as the "publisher of record."

Once an ISBN publisher prefix and block of numbers have been assigned to a publisher by Bowker, the publisher assigns ISBNs to its books. A publisher cannot resell, reassign, transfer or split its ISBNs among other publishers.

CHAPTER 35
Understanding your copyrights

A copyright determines who has the right to copy what you write. Millions of words have been written on the subject, and I see no reason to add a million more. The quick explanation is that nobody has the right to copy your words without permission until 70 years after you die. If *you* copy this book 60 years after I die, without permission from me or my agent or estate, I can come back and sue you. You should be safe around 2102. Until then, these words are mine!

NOTE: I AM NOT AN ATTORNEY. THIS BRIEF SECTION IS BE-LIEVED TO BE ACCURATE, BUT BEFORE YOU DO ANYTHING BASED ON WHAT YOU READ HERE, YOU CAN ASK A QUAL-IFIED ATTORNEY OR THE COPYRIGHT OFFICE.

It is commonly believed that a creative work must be registered with the government to be protected by copyright. That's not true. Your precious work is legally protected from copycats from the moment of creation without your having to fill out any forms or having to pay even one penny to the Feds. Your work is copyrighted even if you don't put the © copyright symbol on it.

However, there are still advantages to going through a formal copyright registration, particularly if you end up suing for copyright infringement.

Copyright is a form of protection, grounded in the U.S. Constitution and granted by law for original works of authorship such as poetry, novels, movies, songs, computer software and architecture, fixed in a *tangible medium of expression*. Copyright covers both published and unpublished works.

➜ Your work is under copyright protection the moment it is created and fixed in a tangible form that is perceptible either directly or with the aid of a device. That means that what you put on a website or blog *is* copyrighted.

Copyright does not protect facts, ideas, discoveries, systems, or methods of operation, although it may protect the way they are expressed.

Copyright protects original works of authorship, while a *patent* protects inventions or discoveries. A *trademark* protects words, phrases, symbols or designs identifying the source of the goods or services of one entity and distinguishing them from those of others. A book's title *can't* be copyrighted, but it can sometimes be protected as a trademark.

Copyright registration is voluntary. Many people choose to register their works because they want to have the facts of their copyright as a public record and have a certificate of registration. Registered works may be eligible for statutory damages and attorney's fees in successful litigation. If registration occurs within five years of publication, it is considered *prima facie* evidence in a court of law. Registration within 90 days gives you the most protection.

➜ The practice of mailing a copy of your own work to yourself is sometimes called a "**poor man's copyright**." There is no provision in the copyright law regarding this type of protection, and it is not a substitute for registration. It probably won't be useful in a lawsuit because it is so easily faked by mailing an empty envelope and inserting a document later.

The United States has copyright relations with most countries and most countries honor others' citizens' copyrights.

The U.S. Copyright Office changed its fees in 2009. Thanks to cost savings achieved through increased office automation, some fees remained the same or decreased. Other fees—mostly for services requiring manual labor—went up.

➡ The fee for filing a copyright application online, using the new electronic Copyright Office (eCO), is just $35. Self-publishing companies often charge much more to get a copyright. CrossBooks charges $204. Schiel & Denver charges $250! It takes less than 15 minutes to register online. The fee is $50 if you register with a paper application.

More than 50 percent of copyright claims are now being submitted through eCO. The waiting time to receive certificates is much shorter for users of eCO than for those who submit paper applications.

In addition to a lower filing fee and the fastest processing time, advantages of electronic filing include the ability to track the status of claims online, to pay by credit or debit card, and to upload some creative works electronically.

Whether you register online or on paper, the Library of Congress still requires a real book to be sent in (except for e-books that don't exist on paper).

You must send what the Library calls the "best edition" of your work. The "best edition" is determined based on expected durability, not luxury. For example, if you publish two hardbound versions of a book, one a trade edition printed on acid-free paper and the other a specially bound edition printed on average paper, the first will be the best edition because the type of paper is more important than the binding.

If you file your application online using eCO eService, you may pay by credit card. Credit cards are not accepted for registration through the mail, but may be used for registrations that are filed in person in the Copyright Office in Washington.

➜ If you register within five years of publication, and have to sue someone for copyright violation, a court should recognize the validity of the copyright and the facts on the certificate. If you register within three months of publication, you can sue for statutory damages and attorney's fee. Later registration may limit your payment to the actual loss—which could be three dollars.

You may register unpublished works as a collection on one application, with one title for the entire collection. It is not necessary to list the individual titles in your collection. Published works may be registered as a collection only if they were actually first published as a collection.

There is no legal requirement that the author be identified by his or her real name on the application form. If filing under a pen name, check the "Pseudonymous" box when giving information about the author.

When you register your claim to copyright a work with the U.S. Copyright Office, you are making a *public record*. All the information you provide on your copyright registration is available to the public and will be on the Internet.

The length of time the Copyright Office requires to process an application varies depending on the number of applications the Office is handling at the time of submission and any questions associated with the application. Ninety percent of online filers should receive a certificate of registration within six months of submission. A third should receive a certificate within ten weeks of submission.

➜ Regardless of the time needed to issue a certificate, the effective date of registration is the day the Copyright Office receives a complete submission in acceptable form. You do not need to wait for a certificate to publish your book.

➜ By custom (not by law), if you publish a book during the last three or four months of the year, you can use a copyright date of the next year. This makes the book seem to be a year fresher as it ages. However, DON'T register it until the year printed in the book.

You may make a new copyright registration for a book if you make "substantial and creative" changes. Simply making spelling corrections throughout a book would not warrant a new registration, but adding another chapter would.

Copyrighting e-books

As of mid-2011, the Copyright Office had not yet devised a procedure for issuing copyrights to books that exist only in electronic form. If you publish an e-book, print out the text and submit the printed material to Washington. The copyright protects content, regardless of format.

Copyright Office website:
www.copyright.gov
Electronic Copyright Office:
w**ww.copyright.gov/eco/notice.html**

Physical Address:
 U.S. Copyright Office
101 Independence Ave. S.E.
Washington, D.C. 20559-6000
Phone: 202-707-3000

(This chapter includes material provided by the U.S. Copyright Office. The author of this book does not claim copyright.)

Your book can be in the world's largest library

The Library of Congress ("LOC" or "LC") is the oldest federal cultural institution in the United States and serves as the research arm of Congress.

It is also the largest library in the world, with more than 33 million books and other print materials, 3 million recordings, 12.5 million photographs, 5.3 million maps, 6 million pieces of sheet music and 63 million manuscripts.

The Library's mission is to make resources available and useful to Congress and the American people and to sustain and preserve a universal collection of knowledge and creativity for future generations.

If you pay $35 to copyright your book, a copy of it may reside forever in the Library of Congress. Your parents should be proud of you. Actually your book will be there until it rots or until a future librarian decides to clear it out to make space for something newer or more important.

◆The LOC was founded in 1800. In 1814, British troops burned the Capitol building (where the Library was then housed) and destroyed about 3,000 books.

◆The LOC has about 145 million items on approximately 750 miles of shelves.

◆Each workday, the LOC receives about 22,000 items and adds approximately 10,000 items to its collections. The majority of the items are received through the copyright registration process, because the LOC is home to the U.S. Copyright Office.

◆ The LOC has materials in nearly 500 languages, and approximately half of the Library's book and serial collections are in languages other than English.

◆ The LOC contains the world's largest law library, with over 2.5 million volumes.

CHAPTER 36
Selling on Amazon.com is probably much easier than you think it is

People outside the publishing business and newbies to self-publishing may be amazed when they learn that your new book is being sold on the Amazon website. In truth, it's actually quite easy to get your books on the Amazon.com site. With most self-publishing companies, within a few days after you approve a proof of your book, it will be available on Amazon. You don't even have to contact Amazon.

Amazon can be inexplicably weird. The company will make changes without notice and for no apparent reason. It can be very hard to reach someone to ask about a change or to make a correction. Sometimes, your effort to correct an error will make the problem even worse. Sometimes, it's more effective to ask your publisher or printer to resubmit the information about your book and this will correct an error on Amazon.com. Sometimes, if you do nothing but wait a couple of days, a problem will be corrected without your having to complain.

Amazon's pricing policies are particularly perplexing. Sometimes, Amazon discounts a book; sometimes it doesn't. Sometimes, a discount will mysteriously disappear and then reappear. You can assume Amazon will sell more copies for you when they charge lower prices. Fortunately, the prices they charge don't affect the money you get paid, as long as you don't change the cover price or the discount rate.

There are several books devoted to selling on Amazon.com. I see no point in duplicating them, but I'll offer some help.

◆Encourage customers to take advantage of the $30 worth of free books they get by opening an Amazon Visa card account.

◆Distribute bookmarks or business cards with your cover on the front and "Available at Amazon.com."

◆In any discussion about the book, whether it's with a neighbor or a TV show host, conclude by saying the book is available at Amazon.com and Barnes & Noble stores and online.

◆Take advantage of the expert knowledge available at **www.amazonsellercommunity.com/forums/index.jspa**

◆The description field on your Amazon book page has the capacity for about 500 words, so *use* your space.

◆Upload an image of the back cover so its content can help you to sell more books. Upload the table of contents, too.

◆Amazon's sales ranking is cryptic, confusing, convoluted, confounding, complicated and not particularly useful. Amazon says, "The calculation is based on sales and is updated each hour to reflect recent and historical sales of every item sold." The lower the number, the better the book was selling *at a particular moment*. ➔When your book first goes on sale, its sales ranking will probably be around nine million—which looks pathetic. By ordering three to six books, you can make a major improvement in your ranking, and have some books to give away or send out to be reviewed.

◆Encourage people who like your book to post online reviews, preferably with five-star ratings.

◆Provide links from your websites to the pages on Amazon that sell your books.

◆Provide links in your email signatures to the pages on Amazon that sell your books.

◆Amazon will publish basic information and a cover image provided by your publisher or printer. If you like, you can enhance your listing at little or no expense to make a stronger "sales pitch" while prospective customers are considering your book. You can easily add descriptive content and images to persuade browsers to become purchasers. Here are the most important items you can put on your book's "product detail page" to supplement or replace the basic information.

- **Cover Art:** Since people judge a book by its cover, let them see the best possible cover. If you've changed your cover design since the original Amazon listing appeared, you can upload a new version. You can also submit a "fake" square cover which will show up bigger than other book covers. See the next page.
- **Description:** This is your chance to convince browsers to become buyers. Make a strong pitch, possibly using promotional copy from your cover or press release.
- **Review Excerpts:** Shoppers want to know what others have said about your book. You can post reviews from both professional and amateur critics.

◆The fastest way to add descriptive content is through Amazon's Book Content Update Form at
www.amazon.com/gp/content-form/?ie=UTF8&product=books

➜ ◆Here's a good trick to make your book more visible on Amazon.com and other websites. Sites establish a maximum size for the "thumbnail" book images they display. Most books are vertical, and *waste available horizontal space*. If you design a "fake" square version of your cover and upload it as a replacement for your "real" cover, you can fill the available space and have a competitive advantage. The Amazon display space can be as little as 115 pixels square. A typical vertical book shows up as only 75 pixels wide and wastes about ONE THIRD of the available real estate. Compare the two thumbnails to the right. Which would catch your eye on a crowded page with competing books? (They're both fine books, by the way.)

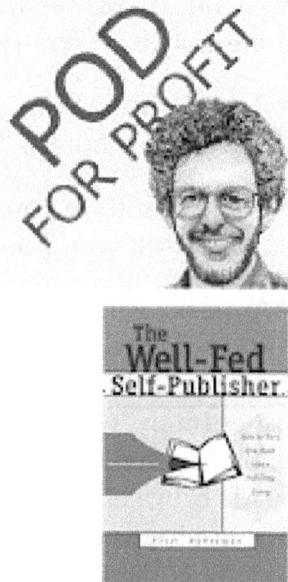

◆Amazon's **Search Inside!** program allows shoppers to view book interiors, not just covers and descriptions. When people search for books on Amazon, results include the actual words from *inside* participating books—not just the author, title, and keywords supplied by the publisher—to show the best possible selection. This lets shoppers discover books that they don't know exist, or that might not show up in other searches.

- With Search Inside, shoppers can also browse sample pages and do additional searches inside a particular book to confirm that the title is just what they're looking for. This close inspection could help sell more books.
- You can join at **www.amazon.com/gp/sitb/publish** or your publishing company can set it up for you. Some companies will set you up for Search Inside for an extra

fee. CreateSpace, which is owned by Amazon, does it automatically, and for free.

- Make your decision carefully. Amazon says that books that can be searched online sell better than books that can't be searched. But it's possible that you will lose sales if people can find the information they need by quickly looking inside your book and not purchasing it.
- If you sign up, you must stay in the program for at least three years and must provide 90 days' notice to cancel.

◆Amazon provides book reviews and comments from a variety of sources. Publishers and authors provide the primary descriptive content and review excerpts that appear for their titles. Amazon also licenses some reviews from other sources such as *Midwest Book Review*. There are also reviews provided by Amazon's own staff, as well as by Amazon customers. Amazon says that "profane or spurious comments are promptly removed." If you feel that a customer review falls outside of the guidelines, you can email **community-help@amazon.com**.

◆To submit your book for possible review, send it via the U.S. Postal Service to:
Amazon.com
Attn: Editorial - [Product & Category]
701 Fifth Avenue
Suite 1500
Seattle WA 98104
Refer to Amazon's list of subject areas to determine which category is best for your book. Indicating a category will ensure that your request is processed as quickly as possible.

◆If you find errors on you book's product detail page, you can request corrections with the **Online Catalog Update Form** which is accessible through the **Product Details** section, mid-

way down each book's detail page. This form will allow you to correct errors or omissions in many fields. See:
www.amazon.com/gp/help/customer/display.html?nodeId =13685621

➔◆Many self-published authors assume that they must offer Amazon a 55% discount off the cover price on their books. While Amazon will undoubtedly be glad to accept this offer, there is no need to be so generous. Twenty percent is adequate. In fact, when Amazon offers a discount, they usually end up with as little as 10% gross profit before they pay credit card fees and other expenses.

◆If you allow only a 20% discount on inexpensive books (perhaps $15.95 or less), Amazon *may* tack on a "sourcing fee" of a few dollars. Strangely, with one of my books, Amazon added a $2 fee and removed it after four days. Later on, two other books of mine had $5 sourcing fees for about a week, and then those fees disappeared. I have no idea why. It's hard to figure Amazon out.

◆If you've written a nonfiction book, particularly a how-to, you are probably an expert on something. If you're willing to give away a little piece of your knowledge, the freebie may turn into book sales. Amazon has a program called "**So You'd Like To...**" **guides** which allows you to publish advice and information, and to plug your own books. You can sign up at
www.amazon.com/gp/richpub/syltguides/create
Your guide must include at least three books sold by Amazon. Whatever you select as the first three books (and the first one should certainly be yours), will become the featured items that appear at the top of your published guide.

Listmania is a somewhat similar feature where you can post a list of favorite books that deal with a specific topic. Go to your Profile page at **www.amazon.com/gp/pdp/profile**.

Click the **Edit Your Profile** button on the top right-hand corner of the page. Click the **Lists** tab in the **Contributions** section of **Your Profile**. Click on **Create your first one now** and continue.

Amazon has several ways to publish your book— not just sell it.

①Amazon's **CreateSpace** do-it-yourself printing business offers a variety of packages and à la carte services for authors. Upfront costs range from nothing to $4,999.
See **www.Createspace.com.**
②Amazon lets you publish books for its **Kindle** e-book reader, and other devices with Kindle e-reading apps.
Info is at **http://dtp.amazon.com.**
③Amazon Encore re-publishes physical books and Kindle editions of books that have sold well on Amazon. See
www.amazon.com/gp/feature.html?ie=UTF8&docId=1000 373401
④Amazon is also developing a family of imprints specializing in such genres as chick-lit and mystery. See
www.amazon.com/gp/feature.html?ie=UTF8&docId=1000 664761

◆Amazon's **Author Central** is a powerful and *free* service intended to help authors to reach more readers, to promote books, and to build a better Amazon bookstore.

At Author Central, you can give readers the most up-to-date information about yourself and your work. You can view and edit your bibliography, add a photo and biography to a personal profile and connect with readers using a blog hosted by Amazon and links to external blogs. Author Central makes it easy for customers to find favorite authors and to discover new authors. Author Central also helps you to enroll your books in programs like Search Inside the Book and Kindle.

You join at **https://authorcentral.amazon.com/gp/join**

In late 2010, Amazon began offering sales data from Nielsen BookScan through Author Central. The data can be revealing, and exciting or horrifying. BookScan combines sales reported by multiple sellers, including Barnes & Noble, Amazon, Target and Buy.Com. Some retailers, including Walmart and Sam's Club, do not participate.

Once you are part of Author Central, a search for your name will bring up your books as well as a link to your "Author Page" on Amazon, where prospective readers can find out more about you and your books. People reading about one of your books can click to go to your "Author Page" and will see your other books.

Michael N Marcus **amazon**.com *Prime*

Become a Real October 15, 2009 ★★★★★ (13) $19.95	Get the Most Out November 1, 2010 ★★★★★ (1) $17.95	Stories I'd Tell My November 1, 2010 ★★★★★ (4) $15.95	Phone Systems & February 1, 2009 ★★★★☆ (2) $19.95
Stupid, Sloppy, March 1, 2010 ★★★★★ (2) $10.95	I Only Flunk My I December 1, 2008 ★★★★★ (8) $15.95	the AbleComm Gui March 1, 2009 $14.95	Independent Self- December 15, 2010 $19.95

Biography

Personal website:
www.MichaelMarc.us

Publishing websites:
www.SilverSandsBooks.com
www.Self-Pub.info

(This chapter includes material provided by Amazon.com. The author of this book does not claim copyright.)

CHAPTER 37
Selling your books yourself

◆On a 300-page, $18 book sold from a self-publishing company's website, you'll probably make 50% ($9). Expect few sales, because of limited site traffic.

◆When your publisher sells through Amazon.com and other booksellers, you'll probably collect 10% ($1.80).

◆If you are an independent self-publisher selling that $18 book through an online bookseller, you can make about $10. While this is better than what you could get by using a traditional publisher, there are ways to make more money.

◆You can probably buy books for $9 each from your self-publishing company. If you sell directly to readers, you keep what would normally go to the booksellers. You end up with $9 of the $18—if you can get your customers to pay for shipping, as they often do with Amazon or B&N.

◆If you buy books right from Lightning Source, you'll pay $4.80 plus shipping, and keep about $12 from the $18. The cost from CreateSpace is $4,45, so you can keep a bit more.

◆Even if you discount the price by a few dollars or pay for shipping to customers, you could still make more than you normally would, and you'll get paid immediately.

How do you reach customers directly? There are several ways. They don't apply to every book, and they probably should not replace Amazon and B&N, but they could be a supplement. You can try to: ◆Sell from your websites and blogs. ◆Sell during or after speeches. ◆Sell at flea markets. ◆Sell to friends, neighbors and business associates. ◆Sell at trade shows and conventions. ◆Sell at book fairs, craft fairs, festivals or events that tie in with your subject, such as boat shows or auto races. ◆Ring doorbells (just kidding).

Writer/blogger Sonia Marsh said, "Known experts should self-publish. Generally, they get $20,000 per speaking gig and sell 700 copies of a book after the gig." I have no idea where she got her data. But even if her numbers are inflated *ten times*, the money is still impressive for an hour's work.

If you are going to sell, you'd better be prepared to accept credit cards. Some in-person purchasers may pay cash, and you may gamble by accepting checks or a promise for future payment, but most book sales are done with credit cards.

You need a *merchant account*. You can get one from a bank, warehouse club or merchant service provider. You will probably pay the company between 2% and 5% of each transaction. There may be other fees. Transactions, where you don't actually see the card cost extra. If every sale will be processed at your office or home, you can use a PC. For in-person sales, you will need a terminal or PC software. You can get a wireless terminal for use where there is no telephone connection from **www.MerchantExpress.com**. They can even enable you to use a laptop for wireless charge authorizations.

Information on accepting credit cards and evaluations of many merchant service companies is at **www.100best-merchant-accounts.com**. It's also possible to process online sales by accepting payments through PayPal. It may be less expensive than credit cards, but some people don't like PayPal.

➔ If you sell in-person, you'll probably have to collect and remit sales tax. It's an ISPITA if you sell in several states.

Many thousands of books reach readers without booksellers. They are distributed—sometimes for free—by entities that want information or opinions circulated. These "special sales" can generate high profits, with no risk of returns.

AN INSIDER'S LOOK AT SELLING BOOKS OUTSIDE THE BOOKSTORE

HOW TO MAKE REAL MONEY SELLING BOOKS

(without worrying About Returns)

A COMPLETE GUIDE TO THE BOOK PUBLISHERS' WORLD OF SPECIAL SALES

BRIAN JUD

FROM THE BEST-SELLING AUTHOR OF BEYOND THE BOOKSTORE

A book you've already written may be perfect for use by an association, corporation, government, charity, foundation, university or a political party. Perhaps a book you've written needs just slight changes and perhaps a new title and cover to become perfect. Maybe the information in your book is fine, but the book needs a new point of view or emphasis to let you make a deal.

If you want to pursue the special sales market, get a copy of Brian Jud's *How to Make Real Money Selling Books*. It includes a huge number of possible purchasers, pus step-by-step instructions for making a sale.

Data weighs much less than paper

I had planned to get a big Kindle e-reader, particularly for newspapers.

I currently subscribe to four daily printed newspapers and read four or more online. Each Monday morning, I schlep a huge blue tub out to the end of my driveway, filled with 50 pounds of paper for recycling.

Lots of it, such as the sports sections, ad sections for distant supermarkets, and multiple copies of *Parade* magazine, are never read and are a complete waste of paper, ink, staples and energy. Getting these papers on a Kindle would be much greener and easier to live with. I just had to convince my wife to go along.

Alas, the iPad made the Kindle obsolete in my eyes. I'll talk more about iPads in the next chapter.

CHAPTER 38
E-books: even greener than POD

Print-On-Demand has the potential to eliminate much of the waste and inefficiency of traditional publishing, But e-books (the "e" stands for "electronic") go even further. By existing only as data files, e-books take up no space in warehouses, trucks, stores or homes, and require no paper, glue or ink to make. They're more convenient to carry, and have features not possible with books made from trees.

E-books (and ebooks and Ebooks—the terminology is not yet standardized) can be read on a computer, a cellphone, an iPod Touch, an iPad or on dedicated devices known as e-book *readers*.

E-books can be downloaded in less than a minute and are available at any time of any day. Many are free. Many are bargains. Most are less expensive than the paper versions, but a few cost more. Some are not available on paper. Some e-books are downloaded to a PC. Some can be wirelessly sent to an e-book reader, an iPod, an iPad or a cellphone. Some are down-loaded to a PC and then transferred to an e-book reader.

Some new-media fanatics are eagerly replacing their home libraries with e-book files, much as they replaced CDs with data on MP3 music players and they downloaded movies in-stead of buying DVDs. Others are keeping traditional books, but buying new books in electronic form whenever possible.

Others, like yours truly, are being selective (or noncom-mittal), buying both e-books and p-books (paper books).

E-publishing is an extremely efficient method of publish-ing, with no expense for physical media, no energy used to transport the "publications," no need for warehouses, almost no waiting before reading, and low or even no cost for the books.

Most e-books are downloaded immediately but some are sent by email a little later, after placing an order.

Opinion is divided on whether e-books will completely re-place books made from dead trees. For now, e-books are an alternate reading format for geeks, greenies, the storage-de-prived and a few others—but popularity is growing rapidly.

Many e-reading devices have been announced, but few people paid attention until Sony and Amazon got into the market. They have the clout, the money and the marketing expertise to greatly increase the use of e-books. Apple gave the e-book business a huge boost, too, selling more than two mil-lion multi-function iPads in just two months.

Most of the first e-books were written for small, specia-lized audiences, particularly in technical fields. Lots of them were instruction manuals on CD or online. The subject matter soon broadened to include a large number of "public domain" books with expired copyrights and no need to pay authors.

E-books: even greener than POD

As more readers accepted e-books, more writers published online e-books as either free or paid-for downloads. Unauthorized e-books have also been published without permission..

Some authors are very enthusiastic about e-books. Stephen King wrote *UR*, a novella, exclusively for Amazon's Kindle. Other authors are not so eager to participate. J.K Rowling, author of the Harry Potter series, long opposed e-versions of her books, but finally changed her mind in mid-2011.

E-books are made in about a dozen different formats, some for viewing on a PC screen, some for portable e-book readers, some for cellphones, and some that work on several kinds of devices. Some book titles are made in just one format, but many are made in multiple formats. ➜**To reach the biggest potential audience, you should offer your books in Kindle, EPUB and PDF formats.**

Some people say that the "e-ink" used in some ereaders makes them nicer to read than PCs or cellphones, and use less power. However, they may not work in the dark as an iPad will. An iPad is hard to view in bright sunlight, and reflections can be annoying. I've learned to live with them.

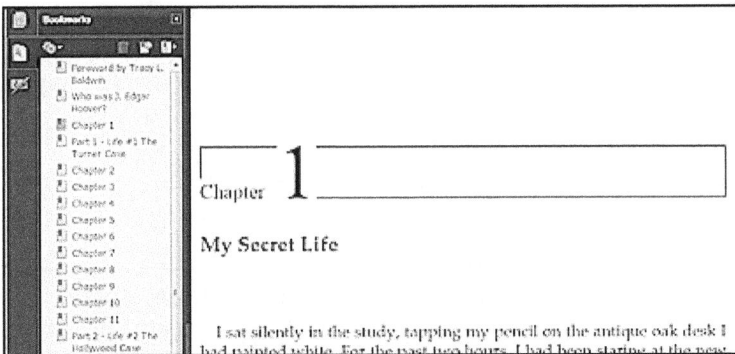

⬆Here's what a page from an e-book looks like in Adobe PDF format. This is *Secrets of an Undercover Agent* by Bethany K. Scanlon. Of course, when *you* read it, it can be as wide as your PC screen or as narrow as a cellphone screen.

ALICE'S ADVENTURES IN WONDERLAND

Lewis Carroll

*THE MILLENNIUM FULCRUM
EDITION 3.0*

CHAPTER I
Down the Rabbit-Hole

Alice was beginning to get very tired of sitting by her sister on the bank, and of having nothing to do: once or twice she had peeped into the book her sister was reading, but it had no pictures or conversations in it, 'and what is the use of a book,' thought Alice 'without pictures or conversation?'

So she was considering in her own mind (as well as she could, for the hot day made her feel very sleepy and stupid), whether the pleasure of making a daisy-chain would be worth the trouble of getting up and picking the daisies, when suddenly a White Rabbit with pink eyes ran close by her.

Th[e]
in
mu
say
be
aft[e]

Kindle's display flexibility allows you to choose type style and size, and page width. This can enhance reading, but the ebook page may be very different from the printed page.

ought to have wondered at this, but at

the more was the pity.

"Well, then," said he, "this is the berth for me. Here you, matey," he cried to the man who trund-led the barrow; "bring up alongside and help up my chest. I'll stay here a bit," he continued.

Kindle's display flexibility can produce very ugly results. This is part of *Treasure Island* by Robert Louis Stevenson.

One Saturday night a cousin persuaded Viktoria to widen her search by going to a discotheque in Hicksville. After a few minutes of nervous anticipation, posing on the "meat rack" at the edge of the dance floor, she apparently passed inspection and was asked to dance by a good-looking American.

He was Richard D'Onofrio, a recently divorced ex-marine. Richard had tattoos, but a slight build. He was polite and gentle and seemed comforting, not macho. He worked in Manhattan as a parking enforcement agent and lived in an apartment in Westbury—not far from Viktoria's home in Syosset.

Richard and Viktoria had several dances, several drinks and several kisses. He asked for her phone number. She was charmed by his chivalry, silly jokes and good looks—and impressed by his apparently secure government job. Richard seemed like excellent husband material (at least based on their two-hour relationship).

Viktoria borrowed a pen from a girl she knew and wrote down her name and phone number on an expired dollar-off coupon for Subway that she found in her purse. She gave it to Richard, but doubted that she would be called by the American. She thought that no girl—especially a non-citizen who barely spoke English—could be that lucky the first time she went out seriously looking for a man.

He called her the following Wednesday night and they met for coffee at the Athenian Diner in Syosset on Thursd[...] of them had to go [...]

Coffee becam[...] brunch time and

Preface: **Why does this book exist?**

♦ To provide the information people need to select phone equipment and services for professional offices, small businesses and homes
♦ To help people use the equipment properly, to get the most out of it, and to keep it working
♦ To help people diagnose trouble and make simple repairs
♦ To help phone people understand computer people
♦ To help the people who sell phone equipment

A hundred years ago, telephones were simple. If you wanted to call someone, you picked up the receiver, cranked the crank, and waited for the nice lady to say, "Operator, may I help you?" Then you said some-thing like, "I want to talk to Daddy," or "I need the doctor," and in a few seconds you were connect-ed. You didn't even need to know the phone numbers.

For equipment, maybe your family could choose between an oak box that went on the kitchen wall, or a metal candlestick model that sat on the hall table. If you lived in a high-tech area, maybe you could get a dial instead of a crank.

Regardless of the telephone style, you paid to rent it month after month, and there was just one company in your town that you could do business with, and that company owned "your" phone.

Today the choices seem endless. Phones can be analog or digital, rotary or touch-tone, plain or fancy, corded,

A PDF ebook can perfectly reproduce the image of a printed page, complete with the original fonts and graphics—all in the right places. Kindle and ePub books may cause graphic images to move. This is from *Telecom Reference ebook*, another book I wrote.

navigating
the BIBLE II

Translation

Navigating the Bible

Exodus » Chapter 12

The Passover Described

12:1 God said to Moses and Aaron in Egypt:

12:2 This month shall be the head month to you. It shall be the first month of the year.

12:3 Speak to the entire community of Israel, saying: On the tenth of this month, every man must take a lamb for each extended family, a lamb for each household.

12:4 If the household is too small for a lamb, then he and a close neighbor can obtain a [lamb together], as long as it is for specifically designated individuals. Individuals shall be designated for a lamb according to how much each one will eat.

12:5 You must have a flawless young animal, a one-year-old male. You can take it from the sheep or from the goats.

12:6 Hold it in safekeeping until the fourteenth day of this month.

The entire community of Israel shall then slaughter [their sacrifices] in the afternoon.

12:7 They must take the blood and place it on the two doorposts and on the beam above the door of the houses in which they will eat [the sacrifice].

12:8 Eat the [sacrificial] meat during the night, roasted over fire. Eat it with matzah and bitter herbs.

12:9 Do not eat it raw or cooked in water, but only roasted over fire including its head, its legs, and its internal organs.

12:10 Do not leave any of it over until morning. Anything that is left over until morning must be burned in fire.

12:11 You must eat it with your waist belted, your shoes on your feet, and your staff in your hand, and you must eat it in haste. It is the Passover (*Pesach*) offering to God.

12:12 I will pass through Egypt on that night, and I will kill every first-born in Egypt, man and beast. I will perform acts of judgment against all the gods of Egypt. I [alone] am God.

Unlike my PDF books, this Bible PDF from ORT.org is interactive. It has contents links on the left of each page as well as hyperlinks within the text to take the reader to relevant commentary.

your homes cleared of all leaven. Whoever eats leaven

CHAPTER III

JONATHAN HARKER'S JOURNAL—*(continued)*

When I found that I was a prisoner a sort of wild feeling came over me. I rushed up and down the stairs, trying every door and peering out of every window I could find; but after a little the conviction of my helplessness overpowered all other feelings. When I look back after a few hours I think I must have been mad for the time, for I behaved much as a rat does in a trap. When, however, the conviction had come to me that I was helpless I sat down quietly—as quietly as I have ever done anything in my life—and began to think over what was best to be done. I am thinking still, and as yet have come to no definite conclusion. Of one thing only am I certain: that it is no use making my ideas known to the Count. He knows well that I am imprisoned; and as he has done it himself, and has doubtless his own motives for it, he would only deceive me if I trusted him fully with the facts. So far as I can see, my only plan will be to keep my knowledge and my fears to myself, and my eyes open. I am, I know, either being deceived, like a baby, by my own fears, or else I am in desperate straits; and if the latter be so, I need, and shall need, all my brains to get through. I had hardly come to this conclusion when I heard the great door below shut, and knew that the Count had returned. He did not come at once into the library, so I went cautiously to my own room and found him making the bed. This was odd, but only confirmed what I had all along thought—that there were no servants in the house. When later I saw him through the chink of the hinges of the door laying the table in the dining-room, I was assured of it; for if he does himself all these menial offices, surely it is proof that there is no one else to do them. This gave me a fright, for if there is no one else in the castle, it must have been the Count himself who was the driver of the coach that brought me here. This is a terrible thought; for if so, what does it mean that he could control the wolves, as he did, by only holding up his hand in silence? How was it that all the people at Bistritz and on the coach had some terrible fear for me? What meant the giving of the crucifix, of the garlic, of the wild rose, of the mountain ash?[7] Bless that good, good woman who hung the crucifix round my neck! for it is a comfort and a strength to me whenever I touch it. It is odd that a thing which I have been taught to regard with disfavour and as idolatrous should in a time of loneliness and trouble be of help. Is it that there is something in the essence of the thing itself, or that it is a medium, a tangible help, in conveying memories of sympathy and comfort? Some time, if it may be, I must examine this matter and try to make up my mind about it. In the meantime I must find out all I can about Count Dracula, as it may help me to understand. Tonight he may talk of himself

This is an EPUB-formatted version of Bram Stoker's *Dracula*. I think it's hard to read. An EPUB "page" is simply the amount of content that will fit on a single screen, which varies with screen size, and whether you are viewing in "landscape" or "portrait" mode.

What's great about ebooks?

◆An e-book reader, filled with thousands of books, is compact, lightweight, easy to carry or store.

◆E-books are generally less expensive than p-books (printed-on-paper books), and many are free.

◆The production of e-books does not consume paper, ink, glue, staples, etc. There is no packaging.

◆Text can be searched, just like in a document on a PC or website. You can look for a specific word or phrase.

◆Some e-book readers can be read in total darkness.

◆An e-book can open automatically to the last page you were reading.

◆E-book downloads usually take just a few seconds.

◆Text-to-speech software can read the book to you via a speaker or headphones.

◆There is no cost for manufacturing, shipping or storing ebooks, so there is no cost pressure for them to go out-of-print even if sales are low.

◆Type size can be adjusted, and sometimes different typefaces can be selected for the most comfortable reading.

◆You can highlight text and insert "electronic bookmarks."

◆You may be able to jump from text to a dictionary or a webpage.

◆Free backups may be available if your reader is stolen, lost or damaged.

◆It can be easy and inexpensive to publish an ebook.

◆E-books can be easily updated and avoid the problem caused by a large inventory of obsolete printed books.

◆Free or discounted e-book excerpts can promote the purchase of complete e-books or p-books.

◆E-books don't get eaten by mice or suffer from mildew.

◆Doggie drool can't wrinkle the pages of an e-book.

What's not so great about ebooks?

◆The writer has less control over the appearance of an e-book than with a p-book. Some e-books look better in one format than in others. Photos, charts, and drawings may shift position on a page or even appear on a different page, or not look as good as on paper. It may take time to experiment before you like the way your book looks.

◆E-readers are more fragile than printed books.

◆E-readers require electrical power. Sooner or later, you'll have to recharge or replace batteries.

◆Some e-readers are difficult to read in bright light.

◆Many p-Books are not available in e-book form.

◆Some e-books are released after the p-book version.

◆E-book readers and other reading devices like cellphones and iPods are more likely to be stolen than p-Books.

◆The e-book you want to read may not be available in the format required by your reader.

◆While a printed book could probably be read 1,000 years from now if it still exists, today's e-book formats may vanish in a few decades.

◆E-readers are not biodegradable. P-books usually are.

◆"Digital Rights Management" may limit your ability to lend, give or sell an ebook you bought.

◆Authors and publishers may suffer from easy hacking of their e-books.

◆You can't build an attractive library on your shelves as with p-books.

◆If you fall asleep while using an e-book reader and drop it on the floor, it may get broken.

◆If an ebook is stolen or damaged, you lose your library unless you have backed it up or you can download again.

◆E-books can't be used to keep a door open or start a fire.

How to publish your e-book

You may produce an e-book without realizing it. A Word document that's formatted to become a p-book is actually an e-book. A PDF that you prepare for your printer, or distribute to reviewers, is an even better e-book than the Word doc is.

There are many paths to e-book publication, with varying costs, distribution venues and revenue streams. As with publishing on paper, you can do all, some or none of the work yourself.

The simplest way to publish an e-book is to arrange for a self-publishing company to do it. Some publishers include e-books in several or all of their packages, others offer e-book options, and some publishers publish on paper only.

- iUniverse provides e-books at no additional charge. Most e-books will sell for $9.99 and pay the author a 50% royalty, based on the wholesale price.
- Outskirts Press includes e-books only with its most expensive ($999) Diamond package—but will do Kindle formatting for anyone.
- Infinity Publishing provides e-book production as an optional service. The setup fee is $199. Authors receive a 50% royalty on the wholesale price.

It's pretty easy to distribute your own short e-book, such as a sample chapter. You can display the full text and not require downloading—people can read online, and copy if they want to. Just put the text on a website you already control. You can use text right from a word processor converted to HTML (hypertext markup language), or make a PDF e-book that maintains your formatting and looks more like a printed book.

A large sampler or complete book should be uploaded as a file and have a link for downloading. You can also upload a file to a free hosting service such as **www.mediafire.com** and link to it from your website or blog. This is OK for freebies. There are ways to collect money for your work from your own website, although these ways are not for beginners.

If you want to make it easier to get paid for your work and to increase the chance of people finding your book by accident, you can use the services of a website that exists to distribute e-Books, like **www.smashwords.com, www.ebookmall.com, www.manybooks.net** or **www.feedbooks.com.**

Smashwords is popular, highly regarded and does not charge authors in advance for publishing and distributing. It publishes in formats for any e-reading device, including the Amazon Kindle, iPhone, iPod Touch, iPad, Sony Reader, Barnes & Noble Nook, PCs and others. As a Smashwords author, you gain access to free, do-it-yourself sales and marketing tools to help you promote your book. You receive up to 85% of the net sales proceeds from your book.

Smashwords e-books are sold on Smashwords.com, plus Apple, Barnes & Noble, Sony and Kobo and were expected to be available on Amazon. Books are also distributed into the catalogs of mobile e-reading apps. Additionally, Smashwords books are promoted by affiliates. Authors make a little less money (70.5%) on sales through affiliate websites.

Although the Smashwords website provides extensive help, I was not able to smash my words successfully. As a first-year baby boomer, I may simply be too old. Although I am skilled in such ancient technology as changing spark plugs, developing film and soldering wires, perhaps e-book formatting is best done by younger geeks.

Amazon's Digital Text Platform (perhaps not coincidentally) shares initials with Desk-Top Publishing. It's a free and relatively easy way to upload books for availability both on Kindle readers, and competing devices like the iPad and Android phones with Kindle apps. It costs nothing to make a book available, and you can collect about 70% of the selling price.

Books can be uploaded as unmodified Word documents, but it's better to convert to HTML so your table of contents can have links to chapter beginnings. **http://dtp.amazon.com**

Information on B&N's similar free PubIt! e-book publishing service is up ahead.

➔ **Lulu** has an e-book publishing system that's free and extremely easy to use for PDF-formatted books. On an e-book that sells for $5 on the Lulu website, you keep $4. Lulu is also a "certified aggregator" (agent) for Apple. Under a typical deal, Apple retains 30% of all revenue from sales on the iBookstore. The publisher (i.e., you) receives 80% of the remaining revenue and Lulu receives 20%. So, when an e-book sells for $9.99 on the iBookstore, you receive $5.60. Lulu charges $99 to convert a book with up to 250 pages. The fee is $199 for 251 to 500 pages. (You can pay $100 to add one page. OUCH.) There may be an extra charge for complicated work.

Apple uses the open EPUB book format. When you convert a book to ePub, the result is a single block of flowable text and images. On eReaders, an EPUB "page" is simply the amount of content that will fit on a single screen, which of course varies depending on the screen size, and whether you are viewing in "landscape" or "portrait" mode. Part of converting to EPUB involves removing much of the page-based formatting (page numbers, headers and footers, page breaks, etc.) which is not relevant in the Apple e-reading context.

Books which are largely text are the best candidates for conversion to EPUB format. Books with many charts, tables, and images can be converted, but the process will take longer, is more expensive, and may not yield optimal results. Large tables and images that fit fine on a printed page may be broken across screens on a small mobile reading gadget.

My ebook Odyssey

In late 2010, I started making most of my books available in the PDF format, because it was extremely easy to do, cost me nothing, and the PDF pages perfectly represent the look of my printed pages. I also produced several ebooks that may never become ebooks.

I was reluctant to publish in the "MOBI" format used by Kindles, and the "EPUB" format used by B&N Nooks, Sony Readers and other devices.

Unlike my beloved PDFs, those other formats "reflow" the text to fit the size of the display and the desires of the reader, and can terribly distort the image desired by the page designer (i.e., me).

With a novel or other book that is all or mostly text, that's no big deal. My books, however, tend to have lots of graphic images, and I was horrified by the prospect of them showing up in the wrong places.

MOBI and EPUB books are reformatted to remove page numbering and headers (which I can live without), but I hate the way the pages look when readers enlarge the type on narrow pages, causing terrible word spacing.

So, what to do?

Since my PDF books are readable on iPads, it seemed logical to devote my first non-PDF effort to providing reading material for the Kindle community.

My book that seemed least likely to suffer from reflowing is *Stories I'd Tell My Children (but maybe not until they're adults)*.

Business Week reported that about 8 million Kindles were sold in 2010. If I could have books on just 1% of them,

I'd be a very happy guy. One tenth of 1% would be just fine, too.

I was not able to format my own Kindle book with Smashwords, Amazon's own Digital Text Platform (DTP) and other services. There are many services that will make Kindle conversions for money. Prices vary greatly, and each service's website is filled with glowing testimonials.

◆I had heard good things about Joshua Tallent's **KindleFormatting.com** and even mentioned him in several of my books about self-publishing, and assumed I'd use his service—but there was a multi-month wait.

◆In 2010, **Outskirts Press** made an intriguing announcement. They would provide publishing services (including Kindle conversion) on an à la carte basis to people who do not buy their publishing packages, and their fee for Kindling is just $135 for outsiders like me (package customers pay 25% less).On books priced from $2.99 to $9.99, the author revenue is 70%. Each $7.99 book I'd sell would net me $5.59—a nice chunk.

Because I have so often been displeased with the Outskirts products and procedures, I was dubious about their conversion process. I also did not like having to pay in advance—before I know how good or bad their work would be. Frankly, I expected them to do a bad job, and assumed that I would have blown the $135 with nothing to show for it but another blog post condemning Outskirts.

Alas, it was not meant to be.

Outskirts is difficult to communicate with. Phone calls go to robots and emails are often ignored. But, much worse was the fact that the company had not properly thought through the procedure for doing Kindle conversions for people who don't buy publishing packages. Their system is based on converting files already on-hand for making p-books, and they had no system in place for me to upload my book files. My questions got vague answers. Although I was prepared to—and hoped to—say nice things about the company, it became clear that Outskirts was afraid to have me as a customer.

We never did a deal, and there was another problem. Although Kindle books are readable on iPads with a Kindle app, Kindle books were not sold on Apple's bookstore site.

◆I also considered paying **Lulu** to do the conversion for an EPUB-formatted book for Apple's iBookstore. Apple takes a 30% commission. With a $7.99 ebook, I'd make $4.47. That's OK, but significantly less than the $5.59 I'd make on Kindle books.

Lulu charges $99 for EPUB conversions of books with up to 250 pages. If you add *just one page* (or if you add 250 pages) the price goes up to $199. My book has 318 pages, so the price would be $199—and I still would not have a book readable on the Kindle. That's a potential deal-killer.

Lulu warns that:

①"The EPUB conversion takes 6-8 weeks. In some instances conversion may take longer." That's a potential deal-killer.

②"In the case where the complexity of the manuscript file requires work outside the scope of our service, we reserve the right to . . . do the conversion with a minimum charge of $100 an hour." That's a potential deal-killer.

③"As there is a great deal of work done to evaluate the files before the full conversion is processed, there are no refunds on this service. In the event more work is needed to convert your file, you may incur additional fees." That's a potential deal-killer.

④"Books which contain lots of charts, formulas, tables, and images can be converted, but the process will take longer, is more expensive, and may not yield optimal results." That's a potential deal-killer.

The fact that I'd been unable to upload a revised file for one of my PDF books for over a month was the final deal-killer.

However, the Lulu e-book publishing system for *PDF* books is free, extremely easy to use, and profitable for the author. The critical weak point about selling PDF books on Lulu's website—or selling any books on Lulu's website—is that approximately zero people go to the site to buy books. It ain't Amazon. If you have books for sale on Lulu.com—and I have nine books there—you will have to *drive* traffic to Lulu.

So, after my detour, I was ready to send my files to Kindle-Formatting.com and wait.

♦The fates, gods and muses were smiling that day, however. I received a press release announcing **eBookIt.com**, and I checked it out. I was impressed by the company's ultra-friendly website, and friendly and competent phone call handling.

Boss Bo Bennett says, "I created eBookIt.com out of my conviction that an author should have an inexpensive, simple, and truly foolproof way to get their book converted to ebook format, and submitted to the major online retailers fast."

I am extremely happy with the company's quality, speed, responsiveness and price (just $149 for multiple formats). The eBookIt website is easy for even a non-geek to use. It's always easy to see what work has been done, what has to be done, and to review communications with the eBookIt staff.

I needed to request multiple changes after I uploaded my file, and the additional work was done promptly, and without any additional charges. That was a pleasant surprise,

After my approval, my e-book was immediately available from the company's website, and it took just a few days to be on sale at Amazon and B&N. After a week, it was available on lots of e-book sites worldwide. I *highly* recommend ebookIt.com

On a book with a $4.99 list price, Amazon pays 70% (i.e. $3.49) to eBookIt. eBookIt keeps 15%, and I get $2.97 per book. That's nearly 40% of the list price, a *nice* chunk of change.

➜ No website that sells e-books has the marketing magnetism that Barnes & Noble, Apple and Amazon have. If you expect to sell e-books from other sites, such as Lulu.com, be prepared to work very hard to send traffic to them.

Amazon Kindle

The Kindle, developed and initially sold only by Amazon.com, is the device that made e-books popular. You can easily and almost instantly download books, blogs, magazines and newspapers to a crisp, high-resolution *electronic paper* display that looks and reads almost like real paper. Unlike the iPad, Kindle lets you read books in bright sunlight, with no screen glare.

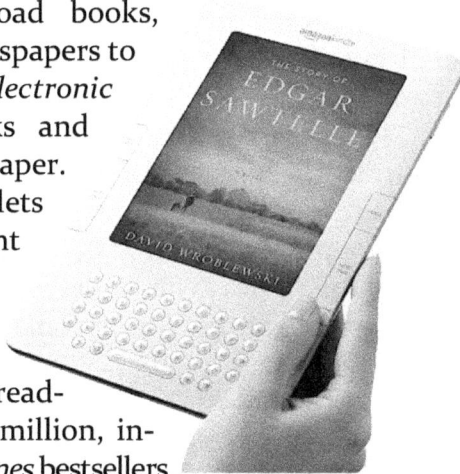

The number of book titles available for Kindle reading is approaching three million, including most *New York Times* bestsellers and most new releases, for $9.99 or less. You can read free sample chapters of many books before deciding whether to buy them. Over a million older books, including many classics, are available for *free*.

Kindle customers can also access newspapers, magazines and blogs—which are delivered automatically either by subscription or individually. Subscription media are delivered wirelessly to Kindles overnight so the latest edition is waiting when customers wake up.

Thousands of blogs are available—and updated wirelessly. Kindle users also can also search the web, Wikipedia, the Kindle Store and documents already stored on the Kindle.

Amazon lets you buy Kindle books once and read them everywhere—on Kindle, iPad, iPod Touch, iPhone, Mac, PC, BlackBerry and Android-based devices. Amazon's "Whispersync" syncs your place across devices, so you can resume reading where you left off. Books you purchase from the Kindle Store are automatically backed up online and can be downloaded again wirelessly for free, anytime.

Kindle owners can use "Amazon Whispernet" to wirelessly shop the Kindle Store, download or receive new content in less than 60 seconds, and read from their library—all without a PC, Wi-Fi hotspot or syncing. Whispernet uses Sprint's 3G data network in all 50 U.S. states. There are no fees or bills for access. Whispernet works only in the U.S., but Kindle content can be downloaded from the web, anywhere.

As with everything in consumer electronics, prices have been dropping and quality has been increasing. The first-generation Kindle was introduced in 2007 and priced at $399. In the summer of 2011, Kindles sold for as little as $114, and $99 seemed likely.

◆Amazon offers a free "app" which enables Kindle books to be wirelessly downloaded and read on the Apple iPad, iPhone and iPod Touch.

◆Joshua Tallent's **www.KindleFormatting.com** has a lot of advice which will help you prepare your document for Amazon. Joshua also provides conversion services, code cleanups, consultation and even screenshots if you don't have your own Kindle and need a photo of your e-book for promotion. The Kindle conversion process will probably make some unexpected changes in your book's format. To minimize unpleasant surprises, read what Joshua has to say before you upload.

Apple iPhones, iPods and iPad

When introduced in 2001, the Apple iPod was a tiny music player from a tiny but respected computer maker—but that was just the beginning. Although the iPod was not the first, last or only device of its type, it quickly became the market leader because of its style, functionality and overall coolness.

In 2007, Apple solidified its market dominance by introducing the iPhone and then the iPod Touch—the equivalent of a phoneless iPhone. The Touches have big, sharp, color "touch screens," suitable for movies, TV shows, podcasts, games and e-books.

The iPad, introduced in 2010, functions as a supersized iPod Touch and is much better for reading books. Its full-color backlit touch screen measures 9.7-inches diagonally, compared to just 3.5 inches for the iPod Touch and iPhone.

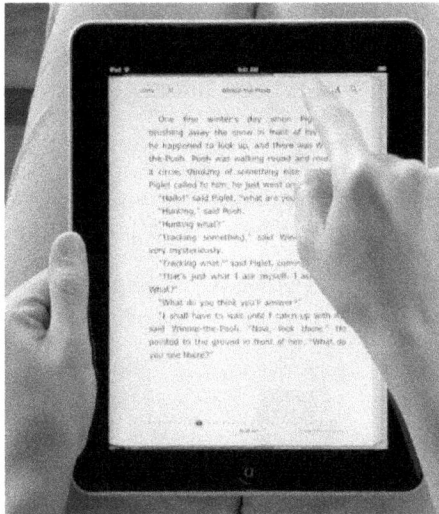

Several models, initially priced from $499, provide different amounts of memory and different connection modes. All models use Wi-Fi, and the more expensive ones also use 3G from AT&T with a fee.

I love my iPad, and use it more than I ever imagined. It's both a tool and a toy. It does much more than a Kindle can, and shortly after I bought it, I gave away my netbook. I've downloaded e-book versions of some of my paper books onto my iPad so I can read them while on a plane, or while waiting for a plane or for a doctor. My iPad also holds some reference works which I have with me most of the time. In some cases I have the same books on my iPad, on my iPod, on a PC, and on a bookshelf. Mainstream iBooks from Apple are generally priced from $9.99 to $14.99, and there are many less expensive books and even free books available.

E-books for iPhones, iPads and iPods are downloaded from Apple's App store, which is a section of the online iTunes store. The iPad comes with a shortcut link to take you there.

The store offers a wide range of both free and paid-for apps, including business, games, reference, entertainment, education and more. Many of the free apps are abridged or limited-function samples which developers and publishers hope will entice users to purchase the full-sized, full-priced versions.

Apple sells e-book downloads and provides free e-books on the App Store within the iTunes Store. ⬇

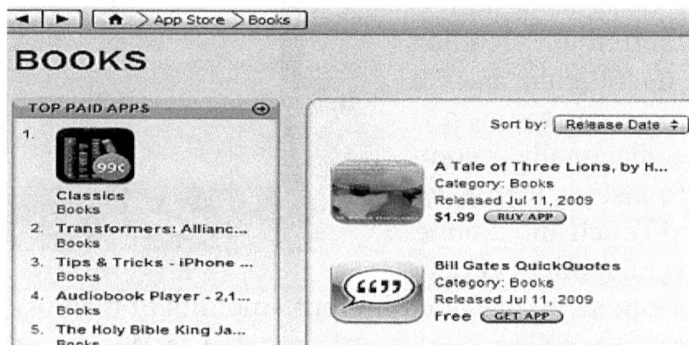

In early 2010, Apple announced that there had been over THREE BILLION DOWNLOADS and hundreds of thousands of apps were available.

Apple allows 70% of revenues from the store to go to the seller of the app, and keeps 30% for itself. The average app price is about $3 and there is a lot of competition among public-domain books where no royalties are paid. You can upload an e-book of plays by Aristophanes or novels by Dickens to sell for $1.00—and lose sales to similar e-books priced at 99 cents.

Uploading a book as an Apple app is more complicated than other forms of e-book publishing. You or your publisher will have to register as an iPhone software developer and pay a one-time fee. Apple says, "You should already have some familiarity with the basics of computer programming in general and the Objective-C language in particular." And "To follow this tutorial, you must have installed the iPhone SDK and developer tools available from the iPhone Dev Center."

If that sounds beyond you (and I readily admit that it's beyond me), you can use your publisher or an independent service company to convert your book files. This field is very fluid, with companies jumping in and out of the business.

Of course, if you make your e-book available on Amazon's Kindle, it can also be downloaded onto Apple iPods, iPads and iPhones without any extra work. Or Blood. Or sweat. Or tears. Or Objective-C language.

Audiobooks

The Apple iTunes store also offers tens of thousands of **audiobooks** ("talking books") with free online previews, author interviews and other features. Book prices start at just 95 cents (less than many songs). Current popular books are generally $11.95 to $17.95, but some are over $20, or even over $30—much more expensive than e-books.

In general, longer books (which mean longer recordings) cost more money. For example, a six-hour talking book could cost $21.95, but an abridged book that runs for less than three hours could sell for $6.95. Some audiobooks are read by their authors, some by famous actors and actresses and some by skilled talkers you've never heard of.

Audiobooks *are* electronic books, but *not* e-books, and authors should be aware of them as a possible additional format for reaching the public and possibly making money. They're great for listening to while driving or while half asleep. You can listen to iTunes audiobooks on your computer, your iPhone, iPod or iPad. It's easy to skip ahead or go back through spoken content and, when you sync your computer and your iPod or iPhone, each one keeps track of where you stopped listening.

This is a selection screen for Apple audiobooks. ⬇

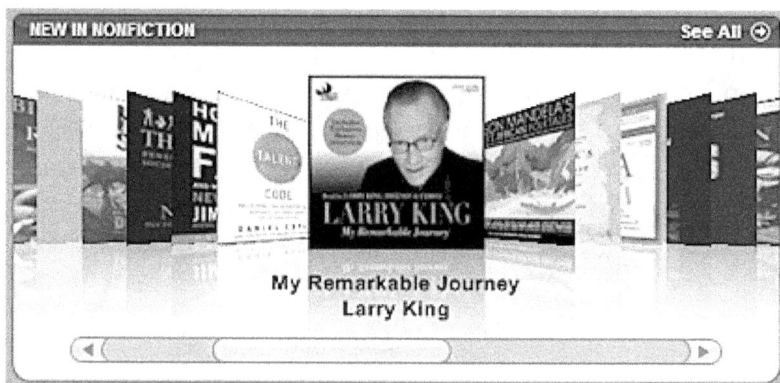

To sell audiobooks through the iTunes store, you or your publisher must become an official "content provider." See **www.apple.com/itunes/contentproviders/faq.html**

Sony Readers

Although the Sony Reader debuted in 2006, before Amazon's Kindle, the Kindle quickly surpassed Sony in reader sales and in available titles. In 2010, Sony brought out its fifth generation, with new technology and styling. These aluminum-bodied Readers have improved touch screens with better clarity, and respond to a finger or stylus.

Gen-5 models use "E Ink Pearl" electronic paper displays, which are readable in direct sunlight.

The screens provide high contrast with 16 levels of gray-scale, so text and images are crisp and easy to see. You can choose Readers with 5-, 6-, or 7-inch screens. Initial prices ranged from $179 to $299.

New technology on all models provides easier reading of PDFs and personal documents. Zoom, adjustable contrast and brightness, as well as automatic multiple page creation can make documents designed for a standard sheet of paper easier to read on a smaller screen. You can use your own photos as screen savers. The "collections functionality" provides book groupings.

The three Readers come with built-in *New Oxford American Dictionary, Second Edition* and *Oxford Dictionary of English*, plus ten translation dictionaries.

Reader Desktop Edition (formerly Reader Library) enables users to synchronize reading among multiple devices, and also provides content management for non-wireless Readers.

Sony's e-book store (**ebookstore.sony.com**) offers over 1.2 million book titles as well as newspaper and magazine content.

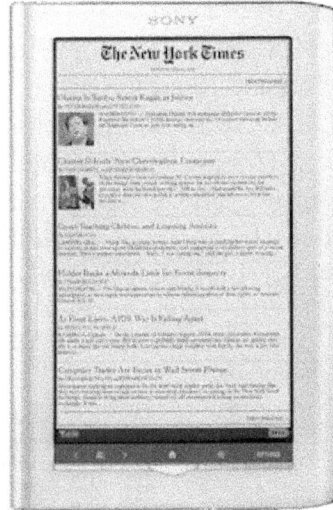

The store's Library Finder provides access to local public libraries to borrow e-books for free.

A set of apps for iPhone and the Android Marketplace extend the Reader experience across multiple portable devices.

Sony offers more than a half-million public-domain books that Google has scanned and digitized, FREE to Sony Reader owners. There are many traditional favorites as well as obscure material and non-English books. People can search the full text of the collection or browse by subject, author or featured titles.

↓Sony e-book Store

Sony provides a section of its website for publishers to establish a relationship for selling e-books from the Sony store at **http://ebookstore.sony.com/publishers**

Barnes & Noble e-bookstore (www.bn.com/ebooks)

claims to be the world's largest e-bookstore, and plans to have "every available e-book" including more than a half-million free public domain books. Free e-book reader software is available for various devices.

E-books: even greener than POD

B&N's top "Nookcolor" e-book read-er was conceived to compete with the iPad and has a 7-inch color touch screen and sells for $249. It provides email, web access and downloads, and it displays books, maga-zines and newspapers via Wi-Fi. You can use office software, play games and play music (but maybe not videos). Built-in storage can hold about 6,000 books, and a memory card can be plugged for more storage. A $199 Nook has a 6-inch grayscale screen *plus* a smaller color screen for touch navigation. It uses 3G wireless as well as Wi-Fi. A 6-inch touch-screen grayscale Wi-Fi-only Nook sells for just $139.

B&N's "PubIt!" (publish it) is an "easy and lucrative" way to distribute e-books through Barnes & Noble.com and the Barnes & Noble e-bookstore. By following simple steps to up-load content in an industry-standard format for e-books, you can reach readers using hundreds of devices including Nook, PC, Mac, iPad, iPod Touch, iPhone, BlackBerry and others.

PubIt! distributes books in the popular EPUB format. If your books aren't available in EPUB, PubIt! Has a free tool to convert Microsoft Word, HTML, RTF, and TXT files into EPUB. It also enables you to preview your titles on a Nook em-ulator before submitting them. ISBNs are not required.

The program is open to authors and publishers worldwide with bank accounts in the United States, and books can be in any language. There are no start-up fees or annual fees. List price must be between $0.99 and $199.99. The publisher (which could be you) gets a royalty of 65% on e-books priced from $2.99 to $9.99, or 40% on e-books priced at or below $2.98, or at or more than $10. (It's simpler than that sounds.)

To keep up with long-time rival B&N, Borders launched **Borders-Get Published** to enable authors to publish and sell e-books through the Borders e-book store and other e-book retailers. Borders was liquidated in July of 2011, as this book was being completed. The Borders e-book program used Kobo technology, but Kobo is independent and will continue in operation without borders.

e-book readers move beyond the geeks

The e-book reader business is expected to become an important product category, and is attracting the attention of additional manufacturers (Acer and HP) and booksellers, as well as major retailers (Walmart, Sears, Target, RadioShack).

When Walmart starts selling a product, it's a good indication that the product is considered acceptable to mainstream America—as when JC Penney started selling thong underwear and when McDonald's entered the bagel business.

(This chapter includes material provided by Amazon, Apple, Sony, B&N, and others. The author of this book does not claim copyright.)

CHAPTER 39
Dealing with the Library of Congress

U ntil recently, books displayed a Library of Congress "catalog number." Now it's called a "control number" ("Library of Congress Control Number," or "LCCN"), and it's important to have one for two reasons:

① It may be difficult to get libraries to buy your book if it does not have an LCCN.

② It makes your book seem more professional, even if you don't care about selling to libraries.

The **Preassigned Control Number** (PCN) program enables the Library of Congress to assign control numbers in advance of publication to those titles that are theoretically *most likely to be acquired by the LOC* as well as to some other categories of books.

The publisher prints the control number in the book to aid cataloging. The PCN links the book to any record that the LOC, other libraries, bibliographic services or book vendors may create. Only U.S. book publishers are eligible to participate in the PCN program.

This program is not for books that have already been published, books for which *Cataloging in Publication* data has been or will be requested (generally not for self-published authors), or e-books.

Publishers must complete and submit an "Application to Participate." When the application has been approved, an account number and password will be emailed to the publisher. Then, the publisher logs on to the PCN system and completes a PCN Application Form for each title that needs a PCN. Based on the information provided by the publisher, LOC staff pre-assigns a control number and the publisher prints it on the copyright page in the following manner:

Library of Congress Control Number: 2007012345.

You can apply at **http://pcn.loc.gov/pcn007.html** or your publisher can do it for you.

You or your publisher should get an email confirmation of the application within a few minutes. If additional information is required, a PCN Publisher Liaison person will send email. Application processing can take about a week, and varies with the volume of requests. I received a control number for this book in a few hours.

If you need to revise the information on your application, don't submit another application. This will slow processing. After you are assigned an account number, you will be able to update book information by clicking on the **Publisher Information Change Request** button on the PCN web page.

There is no charge for a PCN. However, publishers that receive PCNs are obligated to send a complimentary copy of each book to the LOC (address is up ahead). The books are not returnable. ➔Although you can get a PCN for free, if your publisher requests it for you, you may be charged as much as $150.

Published works are assigned an LCCN during the cataloging process *if* they are selected for addition to the LOC's collections. Since there is no guarantee that the LOC will select your book, if you want an LCCN, apply *before* publication.

Complete information about the LCCN process is at **http://pcn.loc.gov/pcn/pcn006.html**

The LCCN doesn't change with each new edition or version, unless you make a major revision or addition. Unlike an ISBN, it doesn't have to change if a book's publisher changes.

The CIP program and PCN program are mutually exclusive. Titles processed in one program can't use the other.

There is no charge for registering for CIP or PCN, but, immediately upon publication, the publisher must send a copy of the "best edition" of the book to which the LCCN was assigned. The "best edition" is the version of the book printed on paper that is expected to last the longest.

Here's where to send your book:
Library of Congress—US Publisher Liaison Division
Preassigned Control Number Program
(*or* Cataloging in Publication Program)
101 Independence Avenue, S.E.
Washington, D.C. 20540-4280

(This chapter includes material provided by the Library of Congress. The author of this book does not claim copyright.)

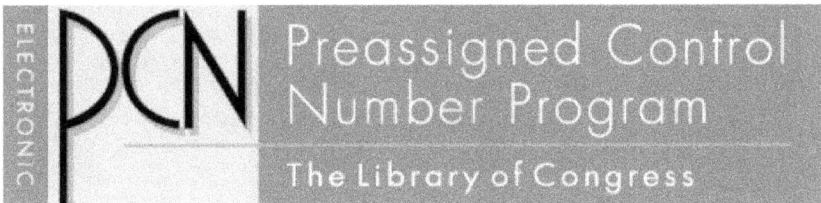

Writing and publishing are addictive. The more you do it, the more you want to do it. The investment is low and the potential rewards are high.

I started my publishing business with the intent to publish *one* book. You are reading number 15, and more are on the way.

CHAPTER 40
Getting out the news: promotion, publicity and press releases

Investigative reporting remains the Holy Grail for news reporters—the goal that wins praises, raises and Pulitzer prizes. But, in truth, most reporting is merely rehashing, replaying and relaying the manufactured news that is distributed by newsmakers who want *publicity*.

These newsmakers range from presidents, bureaucrats and generals who call press conferences or invite reporters to conduct interviews, to the makers of new gadgets who want the public to think that their stuff is wonderful and to buy it or to invest in their companies. Newsmakers also include people like you—authors who want to promote books.

If you read several newspapers, listen to several radio stations, use multiple news websites, or channel-surf between 6 and 7 p.m. you might wonder how and why all of the news media report on the same events.

If the event is a war, forest fire, election or hurricane, it's real news and the duplication makes sense. But if the event is the announcement of a new Toyota, iPod, quarterback or movie deal (or even your new book), it's more like free advertising than news. You're encountering it all over because all of the reporters were fed the same lunch at a press conference, and all of the news editors were fed the same press release.

A press release is a one- or multi-page document that may exist on paper or be sent as email or stored online. It is intended to capture the attention of editors, writers and broadcasters who may regard the information as newsworthy and then will deliver the news to their readers, listeners or viewers. A press release may be all alone, or part of a physical or virtual "press kit" which contains photos, biographies and other promotional materials.

Not just "press"

At one time, all news came from printing *presses*. Now it also comes over the air and through wires and cables. The authoritative *Associated Press Stylebook*, recognizing the diversity of modern media, says that the preferred term for a press release is a "news release." Some people call it a "media release" or even a "PR (Public Relations) release."

However, a press kit is still a *press* kit, even if it exists on a website to provide news for other websites. NBC's "Meet the *Press*," on the air since 1947, frequently has broadcast journalists asking the questions. Reporters for broadcast and online media still carry *press* passes. The White House still has a *press* room. The Associated *Press* is too picky. "Press" hasn't passed.

Not just news

Even if your online press release is completely ignored by the news media, it can still help sell books. As long as a release is available online, its contents are reachable with search engines. Even if the *New York Times* doesn't care about your new book about the effect of atmospheric warming on rodent reproductive cycles, anyone searching for "chipmunk sex" should find out about your book.

In online journalism there's an unfortunate trend to reporting by repetition and reporting by robots—but the trend helps those who want publicity because space has to be filled. Press releases are "read" by robots, which publish them for people and for other robots.

Sometimes human beings *do* read the press releases, but they seldom do the traditional fact-checking that was once an important part of journalism. Accuracy and honesty are assumed and almost anything can be published. If "news" arrives in the proper format, with authentic language, it is almost always believed and is not likely to be challenged by journalists who are competing to publish first. The robots, of course, will put anything online if it contains a few appropriate words.

Not just email

Email has replaced lots of paper and stamps. News release distribution services can quickly email your news to most news media. But lots of email is undelivered or unread or deleted. Sometimes, you should also send your news the old-fashioned way, at least to the important media on your list. A 9×12 manila envelope may be hard to ignore. A FedEx envelope is even harder to ignore.

➡ Remember that the mere publication of your book is not usually sufficiently newsworthy to impress editors and writers. Only the most desperate small-town weekly would publish an article with the headline: "Local Woman Writes Book." Your news release needs a *news hook*. The hook is the main point of your release. It can be a theme, statement, trend or event on which you "hang" your news release. It's also a hook with delicious bait on it that you hope will attract the attention of writers, reporters and editors.

To grab the attention of news people, you have to think and act like one of them. You need to be a partner, not just a salesperson. Think like a news writer, not a book writer. If you were reporting news, what would interest you and your readers? A press release should be newsworthy and read like a news story—not an advertisement. It should adhere to fundamental journalistic standards, using the five W's and one H (Who, What, When, Where, Why and How).

➡️You only have a few seconds to capture the attention of a busy writer or editor. Make your headline interesting, stimulating and clear. Be sure your first paragraph covers all of the important information—and makes people want to read more.

Keep in mind that the customary objective of a news organization, or even one writer, is to make money by informing and entertaining readers. (That's your objective, too.) News organizations do not exist to help you publicize your book, but if you can do something to help them (i.e., provide some news or entertainment), you can work together for mutual benefit.

So, if the actual publication of your book is not the news, what can you say about it that *is* news?

It's great if you can hang your story on a hook that already exists. If an important person just got married, promoted, fired, elected or killed, a book about that person should be newsworthy—especially if you have something new to say.

If your book takes a contrary view, such as that cigarettes are healthy or bathing is unhealthy, that may draw attention.

If your book can help readers save time or money or live better, you should be able to derive a headline and a hook from your newly revealed secrets. But don't reveal *everything* in the release. Your objective is to *sell books*.

The hook for my first humorous memoir was that it took 51 years from conception to completion. The hook for a book I wrote about business phone systems was that most people spend *too little* on their phone equipment.

If your book has local appeal, you'll have a good chance of attracting local media attention. It's often a waste of time and effort to pitch a "local" book to national media.

Press releases can be sent out several times a year through the life of a book, as often as you can think of news events or other hooks to attach it to. Make life easier for other writers and you'll be rewarded.

➜ Make sure your releases are well-written and error-free. Very often, a release will be either published verbatim under the byline of a reporter or quoted extensively. Don't embarrass your media partners with typos, factual errors or sloppy writing. It's important that news writers know they can rely on the material you present to them.

Be relevant. Be targeted. While the major press release services have lists of subscribers at news media who want to receive press releases, they are not the only people who should get your news. It's important to develop your own list, particularly targeting the writers and publications (online and on paper) that are likely to cover your book.

Don't target only book reviewers. Books can be newsworthy for people who write about many subjects.

Study news media. Get familiar with the reporters, writers and editors and the "beats" they cover. If you know what they write about, you'll have a better chance of getting your news distributed, and may get ideas for hooks they will respond to.

Be fun. Even "straight" news can have entertainment value. If your release can make an editor smile, it has a better chance of being used instead of being deleted or shredded.

Be brief. Try to limit your release to the equivalent of two traditional typewritten pages—about 500 words.

Make sure the release has a contact name, phone number and email address for follow-up questions. You may even get interviewed and have your picture taken. One press release I sent out resulted in a full-page story in the *Hartford Courant,* with a huge color photo. It made my parents proud, generated some business and put me in touch with some old friends. The *Connecticut Post* also did a big story about me and my books—but its huge picture was in black-and-white. Oh, well.

If a printed or online news report or book review has errors in it, be cautious about requesting corrections. Sometimes a correction will create worse errors than there were before the correction. Some writers just don't like to be corrected, even if they made stupid mistakes, and will be spiteful.

Help a reporter out

If you've written a book, you're probably an expert on something. Your expertise can lead to publicity if you can reach reporters who need what you know. *Help A Reporter Out* (HARO) is a contact point for tens of thousands of journalists, news sources and businesses. Since its inception, HARO has published more than 60,000 journalist queries and has facilitated nearly 7,000,000 media pitches. HARO is entirely free to sources and journalists. See **www.helpareporter.com**

Choosing a press release distribution service

There are dozens of different companies that you can use to distribute your press releases. Some are free; some have different prices for different "packages," typically between $100 and $1,000. You can spend more, but it should not be necessary.

I've used both PR Newswire and PR Web to distribute releases and have been quite pleased with the results.

Both companies offer packages with different prices, based on distribution and the included photos, audio or video. PR Newswire can even display giant photos in Times Square in Manhattan. The prices at PR Web range from $80 to $360. At PR Newswire, you can spend from $680 to several thousand dollars. If you are interested only in state or regional coverage, you can pay less.

I chose the top-level $360 package from PR Web and was amazed at the performance. Within an hour of the distribution, Google showed many news websites picking up the story about *I Only Flunk My Brightest Students: stories from school and real life.* After a week, there were about **TEN THOUSAND links in media all over the world**. Some of the links were on my own websites or on the sites of stores selling my book, but the vast majority were the results of $360 paid to PR Web.

➔Some PR distribution companies, and therefore the "news" they carry, have more credibility than others. In general, the paid-for services get better pickup than their freebie competitors. Self-publishing companies generally use the less-effective free distribution for their public relations and marketing packages, but they seldom reveal the details. The top companies are probably Business Wire, PR Newswire and PR Web. PR.com is in the second tier, and pretty good.

OOPS! I saw a really silly press release about Lisa Genova, who wrote *Still Alice*. It says, "Lisa gives this advice for everyone who has already self-published their book: Get a website. Network online. Write your own press release and post it free at www.pr.com." Strangely, the release was not sent out by Lisa using PR.com as she advises other writers to do, but by a competitor, SanePR, working for Xlibris. Also strangely, the release carries ads for competing PR distribution companies and ads for people with bad credit.

The release concludes with this bit of idiocy: "Why not get started on that book now? What is your book's name?" That's unprofessional, and unabashed advertising for Xlibris that would instantly turn off any news writer who saw it. **When you pay nothing for a release, you often get what you paid.**

Be ready to take advantage of press coverage

Eighty-year-old New Jerseyan Alfred Pristash wrote a memoir which was published for him by AuthorHouse. Pristash spent 18 months writing the manuscript in longhand, and then dictated it to a son who typed it. The book received extensive and complimentary coverage in NJ.com and in a major New Jersey newspaper. The article mentioned that the book sells for $73.99 and is available at Amazon.com.

I was curious to see how a book from a self-publishing company could possibly justify that high price. Unfortunately, the Amazon page had just basic facts like page count and size. There were no reviews and no information that might convince me to spend $73.99. The AuthorHouse website links for "About the Book," "About the Author" and "Free Preview" contained *nothing.* I did not place an order. ➜ If you are lucky enough to get media coverage of your book, be sure your online presence is ready to back it up and sell some books!

◆ Make your press release as complete as possible, and make it positive without gushing. Don't rush it. Write it as well as you can. Write something that you'd like to read about your book if someone else wrote it. Some "reviewers" are too busy or too lazy to actually read your book, and will merely rewrite or reprint your release. Many websites automatically redistribute press releases.

◆ **You don't have to do your own publicity.** If you don't have the time or temperament to tell the world how great your book is, there are experts you can hire to do it for you, and most self-publishing companies provide publicity both as parts of packages and as optional add-ons.

◆Book publicity is a specialty, and is not the same as publicizing cars, soap or politicians—so pick someone who can demonstrate both experience and success.

◆One company that impressed me is Westwind Communications. See **www.Westwindcos.com/book**.

Carolyn Howard-Johnson

(**www.sharingwithwriters.blogspot.com**) is an award-winning author and a former publicist. With a last name that made me keep thinking about fried clam strips and ice cream, Carolyn serves up a large portion of useful info and advice, even about websites. Her book, *The Frugal Book Promoter: How to Do What Your Publisher Won't*, can empower you to give your book the best possible start in life.

Frugal shows you how to promote your book with powerful but inexpensive or even *free* publicity. Carolyn points out important publicity possibilities that you may not think of, like reviewing other authors' books.

The promotional tips are not just theory—they come from Carolyn's own successful book campaigns. Several ideas will certainly be right for you and your book.

Most new writers have much more time than money, and this book can help you achieve big-buck results with minimum use of your credit cards—and no federal bailout. "Frugal" belongs on every author's shelf, whether you are an independent self-publisher, are using a self-publishing company or a traditional publisher. Here are some of Carolyn's tips:

- **Read, read, read**: Even your junk mail can be useful. My daughter found a flier from the local library in the Sunday paper stuffed between grocery coupons. It mentioned a display done by a local merchant in the library window. My book was displayed in their lobby and I became a seminar speaker for their author series. Rubbish (even spam email) can be valuable.

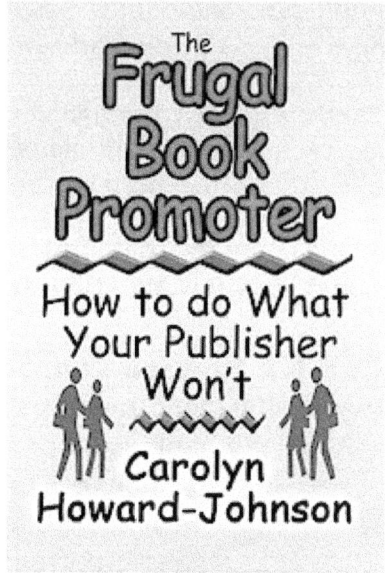

The Frugal Book Promoter

How to do What Your Publisher Won't

Carolyn Howard-Johnson

- **Keep an open mind for promotion ideas:** Look at the different themes in your book. There are angles you can exploit when you're talking to editors. My book, *This is the Place* is romantic and set in Salt Lake City, the site where the winter Olympic games were played in 2002. I found sports desks and feature editors open to it as Olympics fervor grew, and even as it waned.

- **Etiquette counts:** Send thank-you notes to contacts after they've featured you or your book. This happens so rarely they are sure to be impressed and to pay attention to the next idea you have, even if it's just a listing in a calendar for your next book signing.

- **Publicize who you are, what you do:** Reviews aren't the only way to go. Think of angles for human interest stories, not only about your book but about you as its author. Are you very young? Is writing a book a new endeavor for you? Several editors have liked the idea that I wrote my first book at an age when most are thinking of retiring, that I think of myself as an example of the fact that it is never too late to follow a dream.

- **Develop new activities to publicize:** Don't do just book signings. Use your imagination for a spectacular launch. Get charities involved. Think in terms of ways to help your community.
- **Frequency is important:** The editor who ignores your first release may pay more attention to your second or 25th. She will come to view you as a source and call you when she needs to quote an expert. This can work for novels as well as nonfiction. Publicity is like planting bulbs. It proliferates even when you aren't trying.

↓How experts do a press release↓

FOR IMMEDIATE RELEASE
Contact: Tracey Guest, 212-698-7533
tracey.guest@simonandschuster.com

SIMON & SCHUSTER TO PUBLISH BOB WOODWARD'S "OBAMA'S WARS" SEPTEMBER 27, 2010

New York, N.Y., September 7, 2010 -- Simon & Schuster will publish Bob Woodward's book, "OBAMA'S WARS" on September 27, 2010. Excerpts from the 441 page book will appear in *The Washington Post* beginning Monday, September 27. It is Woodward's 16th book, all of which have been published by Simon & Schuster.

Working behind the scenes for 18 months, Woodward has written the most intimate and sweeping portrait of Obama making the critical decisions on the Afghanistan War, the secret war in Pakistan and the worldwide fight against terrorism. Drawing on internal memos, classified documents, meeting notes and hundreds of hours of interviews with most of the key players, including the president, Woodward offers an original, you-are-there account of Obama and his team in this time of turmoil and uncertainty.

Bob Woodward is an associate editor at *The Washington Post*, where he has worked for 39 years. He has shared in two Pulitzer Prizes, first for the *Post's* coverage of the Watergate scandal, and later for coverage of the 9/11 terrorist attacks. Simon & Schuster has published all of Woodward's previous 15 books, beginning in 1974 with the groundbreaking *All the President's Men*, the Watergate reporting story co-authored with Carl Bernstein.

All 15 of Woodward's books have been national bestsellers—and 11 of those have been #1 national nonfiction bestsellers. Editorial Director Alice Mayhew has been the editor on all 16, including "OBAMA'S WARS"—a 36 year editor-author relationship, one of the most enduring in recent American book publishing history. Bob Woodward's previous books include *The War Within, State of Denial, The Secret Man, Plan of Attack, Bush at War, Maestro, Shadow, The Choice, The Agenda, The Commanders, Veil, Wired, The Brethren, The Final Days,* and *All the President's Men.*

OBAMA'S WARS
Bob Woodward
Simon & Schuster
Publication Date: September 27, 2010
Hardcover: 9781439172490, $30.00
Other formats:
CD: 9781442335264, $29.99
eAudio: 9781442335271, $18.95
e-book: 9781439172513, $14.99

CHAPTER 41
Getting book reviews

Most authors dream of getting a rave review in the Sunday *New York Times* book section or a recommendation from Oprah. Actually, almost any review (even a negative one) has the power to help you sell books, and reviews will reach many more potential buyers than the blurbs that are printed on your book cover.

There are two general classes of book reviewers (publications, not the actual people who read and write about what they've read): *prepublication*, and everything else.

Prepublication reviewers expect to receive your book about four months ahead of its publication date. They definitely do not want to receive a book to review if it's already being sold to the public.

In the old days, book reviewers would read *galleys* (or *galley proofs*). Galley proofs get their name from hand-set type. Years ago, a typesetter would prepare a book page by arranging pieces of type into a metal tray called a *galley*. The galleys for a book would be used to print a small number of copies for editing and proofreading, and some would be provided to reviewers and booksellers. After the author and editors marked up the galleys (the pages, not the trays), the typesetter would make corrections and books would be printed and shipped.

Today, it's more common for publishers to provide reviewers with ARCs rather than galleys. ARC has several similar meanings including *Advance Reader Copy, Advance Reading Copy, Advance Review Copy* but not *Advanced* anything. Simon and Schuster has used *Advance Uncorrected Reader's Proof.* The "reader" was presumably the proofreader.

ARCs often do not have the final cover design. The back cover may have blurbs for previous books, and no bar code.

The back cover may include information that will help reviewers and booksellers but will not be on the final book, such as publication date and promotional plans. The ARC may have disclaimers saying that the ARC is not the final version of the book and should not be quoted without verification. There may be a warning that the ARC is the property of the publisher and is not to be sold or duplicated. Many are sold, anyway.

Some review copies are also distributed to magazines that may print excerpts, to libraries, or even to movie producers. Some are given away at trade shows attended by booksellers.

Major publishers may print thousands of ARCs. A self-publishing company might do 100 or fewer. Maybe just six.

It may be tempting to simply distribute an ordinary copy of your book, with a stick-on label that says it's an ARC. For a minimal expense, you can make an alternate version of your cover with an ARC notice actually printed on it. This subterfuge should enhance your credibility so you'll be considered more like one of the big guys, and not just an amateur.

Some publications that require long-in-advance review copies are the *New York Times, Publishers Weekly, Booklist, Library Journal, ForeWord, Kirkus Reviews* and *Independent Publisher.* "I.P." prefers advance copies, but after-publication is also OK. *Kirkus* said it does not review POD or self-published books, but it can't hurt to try. The book business is changing.

Whenever you like—even after publication—you can send review copies to other publications and websites that have book reviews, but it's better to provide them in advance. Even though you can't control the media, by letting potential reviewers know when your book will be on sale and allowing sufficient time for reading and writing, you stand a better chance of having reviews published close to your pub date.

Book review tips (and warnings)

◆Some media and reviewers have policies not to review self-published books, so it's best not to state that you are self-publishing. If your book has a professional logo and proper-sounding publisher's name (not PublishAmerica), there's a chance that you'll be accepted as one of many small presses the reviewer has simply not heard of. If asked if the book is self-published, don't lie, but consider the answer. I sometimes say I'm one of the owners of the company that publishes my books.

◆Most of the time, you will be seeking reviews, but you may actually be approached by a reviewer who wants to read your book. Some people posing as book reviewers are really free-loaders or—less charitably—thieves. They will request a review copy but they have no intention of reviewing the book. They may just want to read it without paying for it, or sell it for whatever they can collect from a used book dealer or a reader—in competition with you. Since your book probably costs less than $10 to print and ship, there is not much point in spending $500 for a detective to check out a possible scammer. But since a whole bunch of $10 books can add up to real money, it pays to do a little bit of detective work yourself.
Unless you know about the reviewer, do not accept a book request by phone or email. Ask for a fax or snail mail on a letterhead. When you get the letter, be wary if the return address is a Post Office box and not a street address. If you've never

heard of the publication, find its website and look for published reviews by the person who contacted you, or request a sample copy, or at least a fax of a review that was published.

♦ If you send a book in response to a request, call in a week or ten days to confirm receipt, offer to answer questions and ask for an approximate publication date.

♦After distributing an online press release, you may get a flattering phone call from the producer of a cable TV show. He'll request a review copy, and tell you that he's considering putting you on an interview show that will be seen by millions. A while after you send the book, you'll get a call from an associate producer who wants to firm up plans. At some point you'll be told that you have to pay thousands of dollars. You are not making news. You are being sold advertising.

♦Don't let a negative review ruin your day or your life. Some reviewers have hidden agendas. (Maybe she is currently writing a competitive book.) Others will dismiss a book which they don't like, regardless of merits. Some will skip around your text and miss important parts or make erroneous assumptions. Some will pan a book simply because it is written for people with more or less knowledge than the reviewer has.

♦If a reviewer made important factual errors, send a note to the publication (not to the reviewer), thanking them for the review and explaining the error. It's too late to change what's been printed, but you may get a printed correction which will give you even more publicity. Online reviews *can* be corrected.

♦It's unusual for a review to be 100% negative. In an overall negative review, you'll probably be able to find a sentence or two that says something good about the book that you can use to help sell.

◆The Midwest Book Review has a big list of book review possibilities. **www.midwestbookreview.com/links/othr_rev.htm** There are also good lists at **www.BookConnector.com**

◆Christy Pinheiro's *The Official Indie Book Reviewer List* provides contact information and guidance to get your book reviewed. It will save you hours or days of research time. The book has over 100 pages and is an inexpensive download at **www.stepbystepselfpublishing.net/book-reviewer-list.html**

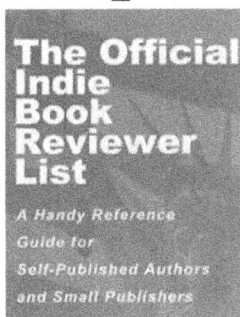

◆NetGalley is an online service for people who read and recommend books. Publishers or authors pay to upload a book PDF and marketing information, and invite contacts to read books online. It's a good, green idea. **www.NetGalley.com.**

A book review sequence:

①Establish your timetable and budget. Unless your book has a *really* tiny niche audience, include the cost to print about 20-100 ARCs, and the cost to package and ship them with your promotional material.

②Design your press package, or packages. The complete package, which will go to the most important media, will include an ARC, a high-quality photo of the cover, a high-quality photo of the author, the author's bio, a press release, reviews of past books (if there were any) and a cover letter. The cover letter (one page, please) should explain why the book exists and should include a brief bio, summary of promotional plans and the vital statistics for the book (ISBN, cover price, page count, trim size), and perhaps a bit about the publisher. This letter should be informative, but not hard-sell. A less-complete package for less-important media would leave out the actual book, but would offer to send one on request. A third level of advance publicity would have the biggest circulation and lowest cost—an email. It should contain the important info and an offer to send an actual book, and should have a link to a website for more information. The site could have a press kit.

③Send out the complete packages to the most important media four months ahead of publication date. These media include national media like the *New York Times*, as well as niche media that are directly related to your title either because of subject, geography or affinity.

④Send out the less-complete packages about two months ahead of publication date.

⑤Send out less-complete packages and email announcements to any media that you think will help you, such as local newspapers and broadcasters (including cable news shows).

⑥Don't forget to send press releases to media that may consider your publication, or the book's contents, to be newsworthy, even if these media don't do actual book reviews.

⑦Follow up on the ARCs you've sent out. It's OK to inquire if the book has been received and to offer to answer questions.

⑧You can continue to send out review copies and solicitations for reviews throughout the life of your book. Try to tie in to a news event that relates to the book, or some news about the book itself, such as an award, a sales milestone, or the book's selection for use in a college course or book club. Peter Bowerman, author of *The Well-Fed Self-Publisher*, recommends sending out 350-400+ review copies over three or four years.

CHAPTER 42
Book blurbs

The second big author's dream is having cover blurbs (endorsements) from famous people who'll say nice things to entice other people to buy books. Often, especially for a new author with a new book, it's just not possible to get cooperation of an expert who will add authority to yours.

That doesn't mean your book has to be "blurbless." There's nothing wrong with asking for and printing blurbs from friends and family, if they're appropriate to your book. Often a blurb from an "ordinary person" who really read your book and with whom prospective readers can identify, will seem more genuine and be more effective than a blurb from a star who spent just ten minutes skimming. Later on, if a celeb falls in love with your words, you can revise the cover to include the new comments.

My book, *I Only Flunk My Brightest Students: stories from school and real life*, deals with *my* life. It made perfect sense to use blurbs from people who know me, rather than a blurb from some distant Nobel Prize winner I'd have to bribe to get a few words from.

The book is funny. Identifying my front cover blurber as "author's classmate since first grade" reinforces the mood.

It's almost a parody of traditional stuffy or irrelevant IDs ("professor of Indo-Eurasian folk medicine at the University of Guatemala," "Miss Tallahassee 1972 Runner-Up," or "Three-Time Northern Utah Senior Citizen Spelling Bee Champion").

A blurb written by a previewer of my *Stories I'd Tell My Children (but maybe not until they're adults)* was so good that there was no need to explain the blurber's background.

> **"This book is so funny that I nearly peed in my pants. My girlfriend didn't think it was funny, so I got a new girlfriend." —Nicholas Santiago**

Don't forget blurbs for the back cover, for the first inside page, for online booksellers, and for your own web pages.

There's nothing wrong with your acting as a writing coach. You can edit blurbs as long as you don't change the meaning. You can even write a blurb and ask someone to "adopt" it.

In some fields of writing, blurbing is corrupt, with authors trading blurbs in order to publicize their own books. Some blurbers dominate their fields. They are like hired guns, or medical experts who will provide an expert opinion at a trial for whichever side will pay the most money. Some experts seem to write more blurbs for other books than complete books under their own names.

On the other hand, plenty of perfectly nice experts and authors refuse to do blurbs because they are just too busy.

I think that the value of blurbs from authors is diminishing, simply because it has become so easy to become an author. Perhaps this book will make the situation even worse.

If you write a book about artistic pickle slicing, a rave blurb from the author of a book about headlight replacement may not accomplish much for you. An endorsement from a Pulitzer Prize winner might mean a lot more, but would be tough to get unless he happens to be your father.

Book blurbs

→Try to get some sincere and well-written blurbs from people who have read your book and know its background and value. That can be more useful than a few perfunctory words from a distant celebrity because readers will be better able to identify with recommendation from "civilians."

If you've written a how-to book, the best blurbs will come from people who have actually been helped by it, not by other authors using your book as a billboard to hawk their books.

Blurbs can go in three places in your book:

◆**The front cover** is where you should put the most impressive blurb—impressive because of content, source or both. You probably won't have much space, maybe just a line or two. It's OK to shorten a blurb, but don't change the meaning. I always get an approval for any changes I make.

◆**The back cover** can probably hold anywhere from three to six blurbs, and they can be longer than what you put on the front cover. Keep in mind that you can show the back cover and its contents on your Amazon page, so take advantage of the opportunity.

◆**The first recto page** inside the book is also blurb territory. Many books label the page "Advance Praise for (book name)." I think that's pushing a bit too hard and prefer a more neutral "What Readers Say" or "Reader Comments."

One page of blurbs should be enough, but some people make a mini-chapter out of them. That seems like a silly and egomaniacal waste of trees. Once you get beyond the first page, the blurbs get pretty weak, or poorly written, or both. Watch out for blurbs that are overwritten or pompous, where the blurber is more impressed with her own words than with the book she's blurbing about.

Brevity and clarity are better than overabundance. You want one to three sentences—not 1,000 words. Don't be afraid to edit. Again, get approval for changes.

Some writers put the same blurbs on the back cover and inside the book. That's silly and obvious padding.

Don't use blurbs from people who have a financial interest in the book. One book I read has a blurb from someone who works for the company that published it. That's tacky. The book also has reviews that promote books written by some of the blurbers. Tit-for-tat is tacky, too.

Tips for better blurbing

♦One prime purpose of a blurb is to borrow credibility from a well-known authority or tastemaker whose authority and taste may be better known than yours. Select your candidates carefully. Even if your college roommate is now a Hollywood star, his fame does not mean he can write a meaningful blurb for your book on tennis, cooking or bathroom remodeling.

♦Don't be too timid to approach famous authors, politicians, business leaders and celebrities, especially if you have something in common which can create a bond. You might be pleasantly surprised. Write a good letter and explain how you think the book relates to the prospective blurber. Find a reason to compliment the candidate. If possible, refer to a time when you were in the same place, perhaps during a speech or a book signing or on an airplane. (I once sat next to Geoffrey Holder.)

♦A good way to find "amateur" blurbers who might write sincere comments about actually benefiting from your book is to observe online communities which are concerned with your subject. If you find articulate people with problems your book solves, offer to send them free advance copies (even PDFs if bound copies are not yet available) in exchange for their comments. You can say that you'd like to know if the book was helpful and how it can be improved. Mention that you might like to quote their comments, but don't guarantee it.

◆Short blurbs are usually better than long blurbs. Humorous blurbs (if appropriate) are often better than serious blurbs.

◆Request blurbs as long in advance as possible—as soon as you have a draft of your book that is good enough to show. The book does not have to be complete. You can probably get by with an introduction, a table of contents, and a few chapters sent as a PDF. If you want a blurb from someone famous, it's probably better to send an ARC (previous chapter) than a PDF.

◆Incorporate good "early" blurbs into your back cover and first page as soon as possible. If other blurbers read them, they may be more likely to write similarly positive comments.

◆Keep in mind that the people you are requesting blurbs from are probably even busier than you are. You can request or suggest that they send their blurb in two weeks, and check with them in three weeks if you have not received it—but don't nag. Even though you will be providing publicity for the blurber, you stand to benefit more from her effort, so respect her presumably hectic schedule.

◆You may be able to speed things along and get a more powerful blurb if you write a few samples that the blurber can use as-is or modify. It's best to customize the blurbs for each target.

◆Don't assume that all potential blurbers will actually deliver, even if they promise to do so. And some of the delivered blurbs may be unsuitable. Always ask for more than you have room for in and on the book—probably twice as much.

◆Blurbs should be as specific as possible and relate to the content, effect and advantages of your book. "Best book I ever read" won't mean much, unless the statement is coming from someone well known for literary taste.

◆After your book goes on sale, you will probably receive unsolicited comments from readers—either as letters, email or comments on booksellers' websites. Ask permission to use the good ones as blurbs. Most readers will be thrilled to see their name on or in your book. Blurbs also go on websites, sell-sheets and press releases.

Space Filler-Upper
A self-published author doesn't have to be a self-designer.

- If you are an independent self-publisher but don't have the time or talent to design your book, there are experts you can hire for the covers or interior or the entire job. They may have better ideas than you do and do better work than you can.
- If you are using a self-publishing company, an independent designer may have better ideas and do better work than the person assigned by your publisher.

You can even split up the work. I generally design and format my books' interiors, but hire a professional artist for the covers.

Book design is a specialty, and is not the same as designing ads, packages or homes—so pick someone who can demonstrate talent, experience and success. I like Marin Bookworks at **www.ThebookDesigner.com, www.vangarde.com** and **www.1106Design.com.**

Although Marin Bookworks can design and format your entire book, the company can also provide a custom design template for you to use. This way you have the beauty of a professional design plus the control of DIY formatting.

CHAPTER 43
One vision of the future for publishing: the Espresso Book Machine

Pundits and predictors have claimed that, at some future time, words will seldom or never be applied to paper. They'll be displayed on the screens of computers, e-book readers and cellphones. Maybe text and images will be transmitted directly to our brains and we won't even have to see to read. Until then, the Espresso Book Machine (EBM) combines the efficiency of electronic publishing with the pleasures of the printed page and a shelf filled with books.

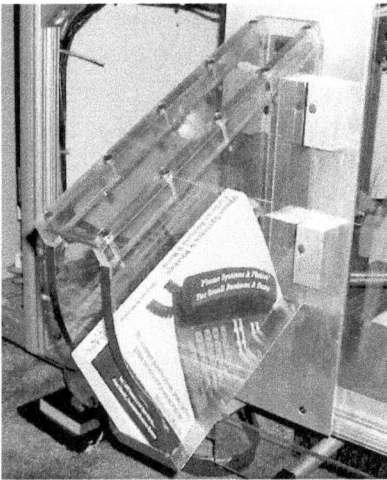

The EBM is a miniaturized book factory combined with a vending machine and is about the size of a large office copier. It contains raw materials (paper, ink and glue) and can quickly print, bind and trim normal-looking paperback books on demand at the point of sale.

The EBM was developed by On Demand Books and was named to *Time Magazine*'s "Best Inventions" list. It provides revolutionary direct-to-reader printing and distribution. It can hold digital files for millions of books, including current titles as well as out-of-print books from publishers of all sizes and types.

Lightning Source, the dominant Print-On-Demand printer, feeds book files to the Espresso network, and Xerox handles EBM installation and maintenance.

Books are printed at the point of sale—primarily bookstores and libraries—not at Lightning's own facilities.

The bookstore business has been in the dumper, but Espresso can make huge changes to help chain stores and mom-and-pops compete against Amazon. It also helps people who want nearly instant gratification but prefer to read on paper instead of on e-book readers, cellphones or computers.

Rather than waiting one to three days to receive a book from an online bookseller, people wait just three or four minutes, and can buy snacks and drinks while they wait.

There's no shipping. No warehousing. No remainders. No markdowns. No returns. No shredding and pulping. No copies becoming obsolete on the shelf. No waiting for special orders. No shipping errors. No shipping delays. No shipping costs.

The Espresso could be a godsend to self-publishing authors who have either been kept out of, or have avoided, bricks-and-mortar bookstores.

It should become as easy to order an instant book as to use a Barnes & Noble computer kiosk to special-order a book.

Some day you may see your freshly printed book pop out of a slot in a Barnes & Noble store, a library, an independent neighborhood bookshop, a restaurant, newsstand, hotel, military base, theme park, airport, aboard a cruise ship or maybe even in a shopping mall between the kiosks for sunglasses and ear piercing.

Chapter 44
Bestselling what?

Lots of writers you've probably never heard of are described as "bestselling authors." Unlike lists of the winners of Oscars, Emmys, Pulitzers and Nobels, there is often no official registry where you can check the validity of the claims. There's an almost endless list of bestseller lists. Unless a publisher provides a detail like "103 weeks on the *New York Times* Bestseller List," it's hard to document or disprove bestseller status.

The *Times*, of course, is the biggie. Other important lists are provided by *USA Today*, Amazon.com, IndieBound, *Publishers Weekly* and Barnes & Noble.

There is often disagreement among the bestseller lists and it may not be obvious how the lists are calculated. For example, online booksellers and "big box" stores may be excluded.

➔A book about flea removal from pregnant three-legged albino Weimaraners could sell exactly one copy and still be the BESTSELLER IN ITS FIELD. There is no law that requires an explanation on the cover or a footnote inside the book.

➔Anyone can call any book a bestseller and the label may help it to achieve more sales—deserved or not deserved.

Keep in mind that even if a book is on a legitimate list, the fact that many were sold does not necessarily mean that it's a good book, or even that buyers have read what they bought.

There are even fudged bestseller labels that are more the result of marketing than of statistics, such as "summertime bestseller" or "underground bestseller."

Amazon's bestseller list has been manipulated by elaborate online campaigns to maximize purchases during a brief time period to temporarily elevate a book to bestseller status.

Since one of my books has been on two Amazon.com bestseller lists, I hereby claim my right to describe myself as a "bestselling author." You can probably make the same claim for yourself and few people will complain.

WHAT IS SUCCESSFUL SELF-PUBLISHING?

Standards for "success" vary for different fields and different people. Here are some of the indicators of success in self-publishing. Choose what makes you happy.

You finish writing your book.
You have a printed copy in your hand.
One copy is sold.
One hundred copies are sold.
One thousand (or one million) copies are sold.
You get your first check.
You get your first good review.
Your book is on a bestseller list.
You are interviewed on TV.
Your picture is on the cover of *Time*.
You are recognized and greeted by strangers
You earn back the cost of publishing.
Your boss gives you a raise.
You get a better job.
You make enough money to quit your day job.
You make enough money to stop writing.
The person you had a crush on years ago—but wasn't interested in you—is now interested in you.

CHAPTER 45
The low standards of PublishAmerica

PublishAmerica ("PA") says that it's a "unique and traditional publishing company." It *is* unique, but since a PA author's advance is just one dollar, and editing and promotion are almost non-existent, it's *not* traditional.

➜ PA has a strange marketing philosophy. It wants authors to provide a mailing list so PA can pester friends and relatives to buy and publicize books.

Jenna Glatzer is a magazine article writer, book author, contributing editor at *Writer's Digest,* and editor-in-chief of *Absolute Write*—an online magazine for writers. In an interview with WBJB radio, she exposed some of the wacky and scary tactics of PublishAmerica.

According to Jenna, "They harass their authors, they start smear campaigns against their authors, they're just an incredibly abusive company." She also said that PA is "built on deception," and has "vindictive, abusive and strange people who have crossed the line."

Jenna discussed author Ken Yarborough, who tried to prove that PA was not selective about accepting manuscripts and did not reject 80% of proposed books, as the company states. Ken submitted a book with the same 30 pages repeated over and over again—and PA accepted it! When Ken revealed what had happened, PA reported him to the police, alleging fraud.

In another case related by Jenna, an author asked PA to lower the retail price of a book to make it more saleable, or to release him from his seven-year contract. PA tried to have him arrested for harassment.

Authors told *Publishers Weekly* that PA "sells books to which it no longer holds the rights;... doesn't pay royalties it owes; engages in slipshod editing and copyediting; sets unreasonable list prices; and makes little effort (and has had little success) in getting books into bookstores."

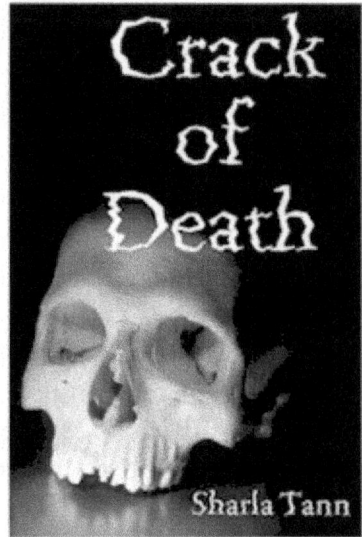

PA's low standards have been exposed by several stings in which it agreed to publish deliberately bad books. *Atlanta Nights* is an assumedly unpublishable collaborative novel created by a group of sci-fi and fantasy authors to test whether PA would accept it. The book was supposedly written by "Travis Tea" (travesty). The *Crack of Death* author was said to be "Sharla Tann" (charlatan), and the book is filled with bad writing, bad grammar, spelling errors, malapropisms, gender shifts, age shifts, name shifts, and more.

FOR THE SEMI-PROFESSIONALS

The next section of the book is for people who want to format their own book pages, either because they decided to operate their own small publishing companies, or because they want more control over a book produced for them by another company.

Even if someone will format pages for you, if you spend some time in this section, you'll have a better understanding of the publishing process, which may help you to get a better book.

(Through 9/11/11, a purchase of the pretty pink Microsoft Wireless Mobile Mouse 4000 generates a $4 donation to the Komen for the Cure breast cancer fund.)

Pick your favorite flavor

Most on-demand book publishers and printers allow you to choose either white or cream ("crème") paper. Traditionally, white is used for non-fiction "how-to" books like this one, with photographs, screen shots and charts—or any book with lots of photos—so the white areas will really be white and not have a color imposed on them.

Some publishing experts say that cream/crème pages are easier on the eyes (less glare) so cream may be a better choice if you don't need white.

◆Cream pages are usually a little bit thicker, and the same number of cream pages will provide a thicker book than white pages. This means that the book's spine will be a tiny bit bigger, so the title can be a tiny bit bigger.. With a 400-page book, you gain a little over $1/16^{th}$ of an inch. With a 200-pager, the difference is insignificant: just over $1/32^{nd}$ of an inch.

◆Sometimes the cream pages are so dark that they make the book pages seem old and yellowed.

◆If you can't decide, ask for samples of printed books with each type of paper.

◆Some typefaces such as Adobe Garamond Pro seem thin or weak, and are more readable on white than on cream paper because of the increased contrast.

CHAPTER 46
Can you really make a book with Microsoft Word? Should you?

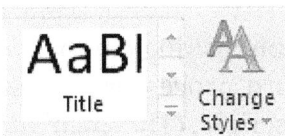

I used Word to make this book, and other books. They don't look too much worse than books composed with Adobe InDesign or Quark Express, which are used by professional designers and a few do-it-yourselfers.

InDesign can provide automatic *kerning* to adjust space within specific letter pairs. For example, InDesign can instantly give you **To** instead of **To**. (Do you see the difference?) With Word, you manually condense the space between letters. It's a lot of work that few folks bother with. I do it for book titles and some chapter names and subheads—but not for body text.

However, the "adult" software can cost as much as $800 and can take a long time to learn how to use properly. (I'm planning to try InDesign for a future book.)

◆ If you've set up your own publishing company and plan to use Lightning Source or CreateSpace to print your books, you will have to submit your text as a PDF file. Info is up ahead.

◆ My books, *Independent Self-Publishing: the complete guide*, and *Get the Most out of a Self-Publishing Company* have more detailed instructions than this book has on using Microsoft Word to format a book, and making PDF conversions.

◆My books cover book page formatting using Microsoft Word 2007 or Word 2010 for a PC, and Windows Vista. If you are using Windows XP or Windows 7 instead of Vista, you may have to make some minor mental modifications because the screen shots I show may not be the same as what your monitor shows. Also, Word 2010 has no "office" button for activating major tasks.

◆ Aaron Shepard's excellent *Perfect Pages* has detailed instructions for using earlier versions of Word, for both PC and Mac. Although it was written before Word 2007 and 2010 came out, a lot of its information will help you with those versions, too. Aaron's newer *POD for Profit* will be a big help for all authors planning to sell books online.

◆You can submit your text to a self-publishing company in almost any format produced by a word processor. Some publishers will accept handwritten manuscripts. (The "man" in "manuscript" means "hand.") Publishers charge extra to type for you.

Self-publishing companies employ designers who will devise a "look" for your book and then format your manuscript to make it book-like, and not just a pile of pages. This service is part of most publishing packages, but it may be an option. You may be able to save hundreds of dollars—and have more control over the look of your book—if you format your own pages.

I'm one of those weird people who think that formatting the interior of a book is fun; but I know it's not fun for all (and maybe not for even *one* other person). However, most writers already own Word and know how to use it. They can quickly learn how to use some of its often-untapped power to produce a manuscript that's nearly ready to become a book.

➔Despite its name, Microsoft Publisher is not suitable for book publishing. Save it for fliers, posters, brochures, newsletters, school projects, signs and birthday cards.

Can you really make a book with Microsoft Word?

I'm going to assume you are starting a new book from scratch, but if you already have some text that you want to make into a book, you can either copy and paste it into a new document to be formatted as a book, or just reformat it.

You have to make some decisions about the appearance of your pages

The first is *justification*. When a text block, which could be a short paragraph or a book, is **justified** (or *full justified*), the lines are all the same width, except for an indented first line or a short last line in a paragraph, just like in this one. ➔ Justified narrow columns often have too much space between words.

Justification has been the standard in publishing for hundreds of years, but it's not the only way of laying out text. There has been an increasing use of **flush-left/ragged-right** text (like this paragraph) in advertising, web pages and magazines. Also called *left-justified*, this style can be used in books when you want an informal look. Magazines and newspapers often mix justified and ragged-right articles to break up the boredom. Sometimes a book that is predominantly justified will have small ragged right sections when the author or designer wants them to have a distinctive look.

The opposite arrangement is **ragged-left/flush-right** (or *flush-right/ragged-left*, or *right-justified*). It's probably not used for full books, but is good for headlines and also for small sections that are intended to stand out from the rest of a page. I sometimes use *rag-left* justification to the left of a photo or chart.

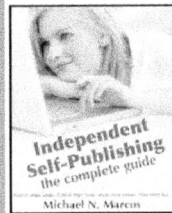

Many amateur webmasters use **centered** type, much too often. It's difficult to read a large centered document. Human brains prefer to return to a fixed starting place at the beginning of each line of type, not to jump around to find the beginning. You can use centered type for a title page, chapter names and subheads, but not for much else. Try not to center more than three consecutive lines. If you are centering, choose words to create a block of text that tapers from narrow to wide or wide to narrow, not one that goes wide, narrow, wide.

If a paragraph or several paragraphs lose their justification setting, highlight with your mouse, then select proper justification from the **Home** tab on Word's ribbon bar.

Justified type can look beautiful, but takes more time and perhaps money to do right. A lot of *very ugly* justified type gets printed, particularly in self-published books.

Watch out for typographical *rivers*, where spaces between words line up above one another.   The eye is drawn to the "negative space," which is ugly and   distracting. You can remove the river by hyphenating and   changing words. (This sample paragraph has an artificial   exaggerated river.)

Justified type has a more formal, polished look. Ragged is obviously less formal, and people can rightfully claim that justified type is abnormal and artificial, but that ragged-right is normal and natural.

Be careful if you are justifying a book that was already completed with ragged-right type. Most lines will expand to the right, but sometimes words that used to fit on one page will migrate onto another page. You may have to change the page numbering for chapter beginnings, or cut words or make illustrations smaller to get what you want. Make sure to check your table of contents and index and modify if necessary.

➜ Sometimes spaces between words look lousy, and you'll have to experiment with hyphenation changes, and perhaps switch to shorter or longer words, or add or subtract words to make things look right. Since you are the book's author, this is your duty and your privilege.

➜ Word has a deeply buried secret setting that can give you better justification. Click on the **Office Button** at the top left of the Word 2007 screen (or **File** in Word 2010) and then click on **Word Options**. Click on **Advanced** on the left of the new window. Then, you scroll down to **Compatibility Options** and then after **Lay out this document as if created in**, click to expand **Layout Options**. Finally, you'll have the opportunity to check **Do full justification the way WordPerfect 6.x for Windows does**.

It seems strange that Microsoft is emulating a once-powerful software competitor.

WordPerfect may have lost the word war to mighty Microsoft, but it apparently developed a better way to justify, which is more like sophisticated publishing software. It can add or reduce space *within* words, not just *between* words. This produces nicer looking pages without the white gaps that Word often introduces when it justifies. Since the WordPerfect method is available in Word, I wonder why it's not active all the time by default. Maybe Microsoft has to pay a nickel to the WordPerfect people every time someone uses this procedure.

This is a subheadline, or breaker headline

It can introduce a section or break up a large expanse of gray. If it has multiple lines, reduce the space between lines.

Another decision for you to make is the size of your **paragraph indentations** (*indents*). Word's default size is a half-inch. That's OK for letters and term papers, but will look too big for most books. I like to use .3-inch, but the decision should be based on your type size, page margins, page size and overall esthetics. I've seen some indents that are so small they are almost invisible. It's nice to break up a gray page with a bit of white.

This is Word's standard half-inch indent. Blah blah blah blah blah blah blah blah blah blah blah blah.

This is my .3-inch indent. Blah blah blah blah blah blah blah blah blah blah blah blah blah blah blah.

This is the too-tiny .1-inch indent. Blah blah blah blah blah blah blah blah blah blah blah blah blah.

Most paragraphs will be indented, but generally not at the beginning of a chapter or section, or after a large white space, or maybe not to the right of or below a photograph. These are aspects of your personal style. Do some experimenting, look at lots of books, and maybe ask for advice or hire a designer. To adjust indent size, open the **Paragraph** dialog box from within the **Home** tab. ⬇

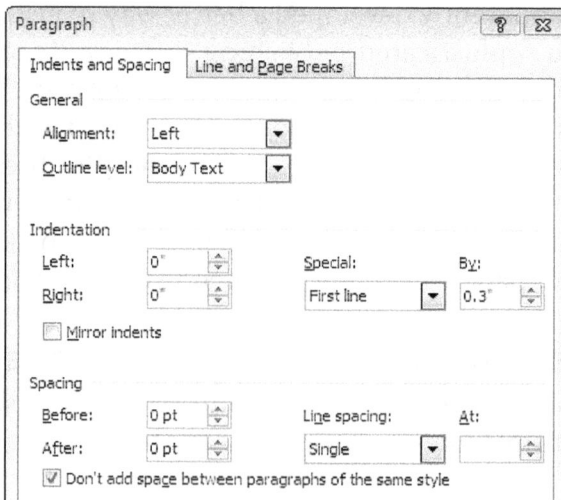

This box is also where you set **Line spacing** (what professionals call *leading*). "Leading" rhymes with "breading," not with "breeding." Unless you have a good reason not to, keep it as

Single as shown in the previous screen shot. This setting can be useful if you have to manipulate the size of a block of text to make it take up more or less space.

This text sample has Word's **default** line spacing. It's set at **1.0 lines.** Compare the text line positioning across the three columns.

This text sample has **vertically expand-** ed type, used when you want to fill a page or a text box, or for artistic effects. It's set at **1.1 lines.**

This text has **vertically compressed** type, used when you must fit in more words, or to keep words from overflowing onto the next page without eliminating words. It's set at **.9 lines.**

Note the excessive word spacing in the center and right columns.
◆It's difficult to get good justification in narrow columns.
◆If you set line spacing at less than .9, you may chop off the bottoms of letters (*descenders*). Be careful.
◆Expansion and compression can be OK for text boxes, captions or an entire book. Don't expand or compress individual pages unless you can make barely perceptible adjustments in line spacing.

At some point—before, during or after you write the body of the book—you'll have to establish a style for it. In this case, style means a set of standards, including margins, typefaces, type sizes, indents, page numbering, headers, footers, subheads, decorations, etc.—all of the little items that make a book look unique, or like another book.

Every book has an interior designer. It might be the author who has never designed anything before, or a skilled professional with years of experience. Someone has to devise (or perhaps copy) a standard for the way your pages will look.

Before you commit to a designer (or to your own design) look through a lot of books and try to understand what makes them appealing or unappealing. After an hour or so, you should develop a sense of what you do like and don't like, what is easy to read, and what slows you down or distracts you. It's OK to copy the style of one book, but it's more fun and more creative to combine elements to develop your personal style.

Try doing some trial pages, with different typefaces, different type sizes, different spacing between chapter headings and body copy, subheads set flush left or centered, and so on.

Once you have decided on your style, make a *style sheet*. I type mine on a temporary "page zero" which I consult until it's deleted when I'm ready to submit the book to the printer.

⬇Here's the style sheet for one of my books. You can adopt or adapt it for your own books.

Body type is 12-pt Constantia
Trebuchet is used for sans serif body type
16-pt Trebuchet bold for chapter titles
14-pt Trebuchet bold for subheads
14-pt Trebuchet regular for headers
No header on first page of a chapter
Chapter titles are flush left, no periods; first word is
    only one with initial cap
Subheads are flush-left
Intro text blocks are 12-pt Trebuchet roman bold with
    about 16 pts above and below
Most text boxes are justified without initial indent, 1.5-
    pt width outside lines, small drop shadow in lower
    right
Text boxes have 14-pt Trebuchet headlines, centered,
    with no space below
Technical terms are set in *italics*, not in quotes
Non-techie terms that are printed or spoken get quote
    marks, not italics
Some screenshots get small borders
Up and down arrows are⬇in bold face
Cellphone, not cell phone. Internet, not internet. web
not Web. Online, not on-line. Drop-down not dropdown.
Bookseller, not book-seller.

Book designer and blogger Joel Friedlander of Marin Book-works (**www.thebookdesigner.com/hire-me**) cautions authors about inexperienced designers and do-it-yourself errors. He warns of these problems:

- **Folios everywhere:** We need folios (page numbers) on most pages, but not on the title page, copyright page, blank pages and advertising pages at the end of the book.
- **Headers and footers on blank pages:** If a page is blank (such as at the end of a chapter), it is not part of the text and doesn't get a header, footer or page number.
- **Odd-numbered pages on the left:** When you open your book, the first page you see is page 1 (even if there is no folio on it). The inside of the front cover—even if something is printed on it—is *not* page 1.
- **Ragged-right (unjustified) typography:** Magazines and websites are often composed with ragged-right lines of text. Unless you are writing an instruction manual or recipe book, stick with justified text for books.

There are thousands of different typefaces ("faces"), and infinite variations including size, bold, italic, roman, etc.

Don't make your book look like a ransom note composed of letters cut out of magazines, or like a ten-year-old's website, with a dozen different typefaces. You can probably get by with just two—or maybe three—faces and their variations. If your book needs a third typeface, choose something that's obviously different from the others. Don't let observant readers assume that you meant to match faces but you goofed.

It's easy to get fooled if you copy text from another source and paste it into a book. I often fail to notice when Times New Roman (TNR) creeps into my Constantia text. The words "Times New Roman" in the previous sentence and in this one are set in Times New Roman. Here's how "Times New Roman" looks in Constantia. It can be tough for typographic beginners to tell the difference with just a few letters. The difference in words or paragraphs should be obvious because Constantia takes up more space.

The numbers are very different in the two faces. Constantia has *ascenders* and *descenders*: 1234567890. These numbers are called *old style figures*, and blend in very nicely with text letters. TNR numbers have uniform height: 1234567890, with no ascenders or descenders. Called *lining numbers*, they are the size of uppercase letters, and POP OUT of text.

Trebuchet is a sans serif face. Georgia has serifs.

"Sans" is the French word for "without." The name of Sanka coffee comes from "without caffeine." "Sans-culottes" means without (fancy) pants.

In a book, it's common to use a **serif face** (with "feet," "flags" and other decorations) for *body copy* and a **sans serif face** for chapter titles and *subheads* (*breaker heads*). No one will arrest you if you challenge tradition, but make sure the typefaces you choose are readable on paper—not just on your PC.

The default typeface in Microsoft Word is **Times New Roman**. It's a condensed (i.e., narrow) face often used to squeeze more letters and words into the narrow columns of newspapers and magazines. Graphics arts professionals advise against using it for books, but it looks OK in bigger sizes, say 12 or 13 points. Some of the pros also caution against using **Arial**, which is the most common typeface on the Internet. Arial looks fine on a PC screen, but, as with most sans serif faces, it may be more difficult to read when used as text in a book. Like TNR, it's said to suffer from overexposure.

I frankly think that the overexposure complaint is a bit of crotchety crankiness from type geeks. Most people who read a book won't care if they see a familiar typeface. On the other hand, with just a little bit of effort, you can make a more interesting selection. **These are some good serif faces for your main text:** Century Schoolbook, Garamond, Palatino, Bookman, Constantia (my choice for this book).

Compare **these words in Trebuchet MS Bold** with **these words in Arial Bold**. I think Trebuchet has a bit more style than Arial. I love the **g** and **|** in Trebuchet. Did you notice the little foot on the bottom of the l?

By the way, a typeface is not the same thing as a *font* (although the terms seem to be merging). Strictly speaking, a typeface is a distinctive design, such as **Franklin Gothic** or **Rockwell** or **MATISSE**. The varieties within each face such as bold, italic or roman (i.e., not italic), are the actual fonts. Rockwell is a typeface. **Rockwell Bold** is a font.

Back when type was cast in metal, a font also indicated a type size. Today, when type images are produced digitally in any desired size, instead of stored in physical type cases, different type sizes are not necessarily considered to be different fonts. It is still common to specify a font being used, as, for example, "***12-pt Verdana Bold Italic.***"

When you think you've decided on typefaces, you also have to decide on the type sizes (height). Type size is expressed in *points*. Each point is equal to $1/72^{nd}$ of an inch. Don't assume that two typefaces of the same point size will really be the same size, because width is also a consideration. A page set in TNR will hold more words than a page set in Constantia or Courier New, even if they are both the same point size.

The quick brown fox in 12-pt (Times New Roman)
The quick brown fox in 12-pt (Constantia)
`The quick brown fox in 12-pt (Courier New)`

Strangely, type that is theoretically the same height, may not be. Here is Times New Roman followed by Adobe Garamond Pro (both enlarged from 12-pt). **88**

Narrow, **Condensed** and compressed type can save space, but may be difficult to read in text sizes.

Most books aimed at general audiences use type in the 10-12 point range. I think 10 points is too small for most books, and the "fly poop"-size type on the backs of credit cards should be illegal. Think about your readers' vision. Large-type books are printed for people with visual impairments, but even simple aging can make bigger letters more appealing.

Wider pages with longer lines of text should have bigger type. The right number of characters per line is probably in the 50–70 range. If you have a big page size, consider using two columns. An 8-inch-wide magazine usually has three columns.

You have to decide on a few more style issues which deal with what goes above and below your normal text. A *header* (also called a *running head)*, not surprisingly, goes up at the top. A *footer*, as you should assume, goes down at the bottom.

Can you really make a book with Microsoft Word?

If you did your homework assignment to examine a bunch of books, you've discovered a variety in what goes up on top of the text.

Many books have the chapter names in headers. You can also include the chapter number in a header, and even your own name. I think it's silly to put the author's name all over the place, but it's often done.

Some books have the titles, chapter names and page numbers at the bottom, and no headers at all.

It's common to have the book title in the verso (left) header. Frankly, this seems pretty silly. Do readers need constant reminders of the title of the book they are reading? If a reader forgets, couldn't he just look at the cover? Despite the lack of logic, I kept up the tradition until this book. I may change my mind again in the future. A self-published author can do that.

Books can have page numbers (*folios*) at the top, bottom, or side. I've recently switched from bottom to side.

Click on the **Insert** tab in the ribbon bar at the top of your Word screen, then click on **Header**. A drop-down menu will appear. You can use any of the choices, but for a book, the top **blank** is probably best. Header spaces will then appear at the top of each page.

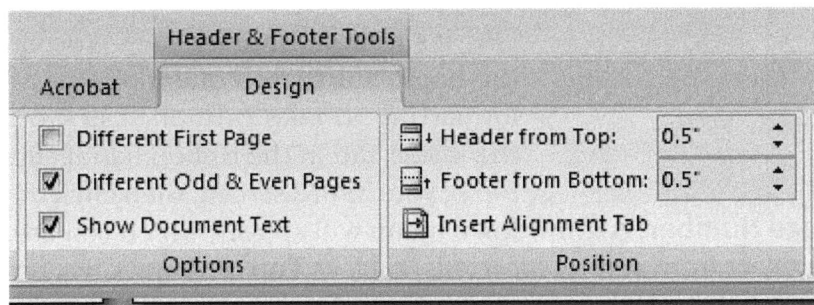

Header & Footer Tools		
Acrobat	Design	
☐ Different First Page		▦ Header from Top: 0.5"
☑ Different Odd & Even Pages		▦ Footer from Bottom: 0.5"
☑ Show Document Text		▣ Insert Alignment Tab
Options		Position

⬆ If verso and recto are different, check **Different Odd & Even Pages** in the **Design/Options** group within **Header & Footer Tools**.

Odd Page Header -Section 11- on't go on every page. Don't put them on the title page, or other front matter.

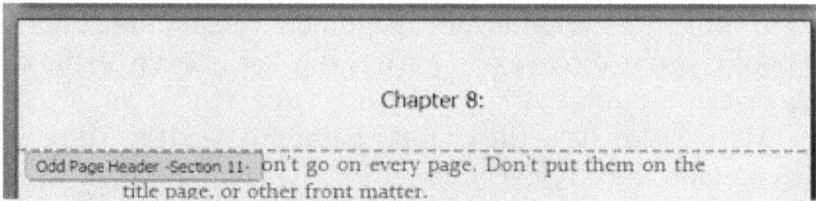

⬆While the header areas are "live," you can type and edit as with normal text. Select the type and justification you want.

Make sure that **Link to Previous** in the ribbon bar is NOT checked unless you are sure you want to use it. It can create big problems and waste a lot of time. ➔The header linking may make more sense if you think of "**Link Previous to This**," not "**Link to Previous**." You can edit the header area any time you want just by doing a left double-click. You can get back into the main text by left double-clicking in the text area. Headers don't go on every page. Don't put them on the title page or on other front matter, or on the first pages of chapters. Sometimes I cheat and use the header space in the front matter or back matter for section titles if space is limited.

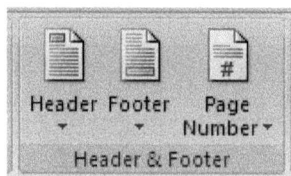

OK, it's almost time to start writing the book, but there's one more bit of formatting to take care of. Click on the **Insert** tab in the ribbon bar at the top of your Word screen, then click on **Page Number**. A drop-down menu will appear, which you use to select from several locations, such as **Top of Page**. Click on the location you want, and a drop-down menu will appear, showing you some style choices. Pick one. You can change it later if you want to.

Next click on **Format Page Numbers**. I recommend that you start with **page zero**, a temporary verso page. It will let you display pages in the proper verso and recto format *and* have the right numbers for constructing the table of contents and index, *and* have a place for notes and to park your style sheet.

Page Number Format

Number format: 1, 2, 3, ...

☐ Include chapter number

Chapter starts with style: Heading 1

Use separator: - (hyphen)

Examples: 1-1, 1-A

Page numbering

○ Continue from previous section

● Start at: 0

OK   Cancel

➔ It's good to have page zero up front while working on the book, but when you've finished writing and correcting, *be sure to delete page zero* before you produce a final PDF for printing.

View your pages as *two-page spreads*, as if you are reading a real book, not as single pages, as if you were typing a term paper or a letter. It's important to see how the text lines up—or doesn't line up—and watch for images that don't look good together and should be repositioned.

Congratulations. Now get to work.

Page Setup

You've completed the setup. Now it's time for your moment of truth. **Are you a writer, or are you not a writer?** The cursor is flashing to tell you it's time to start writing your book. **If you survive the writing, do the index.**

Most nonfiction books need an index. Word can produce an index, but it will be ugly and confusing without intervention.

Highlight the first occurrence of a word that you want to be indexed. Click on the **Reference** tab at the top of your screen, then click on **Mark Entry** from the **Index** group and the **Mark Index Entry** window will open. The word you highlighted will automatically be inserted as the **Main Entry**. You can modify it, for example to change uppercase to lowercase. Insert a cross reference if you like, and indicate whether the term is a subentry of another term. For an important term that's not often used, select **Mark All**. For a common term that you don't want to index always, select **Mark**. When you're through, go to the back of the book and click on **Insert Index**, and begin the agonizing hours of correcting.

→While indexing, Word will show cryptic formatting marks which make pages hard to read. You can make them disappear by clicking on the button with the paragraph symbol within the home tab. It's called a *pilcrow*. Try to use "pilcrow" in conversations, like "Steve's a dumb pilcrow."

Mark Index Entry

Index

Main entry:

Subentry:

Options

○ Cross-reference: See

◉ Current page

○ Page range

Bookmark:

Page number format

☐ Bold

☐ Italic

This dialog box stays open so that you can mark multiple index entries.

Mark | Mark All | Cancel

The weaknesses of Word

①**Word often makes mistakes with hyphens.** Sometimes it seems to guess, or follow a rule based on recognizable patterns rather than consult an internal dictionary. It sometimes makes *bad* guesses. Word 2010 is a little bit better than 2007.

"**The-rapist**" is my favorite abomination sanctioned by Microsoft. I also really like "of-fline" "who-lesaler," "books-tore," "upl-oad," "wastel-and," "proo-freading," "apo-strophe," "li-mited," "identic-al," "firs-thand," "fru-strating," "whe-never," "foo-ter," "miles-tone," "grays-cale," "distri-bute," "percen-tage," "prin-ter," "fami-liarity," "misunders-tanding," "mi-nimize," "sa-les," "me-thod," "libra-rian," "mi-spronounced," and "bet-ween."

Word often assumes that the letter "e" indicates the end of a syllable as in "be-come" and causes errors like "cre-dit" and "se-tup." Word recognizes that "par" is a common syllable, which leads to "par-chment." Maybe Bill Gates retired too soon. Someone has to fix this stuff.

Terms that can have two meanings and can be pronounced in two ways cause problems. Word 2007 won't hyphenate either "Polish" or "polish, and can't distinguish between "min-ute" (the noun) and "minute" (the adjective). It gives you "min-ute" when you want "mi-nute."

Automatic hyphenation can give weird results with proper names, such as "Fe-dex" and "Pa-nasonic."

②**Word often puts too much space between letters.** (normal)
②**Word often puts too much space between letters.** (modified)

Word's "loose" text can make a book look much worse than one designed with real publishing software, and may waste paper. **Examine *each* paragraph *closely*.** If there is too much white space, change some words, force hyphenation, adjust **Character Spacing**—or use all of the tricks—to close up gaps.

Character spacing is in the **Font** tab. Condensing by .1-.5 points often works right. Most letters should *not* touch.

Microsoft Word 2010 and book publishing

Microsoft Word 2010 has improvements which can make book production easier, and make better-looking books.

◆Locating information is faster and easier with the improved Find feature. You view a summary of search results in a single pane, and click to access any result. The improved Navigation Pane shows a visual outline of your document so you can browse, sort and find what you need quickly.

◆With co-authoring, you can share ideas with others at the same time you are editing. You can see who else is available to work on the document and initiate a text or voice conversation without leaving Word.

◆Post your documents online then and access, view and edit them from almost any computer or a Windows cellphone

◆With the Word Web App, you can edit documents in a Web browser when you're away from your office or home.

◆You can apply effects such as shadow, bevel, glow and reflection to your document as easily as applying bold or underline.

◆You can spell-check text that uses visual effects, and add text effects to paragraph styles. Many of the same effects used for images are now available to both text and shapes.

◆Word 2010 offers more options to add visual impact, including dozens of additional SmartArt® Graphics to build elaborate diagrams just by typing a bulleted list.

◆ New picture-editing tools enable you to add effects without additional software. You can adjust color saturation and temperature and use improved tools for easier and more precise cropping and image correction.

◆Word 2010 lets you recover draft versions of recently edited files as easily as opening any file, even if you never saved the document.

◆You can capture and insert screenshots to illustrate your work.

◆The new Backstage™ view replaces the File menu to let you save, share, print and publish documents with a few clicks. With the improved Ribbon, you can access your favorite commands even more quickly by customizing tabs or creating your own.

CHAPTER 47

Getting from a Word doc to a PDF file for printing

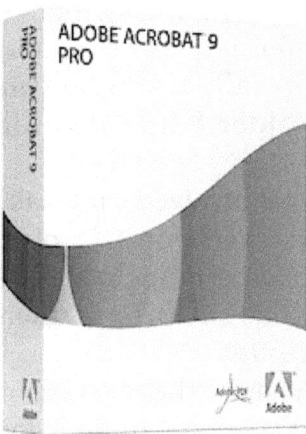

ADOBE ACROBAT 9
PRO

The PDF (Portable Document Format) was developed by Adobe Systems, and is widely used for submission of files to book printers. The PDF conversion can be expensive, inexpensive, or free. The free way is usually not the best way.

If you've heard about the high cost of Adobe's Acrobat software, you may have been relieved to find that your already-paid-for copy of Word has the ability to generate PDF files without spending an extra penny.

The bad news is that you should not use this feature. It's just not as good as the real Adobe software. You should not trust Word's version. Don't waste your time with it. The files it produces probably won't be good enough to produce your book. I tried Word's built-in PDF maker with my first book. It was a disaster and I wasted two weeks with it.

There are also other non-Adobe PDF-making programs. Don't waste your time learning that they do only 84% of what you need. You need the real thing.

As I write this, the current real thing is Adobe Acrobat "X." The list price for it ranges from \$139 to \$1199 (depending on the version) and that's what you'll pay if you order from Adobe's website. Amazon sometimes discounts Acrobat, and sometimes sells it at full price.

➜ You'll probably find some deals for much lower prices, but be careful. There are bootleg copies and OEM versions that are sold with no tech support from Adobe, but that support can be critical to your success.

If someone in your family is a student or an educator, he can get the "education discount" and pay much less than list price and let you borrow it. Do a web search for **educational discounts software.** If you have doubts about saving money this way, consult your rabbi, priest, minister, padre, imam, guru or shaman. **You can save substantially if you buy an older version. The two-generation-older 8 has sold for \$49.99 on eBay.**

If you are not sure that you want to get involved with making PDFs, you can download a free trial version of Acrobat from **www.Adobe.com**. It is not supposed to include tech support, but on two occasions when I needed help, I was taken care of quickly, competently and courteously.

And finally, you can ask a friend who owns the software to make the conversion, or you can pay a company to do it for you. It's inevitable that the first PDFs will reveal errors that were unnoticed when viewed in Word. You'll waste a lot of time waiting until someone else has time to help you if you can't produce your own PDFs. If you are serious about self-publishing, PAY THE MONEY to own Acrobat.

Getting from a Word doc to a PDF file for printing

The following instructions for producing a PDF version of the interior of your book assume that you have installed Adobe Acrobat. There are other methods, but this has worked for me while producing many books.

1. Save your Word file as you normally do.
2. Click on the round **Office** button at the top left of your screen in Word 2007 or **File** in Word 2010.
3. Click on **Print**.
4. Select **Adobe PDF** in the **Printer Name** drop-down menu.

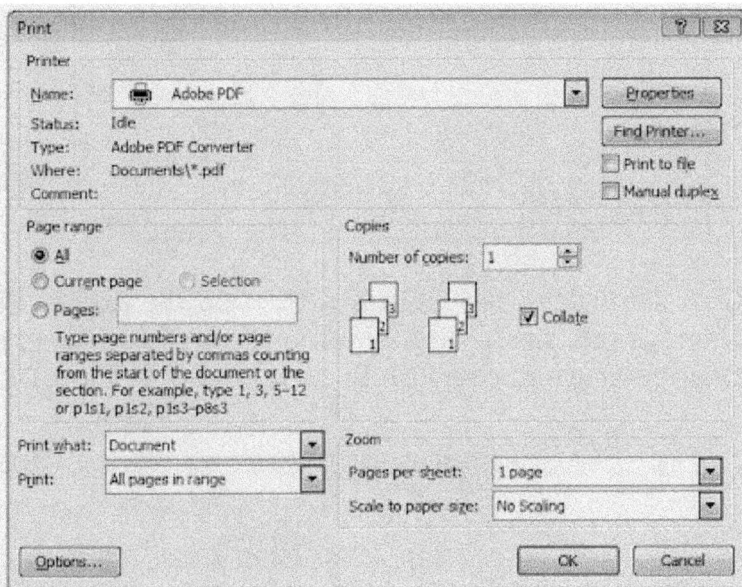

5. Click on **Properties** and then click on **Paper Quality**. Click on **Black & White** and **OK**.

6. Click on **Properties** again and then on the **Adobe PDF Settings** tab. In the first drop-down menu, select **Press Quality**. Leave **Adobe PDF Security** as **None**. Click **OK**.

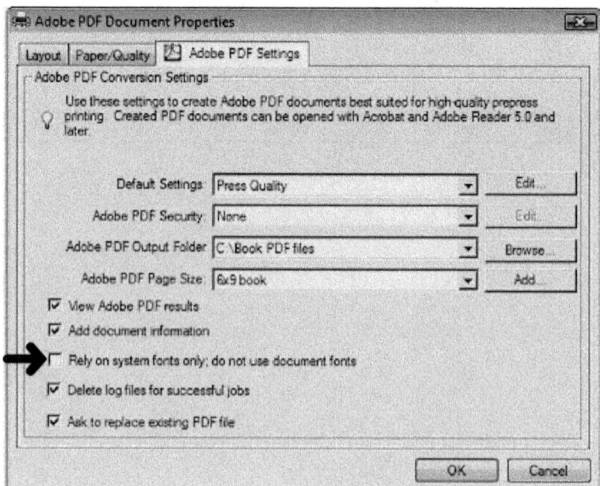

DO NOT CHECK →

7. To the far-right of **Adobe PDF Output Folder**, click on **Browse**. Select the folder where you want to store your PDF files and make sure it is displayed. It can be a previously used folder, or one you created just for PDFs or book files.

Adobe PDF Output Folder | C:\Book PDF files | ▼ | Browse...

8. To the far-right of **Adobe PDF Page Size**, click on **Add**. When the small **Add Custom Paper Size** window opens, enter the page size for your book, type in an appropriate name in the **Paper Names** window, and then click on **Add/Modify**. The window should close.

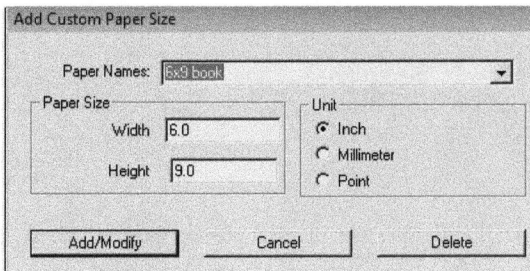

Add Custom Paper Size

Paper Names: 6x9 book

Paper Size
Width: 6.0
Height: 9.0

Unit
• Inch
○ Millimeter
○ Point

Add/Modify | Cancel | Delete

9. Back at the **Adobe PDF Settings** screen, in the **Adobe PDF Page Size** section, make sure your new page size is displayed. ➔➔➔Click to check all boxes EXCEPT **Rely on system fonts only**. It is VERY IMPORTANT that you do NOT check this box so that all of the fonts you've used will be *embedded* in the PDF file and available for printing your book. Click on **OK**.

10. A **Save PDF File As** window should open. Select the file folder where you want to save the PDF file. Type in an appropriate file name. To eliminate confusion, give it a different name than the one you used for the Word file. Click **Save**.

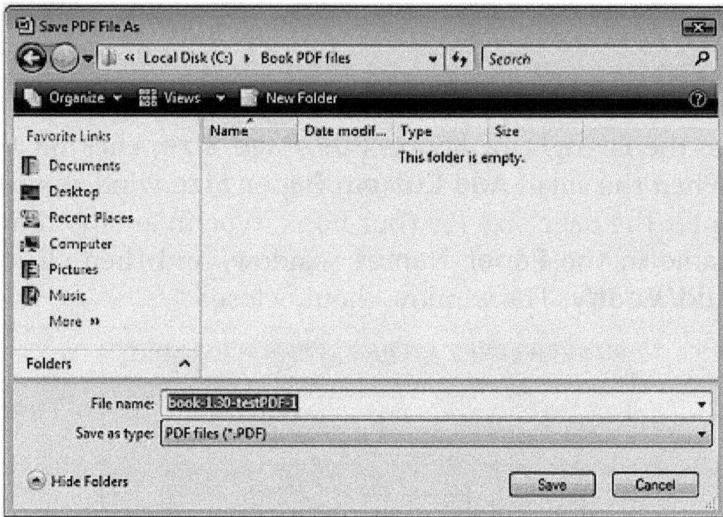

11. You should soon see a small window that shows the progress of the PDF file-making process. It will probably take a minute or two to complete.

12. When the process is complete, a small window should open briefly to tell you it's complete. You should also see an Adobe icon and your file name in your **Taskbar**.

13. It's **very important** that you spend a lot of time going over the "book-like" PDF version of your book because it's highly likely that it will reveal errors, and maybe some bad design decisions, that were not apparent in Word. For a more realistic view of your book, click on **View**, then **Page Display**, then **Two up** to see two-page spreads as in a printed book. It's likely that you will make three or more PDFs before you are satisfied. Your proofreader should also view what you consider to be the final version, and then you can make another final version, or two. You will never have a perfect book, but make the best one you can. ➔NOTE: if your PDF does not show all of your photographs, try saving your Word file as ".doc" instead of ".docx."

14. It's important to confirm that all of the fonts you've used have been correctly incorporated in the PDF. While the document is open, click on **File** and then click on **Properties** from the drop-down menu. A list of the fonts you've used should then scroll down. While the list is filling, you should see **Gathering Font Information** below the list in the window, with a changing percentage number to indicate progress. Don't worry if you don't see 100%. When the list stops scrolling, click **OK**.

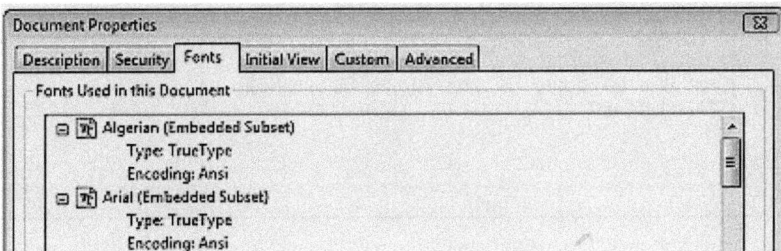

15. Open Adobe Acrobat Distiller. In **Default Settings**, select **PDF/X-1a2001**. Click on **File**, **Open,** and then select the Postscript file that was previously saved. The **Progress Status** bar will show the formation of a new PDF file, one page at a time. It will probably take a few minutes. Distiller will produce a much smaller version of the PostScript file, reduced by about 90%, for much faster transmission over the Internet.

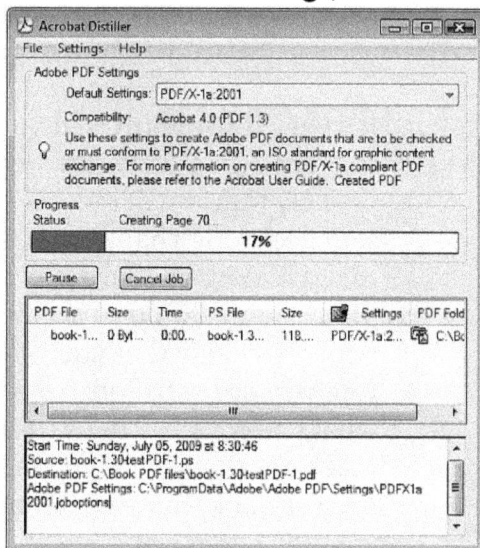

16. When the Distiller has finished creating your new PDF file, "End of Job" will appear at the bottom of the window.

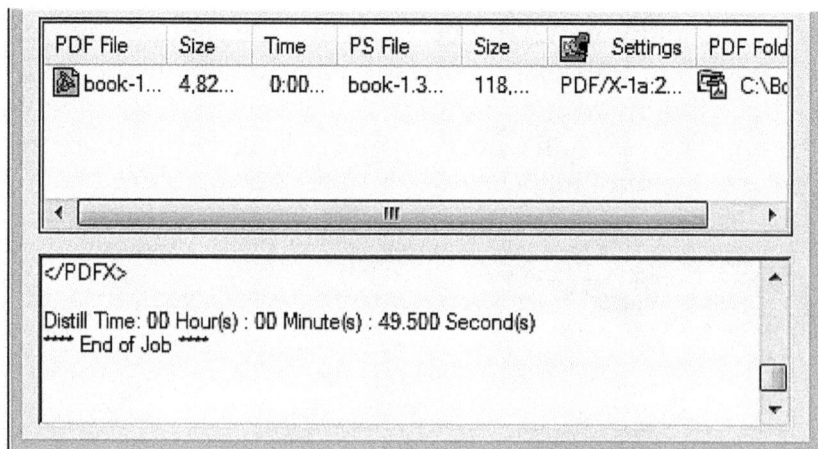

17. Locate the new file in the folder when you are ready to upload it to your printer. There will probably be several files with similar names. For Lightning Source, you will select the smaller Acrobat file, not the large PostScript file.

Name	Date modified	Type	Size
book-1.30-testPDF-1	7/5/2009 8:31 AM	Adobe Acrobat Document	4,826 KB
book-1.30-testPDF-1	7/5/2009 8:04 AM	PostScript File	118,279 KB

WARNING:

Be careful when you try to print a document after you've produced a PDF file. Your PC may try to send the text to Adobe Acrobat instead of to your normal printer. Look at the printer selection before you click "OK" to print.

Design Tip

In the word "warning" up above, I condensed the space around the W by 3 points. If I didn't condense, the letters would look like **WA** instead of **WA**.

The technical term for this kind of condensing is "kerning."

From the moment I picked your book up until I laid it down I was convulsed with laughter.
Someday I intend reading it.
Groucho Marx

CHAPTER 48
What about pictures in your book?

Even the most compelling stories can be boring to look at if there's only black type on white paper. Just like paintings on the wall of a room or a cave, photos—and illustrations, graphs and charts—liven up a book. They can also make it easier to explain things.

In the earliest days of book-making, long before there were printing presses, monastic scribes decorated the pages of bibles and other books with ornate, colorful and sometimes even gilded *illuminations*.

Illuminations could be illustrations inspired by the text, or just decorative borders and initial uppercase letters. It's not known when the first illumination was done, but the earliest surviving illuminated texts from Europe date back to about 400.

Early illumination (and most bookmaking) was limited to religious topics, but later broadened to include secular subjects, and both paper and parchment were used. The invention of the printing press pretty much killed illumination, except for special editions.

Printing predates photography, so early printed pictures were produced by *engraving*. Artists used fine-pointed tools to carve images onto plates which were inked and printed.

Black ink on white paper produces a boring, gray blob. The *New York Times*, known for using few pictures, used to be called "the gray lady." I have a copy of the front page from the day I was born in 1946. It's all gray, with not even one picture.

Ironically, I also have a copy of *The Illustrated News of the World* from the late 19th century. It's filled with beautiful, highly detailed pictures, meticulously engraved by hand. *The Wall Street Journal* still uses engravings, but most newspapers are filled with photographs. Changes in technology, competition and expectations have made color photos commonplace.

Technology has made it much simpler and less expensive to include photos in books. At one time, photographs were printed on special paper in the center sections of books. Today, photos can be printed on any page.

➔ Photo reproduction in a POD book like this one is unpredictable. Some photos look fine with no adjustments. Others, even after lots of tweaking, will look mediocre at best.

Books with color pages are more expensive than black-and-white books—sometimes much more expensive.

➔ If you are going to send a book to a publisher as a PDF file, it should not cost you a penny extra to include all of the pictures you want to have published. If your self-publishing company is going to compose your pages, you can expect to find that there is a maximum number of photos you can include unless you pay extra.

What about pictures in your book?

Even in a book of fiction or poems where no illustration is necessary for explanation or edification, it's nice to break up the type. I like to interrupt the gray about every six to ten pages. Try an appropriate photo or drawing on the first page of each chapter. Readers like to look at pictures, and even a few illustrations can liven up an all-text book.

The words you see here are separated from the photograph by the standard 0.13 inches, found in **Text Wrapping**. Sometimes this results in large gaps between words, such as in much of this paragraph, and may not allow enough space for all of the text that you need to fit in.

The words you see here are separated from the photograph by 0.04 inches (probably too little). This allows you to fit more words in the same space and may reduce spacing between words, which looks better. You can also use *condensing* to tighten up the text. It's in the **Font** dialog box in Word.

♦Clip art photos, illustrations and cartoons are ubiquitous, but be aware that most clip art on CD-ROMs or websites is NOT supposed to be used for commercial purposes—like books.

♦There's no need to risk an embarrassing and expensive lawsuit when high-quality art is available for very low prices. I've been very pleased with **www.Fotolia.com**.

♦Free photos are available at various state and federal government websites ranging from New Jersey to NASA. Military services, the Library of Congress and the White House have plenty of pix. Many corporate websites have excellent free photos, but be sure to follow the rules for using and crediting.

◆When you reduce a photograph to a small size, it's a good idea to sharpen it a bit—but not too much. Look at it closely.

◆By changing the number, size and location of graphic elements, you can increase or decrease your book's page count.

◆Every author needs a portrait, for books, websites, blogs, press kits, posters, etc. Unfortunately, many authors use amateur photos with bad lighting, bad focus and distracting backgrounds.

The price of a portrait shot in a professional photographer's studio can easily be in the $300-$1,000 range, too steep for many writers who don't have a big publisher to pick up the check.

Fortunately, there are good low-cost alternatives that few authors think of—the photo studios inside retail stores such as Sears, Penney, Target and Walmart. While most of their business involves babies and family Christmas cards, they *will* take pictures of solitary adults, often at ridiculously low prices (typically $7.99-$65).

The photographer will be thrilled to have a subject who does not vomit on her, or require funny faces to elicit a smile.

If you're getting one picture, choose a plain white background which can later be altered in Photoshop. Get a CD-ROM, not a bunch of wallet-size prints.

CHAPTER 49
How to make a better book (assorted tips and advice)

Most of this chapter is for using Microsoft Word.

If you're a self-publishing writer, you can avoid possessive apostrophes like George Bernard Shaw, use dashes in place of quotation marks like James Joyce, or shun uppercase letters like e. e. cummings. However, if you are not yet famous, it's better to obey the established rules of writing and publishing. Some ancient rules and customs seem silly or unnecessary in the 21st century, but be sure you have a good reason to break them if you must. I've broken a few and have not yet been arrested or sued. I don't know if my book sales have suffered.

◆Some people think they should compose book with separate data files for each chapter. There's no advantage to doing that in Word, and it will waste time and make it difficult to shift paragraphs or chapters around.

It is very important that you understand and use Word's *section* system.

A section can be one page or hundreds. Typically, it's a chapter or part of a chapter. What

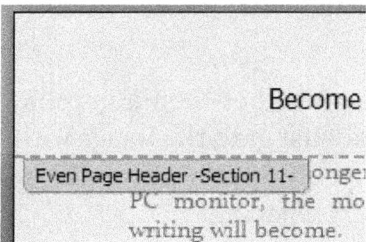

sets one section apart from other sections is its *headers and footers*, which are uniform within a section, even if some material is the same in several or all sections. If you want all of the headers on even-numbered (left, verso) pages to show the book title, type it into one verso header and check **Link to Previous** in the navigation section of the ribbon bar. Be sure that it's

unchecked when you are working on recto headers that will probably be different for each chapter (and section).

To end one section and start a new one, put your cursor just after the last character at the bottom of a page, and click on the **Page Layout** tab at the top of the **ribbon bar**, and then click on **Breaks**. Below the **Breaks** divider, click on **Next Page**. The next page will start a new section. Because of some strange defect, when you do this, the first line on the next page will probably gain an unintended indent or will drop to a lower position and you'll have to fix it.

To find out which section a page is in, do a left double-click in the header area.

◆When you want a page to **end** (especially the last page of a chapter, do NOT just keep tapping the **enter** key. Instead, within the **Insert** tab, click on **Page Break**. You can also accomplish the same thing within the **Page Layout** tab by selecting **Breaks** and then **Page**.

◆If you want to adjust the vertical space between a graphic image and the words above it, you can just grab the image with your cursor and slide it up or down a bit. If you go too far, it will move the text, not just change the spacing.

◆One of the most boring and most important tasks in publishing is to carefully read down the right-hand edge of each page so you can spot and fix improper hyphenations. Word's hyphenation system sometimes makes bad guesses and you'll have to overrule its decisions. Don't be embarrassed by "the-rapist" or "eb-ook."

◆ When you have several graphic elements such as photos or text boxes on a page, use *gridlines* to line them up and to stay within the page borders. Click on the **View** tab and then check the **Gridlines** box. The grid can be annoying, so shut it off when you don't need to use it. You can also use a **table** to contain and align multiple graphics.

◆Don't be afraid to make small violations of your style sheet if the broken rules allow you to make a better-looking book. If you normally allow 24 points between a chapter title and the first sentence, no one will sue you or arrest you and few will notice if you occasionally use 23 points or 25 points. Similarly, if you normally use 16-point type for chapter titles, but by using 15.5 points you can get all of the words in one line instead of two, do it and save some space and some trees.

◆Although Word's type menu has sizes from 8 to 72 points, those are not your only choices. You can force Word to accept almost any size, such as 3, 21 points or 106 points. You're not limited to whole numbers. If 10.5 points is the right size, use it. Tiny sizes are generally used for spaces, not words.

◆The opposite of *italic* is roman. It's not the same Roman as in Times New Roman. You can use Times New Roman roman or *Times New Roman Italic.* ➔VXII is a Times New Roman roman Roman numeral. (I've wanted to type that for years.)

◆On a book cover, you can lessen the impact of a dull word by following it with a word that is strong because of either its meaning or its appearance.

◆Watch out for unexpected changes in line spacing (*leading*). Word has a mind of its own and sometimes makes decisions without consulting you.

◆By default, Word puts 0.13 inches of space to the left and right of a picture you've inserted. You can often improve the look of a page by changing the space so words flow differently. Click on the picture, then **Picture Tools**, **Text Wrapping**, **More Layout Options**, and then adjust the **Distance from text**. You can go as small as .01 inches, but that is probably too tight in most cases. If a photograph or illustration includes its own white borders, you can run text closer than if it has no border and you have to create your own separation. Also, a built-in white border allows you to slide a photo a little bit "too far" into a margin, without losing any of the actual image. ⬇

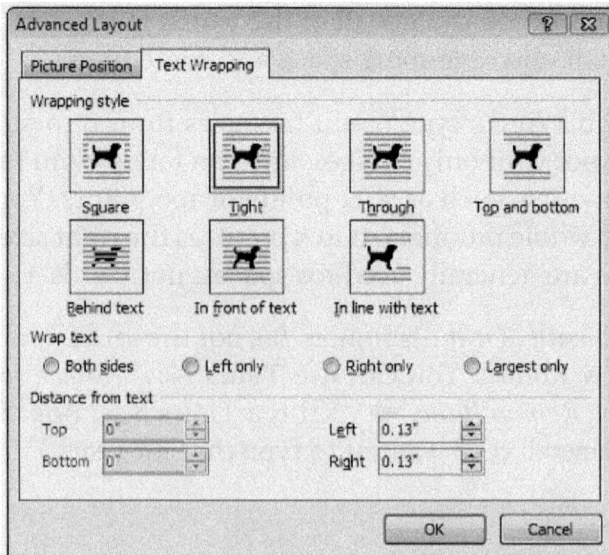

◆You are not limited to straight walls of type adjacent to your

Back in the "gilded age" of the late 19ᵗʰ century, self-publishing was an activity indulged in by wealthy men who produced expensive leather-bound, gilt-edged limited editions for family and friends, and to enhance their personal libraries.

Female writers such as Edith Wharton self-publish-ed because traditional pub-lishers favored men. In 1921 she became the first woman to win the Pulitzer Prize for litera-ture.

Mark Twain is said to have be-come his own publisher because he thought another pub-

graphics. If you click on **Picture Tools** and then click on **Picture Shape** you can select from many op-tions for wrapping your text around an image. Ma-ny shapes will cut into your image, but some work nicely such as the oval I used with tycoon J. P. Mor-gan, shown here. You have more flexibility with **Edit Wrap Points**, in **Text Wrapping**, in **Picture Tools**.

◆Although you can position a graphic image anywhere on a page,

The Espresso Book Machine, a vending machine for books, has the ability to store digital files for hundreds of thousands of titles.
The only inven-tory it needs are paper, ink and glue. In just three or four minutes it can spit out a completely finished high-quality pa-perback book — at the point of sale. There is no ship- ping delay, no ship- ping expense, no markdowns, no returns, no shredding, no obsolete informa-tion being published, no warehousing. Any book store that can afford the machine can provide its patrons with a huge

use your power wisely. Don't be overly cute or too creative. If you want peo-ple to read what you have written, it's best to keep a picture all the way to the left or right. If you put a picture in the middle of text, it will be difficult to read across the picture.

◆If you're not making a color book, color photos and illustra-tions should be converted to black-and-white (also called *mo-nochrome* or *grayscale*) before saving in a file and then insert-ing in your book. Use the TIF format, not the more common JPG, which is used for the web. You can safely reduce the size of an image, but if you try to enlarge it more than a tiny bit, you will lose quality. If you are taking photos or hiring a pho-tographer, the camera should be set for TIF (or RAW and later converted to TIF). If you are buying stock art, select a version with 300 DPI (dots per inch) *resolution*. If you are downloading art from a website, it will most likely be a JPG with lower resolution. I have used many JPGs with no problems in several books. If you can select from several suitable JPG images, pick the *biggest* one, if all else is equal. JPGs should be converted to TIF images. JPG images lose a bit of sharpness each time they are saved after making changes in them. TIFs are "lossless."

◆If you need to scan a photograph or illustration, scan at a resolution of 300 DPI and produce a TIF image. Some scanners will work at 72 DPI unless you change the setting, so pay attention. (The setting may be on the scanner or on your computer screen in the scanner software.) 72 DPI is not good enough for a book. Resolution above 300 DPI is not an improvement. It may slow down your computer and will probably create an oversized file. Make sure your scanned file is a TIF, not a JPG.

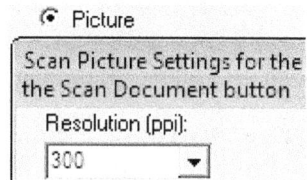

◆Photo quality in a laser-printed POD book will not be as good as in a book that's offset printed on better paper. It should be good enough—and there seem to be improvements in POD about every six months. Lulu can provide better photo quality than Lightning Source, which is used by many publishers.

◆Less-than-optimum (i.e., crappy but necessary) photographs will look less crappy if you keep them as small as possible. It's best to eliminate or replace sub-par photos if you can.

◆Unless there are major problems with a photograph, don't bother adjusting its brightness or contrast until you receive a printed proof. What you see on your screen or coming out of your own printer will not be the same as what gets printed in a book. You may be surprised—pleasantly or otherwise.

◆Photo quality, cover alignment, cover color and other book conditions may vary from print run to print run. Periodically order a copy from a bookseller or from your publisher's online bookstore for quality control. Don't be reluctant to complain. Let your publisher know you have high standards.

◆Word has lots of **picture effects** to manipulate images and to make complex text boxes. You can have frames, shadows, bevel edges, glowing, rotation, warping and more. Word 2010 has more effects than Word 2007. Use them *very* sparingly. Don't crap-up your book.

◆You can change the look of letters with **shadows,** outlines, **emboss-ing and more.** Open the **Font** dialog box, and then click on the **Font** tab.

◆Check for periods that should be inside or outside closing parentheses. Check for double periods..

◆If you copy-and-paste from another document or a web page, you may end up with a hyperlink imbedded in your book text. It can be distracting when you're working on a manuscript, and you may even click on it accidentally and be taken from your book page to a web page. To deactivate it, highlight and right-click on the linked word, then click on **Remove link**. At this point you will be left with ordinary text—at least until wacky Word decides to change it back into a link. If you want to make it obvious that it's a web address, try underlining it and/or use a different font, like this: **www.SilverSandsBooks.com.**

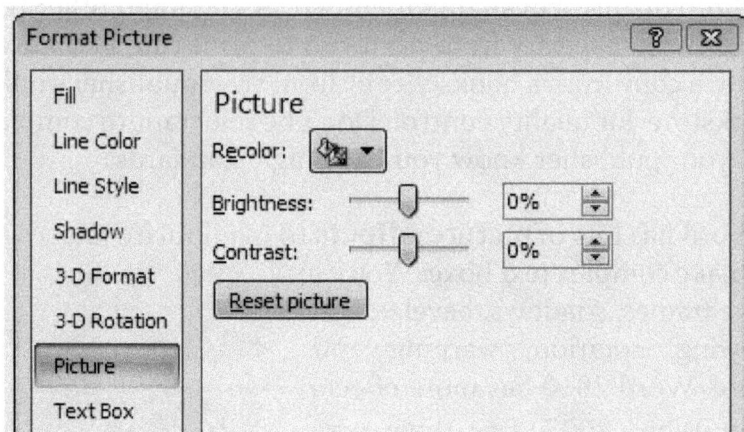

Format Picture	? ⊠
Fill	**Picture**
Line Color	Recolor:
Line Style	Brightness: ——0—— 0%
Shadow	Contrast: ——0—— 0%
3-D Format	
3-D Rotation	Reset picture
Picture	
Text Box	

♦Word has the ability to modify graphic images in the **Format Picture** window ⬆ within **Picture Styles**. You may get better results, and definitely will have more options, with a real graphics program such as Adobe Photoshop Elements or Microsoft Digital Image Pro, or even Microsoft's simple Image Composer.

➔♦If you are the author and formatter and are paying for publication of your book, you have an advantage over most authors. You—not some unknown stranger—have the right to chop out words or add words or substitute words to improve your book.

♦Sometimes the best way to improve the look of a paragraph is to add a word or two, or eliminate a word or two.

♦Sometimes, a word—particularly a brand used as a logo—is chosen because of the way it looks, even if it has no meaning. **AVAYA** is a *word picture*, selected because of the way the letters fit together. Word pictures can work well on book covers.

◆ *Widows* and *orphans* are lonely and need some attention. They make a book look lousy and amateurish. Do your best to eliminate them.

A **widow** is the last line of a paragraph that shows up at the *top* of a page, or at the *top* of a column on a page with multiple columns.

In typography, an **orphan** has two meanings:

(1) An orphan can be a single line of type beginning a paragraph at the *bottom* of a page, or at the *bottom* of a column on a page with multiple columns.

(2) The other kind of orphan is a single word or the final syllable of a hyphenated word on a line by itself.

◆ From the *Chicago Manual of Style*: "A page should not begin with the last line of a paragraph unless it is full measure and should not end with the first line of a new paragraph. Nor should the last word in any paragraph be broken—that is, hyphenated, with the last part of the word beginning a new line."

The following paragraph has an ugly orphan:

When I was in junior high school, if the weather was nice, I rode to school on my bicycle. There was a long hill that was a lot of fun to coast down, even though it could be hard to stop if there was a red traffic light at the bottom. At the end of the day, unfortunately, I had to walk up the steep hill to get to my house.

By making a minor change, I got rid of the orphan, eliminated a line, and did not change the meaning:

When I was in junior high school, if the weather was nice, I rode to school on my bicycle. There was a long hill that was a lot of fun to coast down, even though it could be hard to stop if there was a red traffic light at the bottom. At the end of the day, unfortunately, I had to walk up the steep hill to get home.

◆Be very careful to check the last line in a justified paragraph. Sometimes even two or three words are spread out full-width, and   they'll   look   very   stupid.

    You can just select the line and re-do it as flush-left, or (in Word) tap the **Enter** key after the last word in the line.

Design Tip ✆

Graphics experts frown on the use of <u>underlines</u> in books and recommend *italics* instead if you need to call attention to a word. Sometimes an italic word is too weak, or doesn't look right when it's next to a roman (not italic) word.

Compare these versions of a book title:

❶Become a *Real* Self-publisher

❷Become a <u>Real</u> Self-publisher

In the second case, "<u>Real</u>" looks stronger because it's upright and there are no strange gaps between it and the adjacent roman words because of slanted letters.

Mixes *Look* Weird. *All Italics Look OK.*

If you mix italic and roman type, be careful with slanted letters W, Y, K, and sometimes M. Look at "*k*W" above.

◆If you need to copy text from the web into a Word document, first paste it into Notepad. Notepad will cleanse it by stripping out HTML, links, rules (lines), background colors, table grids, etc. Then just copy from Notepad into Word and do whatever editing is necessary. Notepad is also good for purging extraneous garbage that Word sometime generates without your command or consent, such as horizontal rules.

◆As the author, you also have to be an editor, but not the *only* editor. You won't catch all of your own mistakes, no matter how many times you read through the manuscript and proofs.

◆If you have multiple lines in a chapter title or subhead, don't use all caps or small caps. Also, reduce the space between the lines—especially if there are no descenders.

◆Don't expect Word to do all of your work. Sometimes Word simply lacks the brainpower to properly handle a sentence.
Compare the two highlighted paragraphs:

Because of their limited "character set," emails and web pages, like old typewriters, make double-duty of certain punctuation marks.
⬆Above, generated by Word, the paragraph has an ugly gap at the end of the second line because it couldn't figure out how to break up "punctuation" or make other adjustments. "Punc" would not fit at the end of the second line.

Because of their limited "character set," emails and web pages, like old typewriters, make double-duty of some punctuation marks.
⬆Above, the text looks much better after I substituted the shorter "some" for "certain." The meanings are not identical, but are close enough, and the change solved the spacing problem. You can also make room in a sentence by condensing (kerning) the space between letters. Open the **Font** dialog box, and then click on **Character Spacing.**

◆Make a decision to use either double spacing between paragraphs, or an indent, but not both. The double space is OK for techie books (it looks like a website), but probably not for most other books. It's OK to use a double space between sections of a chapter, as I do in some parts of this book.

①Include lists in your book. People like to read lists.

②Include photos, charts, graphs and cartoons to break up the gray space, to help make your points, or even for amusement.

◆Spend some time investigating the **symbol section** (within the **Insert** tab). It has lots of useful decorations like ✂ which can be used to dress up boring-looking text. It also has fractions, symbols and foreign punctuation marks to make your book more accurate and professional.

☞⊘✂✳

▶Don't overuse decorations◀

☹ ◉ ✿ ⬢●

The symbol section is the source of *ligatures*. They're combinations of consecutive letters that improve appearance and save a little bit of space. In normal text, you can get away with "find" and "floor." But, in large type sizes, such as for a book cover or title page, the ligatures will provide much more attractive type.

find looks much better than find

floor looks much better than floor

You'll also find *subscripts*, *superscripts*, lots of arrows, little cartoons like 📂 and 📁, and much more. Make sure you look in the **Wingdings** collections.

Exposé is better than expose.

Naïve is better than naive. (Word may or

may not do these correctly. You may have to select the symbol manually.)

© **is better than** (c)   **1¾** **is better than** **1-3/4**

3✕4 **is better than** **3x4**

◆Be careful hyphenating names. I think "Fitz-gerald" is OK, but not "Mi-chael" or "Bo-ston."

Justified sans serif type often looks worse than justified serif type because sans serif may have less consistent spacing between words. Also, the decorations on the letters of serif typefaces fill in the spaces in some lines.

Compare it to the same text in the same point size, also set justified, but with a serif typeface⬇

Justified sans serif type often looks worse than justified serif type because sans serif may have less consistent spacing between words. Also, the decorations on the letters of serif typefaces fill in the spaces in some lines.

Serif Spacing
Sans Serif Spacing

Experiment with different typefaces to find the right look for your book.

◆Be alert if you work on your book with more than one PC. Multiple PCs, even if you think they are identical, may have subtle differences which will drive you NUTS. One major problem relates to different fonts being available on the PCs. If PC #2 doesn't have all of the fonts which were used with the book on PC #1, it may substitute other fonts that will cause the text to flow differently. Paragraphs may run longer or shorter than expected, and words may move from one page to the next page—or even to the previous page.

➔ ◆Expect **BIG TROUBLE** if you start a book in Word 2007 and switch to Word 2010. Text may flow onto later pages and you book may grow greatly. **One version of this book had 370 pages in Word 2007, but 436 in Word 2010!**

◆Professional designers frequently adjust the spacing (*leading*) between lines so that facing pages end parallel to each other, except at the end of a chapter. That's much too much work for me. I almost never monkey around with line spacing. I can live with one page in a spread being one line shorter than the other, but usually not two lines. If I have to make an adjustment, I'll usually increase spaces between paragraphs, enlarge or reduce a photo, add or reduce space around a photo, shift a line to the next page, add or remove words, or do other tricks.

◆The end of a line of type, especially in large sizes used for titles and subheads, functions as unintentional punctuation. It's sort of an "unprinted comma" or even an "unprinted period." Readers will slow down or hesitate when they get to the far right. Keep this in mind when you choose your words. Breaking a common phrase construction at the end of a line will encourage readers to ignore the unprinted and implied punctuation and quickly move down to the next word. If the word at the end of the line seems like the last word in a sentence, people will slow down and may miss the impact of your title or headline.

This is an example of spacing that makes people quickly move to the next line.

This is an example of spacing that makes people hesitate at the end of a line.

◆Don't indent the first line below a white space, a chart, a diagram or a photograph; or in the top line of a new paragraph that starts parallel to the top of a graphic element.

➡➡**Sometimes, writers and readers will think words are printed on page but are really in the mind and were not typed. (Did you notice it?)**

➡➡**Sometimes, editors will miss words that are are printed twice, particularly at the end and beginning of successive lines. (Did you notice it?)**

◆While you are experimenting with different possible layouts for pages or covers, it's good to have real words to play around with, even if you have not yet written the text that will ultimately be used. To make a real-looking *dummy* cover or interior page, copy and paste-in what's known as *Greek* text or *Greeking* (although it's really Latin). Do a web search for "lorem ipsum" or go to **www.lipsum.com** and copy and paste.

Here's what it looks like: **Lorem ipsum dolor sit amet.**

In addition to its stand-in function, Lorem Ipsum makes it easier to judge a design because, unless they understand Latin, viewers won't be distracted by reading the content.

◆Headers can be an ISPITA (Industrial Strength Pain In The Ass) to work with in Word. They seem to have minds of their own, jumping chapter borders and changing contents whenever they feel like it, just for spite. One tiny change in a section's start or end point can cause endless headaches and repairs. Wait until you're 99% sure you won't be moving anything around before you put any words into the headers—or avoid headers or let someone else format the interior of your book.

◆Put a bit more space above a subhead than below it, so it better connects to the text that follows it.

◆*Italics* often take up more space than regular (roman) type, and an italic word may make a paragraph need an extra line.

◆If you really want to show off your typography skill, you can use SMALL CAPS for abbreviations and acronyms like FBI, A.M., P.M., RADAR, ETC. to keep them from POPPING out of the text like full-size uppercase letters. They're in the **Font** tab. You'll have to make arbitrary decisions to resolve inconsistencies.

◆Use condensing (kerning) to reduce spaces between letters in large typefaces, particularly on book covers. Some letters should overlap. In the title below, I kerned the "A" and the V" in "HAVE" and the "L" and the "Y" in "UGLY." With MS Word, highlight the text you want to modify. Open the **Font** dialog box and select **Condensed** from the **Character Spacing** drop-down menu. Try different numbers of points.

A SELF-PUBLISHED BOOK DOESN'T HAVE TO BE UGLY

◆Big, expensive signs have misspelled words, typos and bad grammar. Most books have them, too. Look closely.

DINNING ROOM

HOSPITAL BED'S

If you start a paragraph to the right of a photograph, illustration or chart and the first line is approximately even with the top of the graphic, it looks lousy if you indent the first word, even if that is the style for your book. Lorem ipsum dolor sit amet, consectetur adipiscing elit. Sed quam. Do you know if there's a fungus among us?

Your book will look much better if you remove the indent so the first word starts flush-left against the artwork, and there is no gap. Lorem ipsum dolor sit amet, consectetur adipiscing elit. Sed eu quam sit amet nisl placerat lacinia. Proin eget velit quam. Praesent convallis ac erat funky monkey.

If your book is set flush-left/ragged-right and you have text to the left of a photograph, illustration or chart, it will look lousy because of the jagged gaps along a straight vertical border. Lorem ipsum dolor sit amet, consectetur yabbadabba doo adipiscing. Sed quam amet. I love clams.

Your book will look much better if you temporarily change your style. Modify the text to be justified, or perhaps even ragged-left/flush-right. Lorem ipsum dolor sit amet, consectetur adipiscing. Se equam si. My dog has a new pooper scooper. Lorem ipsum dolor sit amet, consectetur adipiscing elit ap

It's important not to have a person or a vehicle looking or traveling "off the page." It's natural for the reader to follow the eyes of the person (or the headlights of the car), so don't direct a reader's eyes away from the book.

If you are using stock photos or clip art, you can easily reverse (*flip*) the photo to keep the readers' eyes focused inside the book. **Be careful of the effects on your flip if you change pages from recto to verso—or vice-verso.** (Sorry—I've wanted to use that line for many years.)

If you use a photo of a well-known person where flipping would be noticeable (such as moving a pimple, wart, tattoo, pierced eyelid, missing tooth or nose ring from the left to the right), you can rearrange a page so the eyes lead into some text instead of off the page.

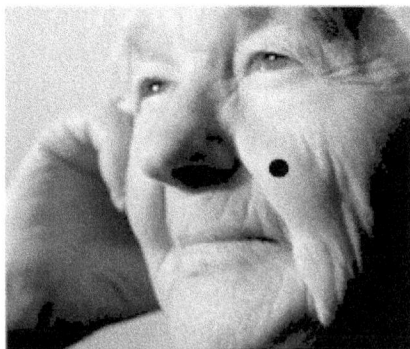

⬆If you flip a photo, watch out for a text reversal in such things as name tags, keyboards, initial jewelry, clocks, wristwatches or signs or license plates in the background. Watch for reversed flags or logos, too. Make sure wedding rings are on the correct hand (usually the left hand in the USA).

Some products, even if made by hundreds of different manufacturers, have standard formats. Don't reverse a telephone and end up with the handset on the right side instead of on the left. On old televisions, knobs were almost always on the right.

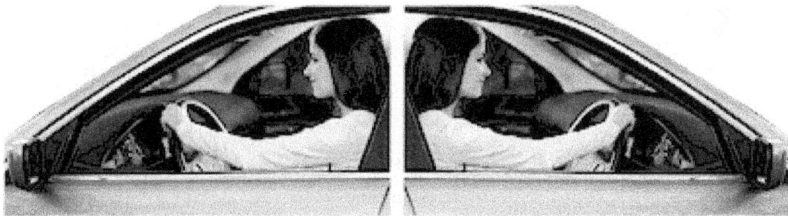

⬆Be careful if you flip a photo of a car or a truck. Remember which side the steering wheel is supposed to be on.

♠NOTE: sometimes a flag is *supposed* to be "backwards." When the American flag is on the right side of an airplane (including Air Force One) or on the right sleeve of a uniform, the stars go on the right. This mimics the way the flag would fly from a mast on a moving ship or when carried into battle.

♠If you are combining photos to make them seem like one picture, pay attention to the background (white is usually safe), and to the scale. If you want people to look like they are next to each other, their heads should be pretty close to the same size if they are adults. I align the eyes to make them parallel, and then adjust the head heights. A tilted head requires extra effort to get it right. In the previous composite, his hand seems too big and they're not looking at the same thing.

⬆ If you are composing an array of people, pay attention to the directions of their gaze, their scale, and other incompatibilities. Try to have similar backgrounds. Look for tiny reversed letters or words if you do a left-right flip.

◆ If your book uses blank spaces to separate paragraphs, you can save space on a page if you reduce the spacing between paragraphs. The default format gives the blank space the same height as a printed line, but you can easily decrease the space if you need to get more text on a page. (You can also increase the space height if you want to fill the page more.)

Put your cursor in the space and change the type size in the drop-down window so you can experiment with different solutions to find what looks best to you.

◆ Don't trust your eyes or your monitor. While fixing up a scan of an old photograph for use in a book, I used a graphics program to simply paint some black over various white spots and streaks in the otherwise solid black background.

Later on, I printed a couple of pages on a color laser printer simply to compare a few different type faces and sizes.

I was horrified to see that the photo that had looked perfect on my LCD monitor had dark black blotches against a grayer background.

It was a scary and valuable lesson, and I'm glad I learned it before the book went to press. Apparently, most LCD monitors just don't have the ability to display the full range of colors that can be printed—or even the colors that can be displayed by a clunky old CRT monitor.

I redid my retouching.

◆A pair of *em dashes* often indicates a parenthetical thought—like this one—in informal writing. A single em dash often functions as a *soft colon*. E.g., "This is our deal—she feeds the dog, I clean up the poop."

Em dashes are not available with regular keyboards, so double hyphens (--) are used as a substitute. Em dashes can be generated automatically with Word (under **Word Options/Proofing/Auto Correct Options/Auto Correct**) or you can select an em dash from **Insert/Symbol**.

The term "em dash" is derived from the width of one *em*, which is a standard spacing in the typographical *points* system with which type sizes are specified.

Years ago, one em was the width of the letter "M" in some specific font. That letter "M" was square—as wide as it was tall. So, in 11-point type, an em dash is 11 points wide, and so on for other type sizes. There is also a shorter *en dash*. In theory, it's longer than a hyphen but shorter than the em, but few people will notice if you use a hyphen instead the en.

Many purists insist that the em dash should be attached to the letters before and after it, like—this, with almost no visible space. Those on that side of the argument include the Oxford University Press and the *Chicago Manual of Style*.

On the other side, the *New York Times* likes to put a space before and after each em dash. I've gone back and forth on this issue, with different styles in different books. As long as I publish my own books, I control my em dashes. You control yours.

◆It's best not to have more than one hyphen in a word, but when a term or phrase already has a hyphen, like self-publishing, it can be hard to avoid. You can try revising the sentence, but the revision may be awkward or too long.

◆As a book evolves before publication, the sentences, paragraphs and pages go through many changes.

Sometimes a word that had been on the end of a line of text and needed a hyphen ends up in the middle of a line and no longer needs a hyphen, but the hyphen's still there.

The problem is most common when hyphens are manually added by the writer, rather than automatically added by the word-processing robot.

Misplacements frequently occur when you change the location or size of an illustration. You'll probably find some of the errant hyphens during regular proofreading, but to be safe you should do a search for hyphens. It may take a long time, and it's boring, but do it.

◆Word allows you to **raise** or **lower** text from its normal position. Open the **Font** dialog box, select the **Character Spacing** tab and use the **Position** drop-down menu and select the number of points for shifting up or down. This can be useful when you want to fit in a non-standard character, like ♫.

◆You're inviting trouble if you have *internal referrals* in a book. You may think you're helping your readers by saying that there's more information about a topic "on page 213" or "in chapter 14." Pages and chapters often migrate as a book evolves, and it's easy to lose track of your referrals. If you send a reader on a wild goose chase to the wrong page or chapter, she'll waste time, get pissed off and you'll look stupid.

It's much safer to say something like "later on in the book."

Similarly, it's dangerous to refer to a photo or illustration "above," "below" or "on this page." You can rewrite the referral so it's vague but truthful. I doubt that anyone will refuse to buy your book because of the lack of page-specific referrals.

→ If you use referrals, put them in **BIG BOLD RED TYPE**, so you can find them easily for checking in the final version. At the end, change to normal type.

◆ Word has some very useful features which are buried so deeply that almost no one ever finds them or uses them. One of my favorites is the **non-breaking hyphen**. It keeps a hyphenated word, phrase or number sequence from being split into pieces on two lines, and possibly gaining an extra hyphen. It's important for web addresses, email addresses and phone numbers. Since a hyphen is a "real" element in an Internet address, you don't want one to be put where it doesn't belong. Put your cursor where you want the hyphen to go, then press **CTRL** plus **SHIFT** plus the hyphen key.

◆ I hate to break up a web address by letting it run on two lines. If a hyphen is added automatically, the address is invalid. If the URL is short, you can pick other words to make it fit nicely. With a long URL, I let the line above run short:
www.this-is-an-example-of-a-long-url.com
Avoid   ugly   justification   before   a   long   URL:
www.this-is-an-example-of-a-long-url.com

◆ After you convert a color picture to grayscale, try sharpening it "lite" or "light" if your graphic software offers it. Photoshop's Auto Sharpen usually works quite well with no tinkering.

◆ Small photos, less than about 150 pixels wide, often get ruined if you try to sharpen them. Save an unmodified version so you can go back to it if your modification is a disaster. Sometimes an "undo" doesn't undo.

◆Word has a cool, built-in trick that lets you easily wrap text around an irregularly shaped object. If all of your photos and illustrations are rectangles, you can ignore this section. But if you have graphics with curves and angles, pay attention.

The feature, called **Edit Wrap Points**, allows you to determine the "borders" of a photograph or a drawing so that the adjacent text can come closer than with the normal borders. This gives a book a more interesting, polished look, and also allows you to fit more text on a page. While it's possible to use the feature with any graphic image, it works best with images that are surrounded by white space which blends into your page. You can use Photoshop to eliminate a distracting background.

This is an example of text butting up against an irregular object within a rectangular white space. The good-looking kid is your humble author when he was about four years old. My wife said she fell in love with me when she saw this picture. I will now insert some "Greek" type to fill in the rest of the space: Lorem ipsum dolor sit amet, consectetur adipiscing elit. Proin eget yabba dabba doo.

This is an example of how text can wrap around my adorable face. Left-click on the photo and then click on the **Picture Tools** at the top of the screen. Then click on **Text Wrapping, Tight**, and **Edit Wrap Points**. The photo will then have a red border which you can nudge with your mouse to follow the face contour. Both photos were set to allow .06-inch text distance instead of the normal 0.13-inch.

◆Don't be afraid to try different software "tools," especially if you already own them. For example, there's a good chance that you may have different graphics programs accumulated over the years.

I've generally used Microsoft's ancient but versatile Image Composer for sharpening photos. While writing a book, I found that the **Auto Sharpen** tool in Photoshop Elements is much better.

Some tools are easier to use than others. I like to use Microsoft Digital Image Pro 10 to remove spots from old photos. I assume I could do it with Photoshop, but I haven't yet figured out how to do it. Like most men, I seldom RTFM, or ask gas station attendants for travel directions.

◆Even the best computerized spell checker is not a substitute for a human editor. The robot can tell if a word is spelled wrong, but not if you used the wrong word. One book that I love to hate says, "for all participates." "Participates" is not a spelling error; it's the wrong word. "Participants" was the right word, but the robot didn't realize it. Neither did the author. There apparently was no editor, and the publisher didn't care.

◆Boldface type is used for chapter titles and subheads, and to attract attention. I sometimes use it with a different typeface **in the middle of text so it will be noticed** as people flip through the pages of the book. If you insert sans serif words in the middle of serif text, reduce its size by half or one point to match the serif type height.

If I want to emphasize a word or phrase, but not attract or distract people who are flipping pages, I use ALL CAPS, which is the typographic equivalent of SHOUTING.

Sometimes I use an <u>underline</u> to call attention to a word rather than to emphasize a concept.

I don't often use *italics* for emphasis, because italics have other uses such as indicating a book title or a technical term. Sometimes I do use italics for a *little bit of emphasis* when I don't want to SHOUT at readers.

◆Beware of oversize spacing between letters.

Trebuchet shows too much space between most of the letters.

Trebuchet looks much better when space around the **T** is condensed by 2.5 points, space around the **r** is condensed by 1.6 points, and the rest of the word is condensed by .4 points. The word still needs some adjustments. This can take a lot of work, but the result is worth it, particularly for large text.

Design Tip ⌐

Be careful with drop cap alignment. The default setting is usually OK, but sometimes the letter will migrate up or down and will have to be repositioned.

Design Tip ⌐

If you make a change in your book's graphic style, be very careful to make *all* of the changes. I changed the drop cap font in one book, and needed *seven* passes to find them all.

Design Tip ⌐

Try to avoid typographical *ladders*, where several consecutive lines end in hyphens. Two consecutive hyphens are usually OK, but more would be ugly. Ladders can be eliminated by shifting, changing, or removing words.

♦As you write, be conscious of your habitual errors, which may increase as you get older. I have many "senior moments" (also known as "brain farts") while typing. Don't laugh at me if you're just 30 years old. The 20-year-olds are laughing at you. It takes just about 15 minutes to go from age 30 to age 50. It takes five minutes to go from 50 to 60.

I'm a proud member of the first cohort of the Baby Boom. I was born in 1946 along with Billy Clinton, Dolly Parton and Donny Trump.

➜In the new system, we are all still middle-aged, and we will remain middle-aged until dirt is shoveled on top of us.

Lately, I've stupidly held down the shift key as I pressed the key to insert an apostrophe, and ended up inserting a colon. I often type "i nthe," "hsould," "nad" and "fro ma." I now tap the Caps Lock key a lot by accident, the semicolon instead of the apostrophe, and the "Page Down" key instead of "delete." I've also degenerated from being the world's fastest six-finger typist to a pretty-good two-finger typist. (I actually have ten fingers but I've never used them all for typing.)

If I live long enough, I'll probably develop even more bad habits which I can't control. I hope sloppy typing is not an early sign of dementia. I guess having to fix typos is better than dying young and perfect. When I start drooling on the keyboard, someone should take it away from me.

Aging Baby Boomer's Low-Tech Secret Weapon

If you remove the Caps Lock key, you can't tap it accidentally.

CHAPTER 51
Why and how to make your book shorter or longer

You can't have just *any* number of pages you want. The number of pages must be divisible by two, even if one or several pages are blank. Each sheet of paper in a book, called a *leaf,* has two sides (i.e., two pages). If your book has 300 pages, it uses 150 leaves. If your book has 301 pages, it uses 151 leaves—and you have one blank page. It's common to have one or more blank page at the end. The *signatures* (large sheets of paper that are printed on before cutting and binding) may dictate that books use multiples of specific numbers, such as 4, 6 or 8. You may need to make adjustments to avoid the blanks.

You probably have a "target" length for your book. You may think that to justify your price, you should be providing at least 300 pages, but you have only 289. Maybe you think a 300-page book will overwhelm some people, but you've come up with 311. Maybe you want to offer more pages than a competitive book. Maybe you want a thicker book so the title printed on the spine will be bigger.

There are many ways to reduce the number of pages without cutting important words, and it's also easy to increase the number of pages even if you have nothing more to say. One obvious method is to use larger or smaller pages.

➔Some of the tricks for increasing or decreasing the page count can also be used to improve the appearance of a book by eliminating orphans or other typographic misfortunes such as having just a few words that take up an entire page at the end of a chapter. The first sentence in this paragraph says "increasing or decreasing." Space could be saved by substituting the word "changing" without significantly altering the meaning.

The first text block shown below is ugly because of the orphaned word "do" on the third line.

The worst-looking book I've ever seen, and a catalog of all of the things you shouldn't do.

By simply changing from 15-pt type to 14.5, the orphan disappears, and a line of type is eliminated:

The worst-looking book I've ever seen, and a catalog of all of the things you shouldn't do.

Kerning can save space, too. Instructions are ahead.

The worst-looking book I've ever seen, and a catalog of all of the things you shouldn't do.

◆Use smaller-sized type, either in the whole book or in sections like the table of contents, bibliography or index. Even a one-point difference can save pages. Don't sacrifice readability.

◆Take advantage of shorter words and contractions. "Pasta" takes up less space than "macaroni" or "spaghetti." "Group" and "club" are shorter than "organization." ➔Sometimes eliminating just one or two characters can eliminate a page.

◆Remove some words. Any page can probably give up a few.

◆Change to different margins. Even using 1/16 of an inch less can save many pages.

◆Use fewer or smaller photos, or pack type closer to them.

◆Use a narrower typeface like Arial Narrow or Gil Sans Condensed for tables or captions, but not for regular text.

◆Make bulleted lists flush-left instead of indented.

◆Use condensing (kerning) to reduce spaces between letters, particularly in large type faces. This may eliminate a line. Highlight the text you want to modify. Open the **Font** dialog box and select **Condensed** from the **Character Spacing** drop-down menu. Try different numbers of points.

Sample Text, normal.
Sample Text, condensed 1.2 pts

It's equally easy to "pad" or stretch a book to add pages. I am morally opposed to having more pages than necessary because it's wasteful and dishonest; and I've criticized authors whose books use extra paper. On the other hand, I would rather see a page with words on it than a blank page that a printer added because of technical requirements; and I recognize that a bigger book may sell better and therefore be more likely to deliver an important message.

Don't be obvious if you have to stretch a book. Don't use 16-pt type instead of 11. It didn't fool your history teacher who wanted ten pages about Abraham Lincoln and you only had enough words to fill nine pages with normal-sized letters. You won't fool people who review or buy your book, either. If you have to stretch, use a combination of techniques, in moderation. Don't use one in excess. Try some of these:

◆Always start chapters on a recto page.

◆Put more white space around photos, charts, tables and illustrations.

◆Use *pull-quotes* (also known as *lift-quotes* or *call-quotes*). A pull-quote is a block of text printed in a distinctive typeface and inserted in the page with the main text wrapped around it. A *text box* is used to hold a pull-quote.

Vestibulum ante ipsum primis in faucibus orci luctus et ultrices posuere cubilia Curae; Aenean id porta dolor. Pellentesque malesuada risus id urna blandit molestie egestas massa lobortis. Maecenas sol-

> **This is a sample of a pull-quote. It can be useful and attractive, and can increase your number of pages. If your text is set in one column, don't put a pull-quote in the center. It will be difficult to read across it. Put it on one side.**

licitudin magna vel arcu imperdiet vitae ultrices arcu elementum. Phasellus nec nunc eros, quis pellentesque neque. Sed tellus orci, viverra vel iaculis a, rhoncus et lectus. Praesent dictum, eros vitae eleifend vestibulumibh. The silly dog ate poop.

Vestibulum ante ipsum primis in faucibus orci luctus et ultrices posuere cubilia Curae; Aenean id porta Pellentesque malesuada risus id urna at mattis. Maece nas sollici

> **If your text is set in two columns, it's OK to center a pull-quote. It may be hard to remove ugly gaps in the text around it.**

tudin magna vel arcu im perdiet vitae nunc. Aenean iaculis ornare dignissim. Quisque accum ante ipsum primis in faucibus orci. Un-oh, I stepped on the cat's tail. Waaaaah!

◆Use bulleted lists, instead of paragraphs with many items separated by commas.

◆Increase the spacing between lines in a list.

◆Spell out some names instead of using initials: "John Pierpont Morgan" takes up more space than "J. P. Morgan."

◆Include a summary at the beginning or end of chapters or sections. This is common in instructional books.

◆Include a bibliography, listing additional resources.

◆Put an order form in the back of the book. Include your other books if you have any.

◆On facing pages that act as a unified spread you can have more space above and below the text than on other pages.

◆Start chapters in the middle of a page rather than at the top.

◆Put quotes or helpful hints on individual pages.

◆Break up paragraphs into smaller paragraphs.

◆Add some words. ◆Use longer words.

◆Define technical terms when you introduce them.

◆Have more front matter and back matter.

◆If you just want a bigger spine to print your title on but don't care about more pages, use thicker paper. Cream (a/k/a "crème") is usually a little bit thicker than white.

◆Add more photos, charts, tables and illustrations.

◆Make photos, charts, tables and illustrations larger

A *drop cap* is an oversized letter that begins a paragraph. It can dress up a dull page, introduce an important point, and can stretch out your book a bit.

U se drop caps sparingly. Don't put them all over the place or have them close together like I did here.

Space Filler-Upper 🗁

Proofread in multiple formats: on screen in word processing, on screen in PDF, on a paper printout and in a bound book from your publisher. Different errors will show up in each format.

You can save money and time if you have early proofs made by your local UPS or FedEx store instead of by your printer or publisher.

Lightning Source charges $70 to make a change and send a proof. If you make a lot of revisions, those charges can add up to a big number!

You can get less-expensive bound proofs from Lulu or CreateSpace—but they may not look exactly like what Lightning Source will print.

Design Tip 🖱

Be careful if you use a typeface like Constantia, which has shorter-than-normal "oldstyle figures": 0123456789. You can have a problem if you have a reference to a zero (0), which looks like the letter "o." Temporarily switch to another compatible face like Century Schoolbook (0).

Also, if you use a typeface like Constantia, consider changing faces temporarily when numbers have to go along with letters in a term. **Microsoft Word 2010** looks weird compared to **Microsoft Word 2010. Yale '12** looks weird compared to **Yale '12**. I plugged in Century, again.

To judge typeface compatibility, enlarge to 300%. Compare the following numbers from Constantia, Garamond and Century. Garamond has thinner strokes and is a bad match for Constantia.

o 0 0

CHAPTER 52
Are you a lowly amateur or a near-professional?

One of the most obvious indicators of a novice or inexperienced bookmaker is the appearance of typography from the Internet and ancient typewriters.

There is no single person who can be identified as the inventor of the typewriter. Various typing devices appeared in the 18th and 19th centuries, and they became pretty common in the mid-1800s. In 1935 IBM introduced the first commercially successful electric typewriter in the United States.

The early typewriters provided the same width for all letters and punctuation marks, regardless of size. With their *fixed-width* letters, an "**i**" was as wide as a "**w**," as in Courier New type, which mimics old typewriters.

There was too much space around narrow letters and too little space around the wide ones. This made typewritten documents noticeably different and graphically inferior to those produced by typesetting—which permitted different widths as needed. After years of research, and a delay caused by World

War II, IBM introduced the "Executive" typewriter with *proportional spacing* in 1946.

Although the Executives and the Selectrics that followed in the 1960s became very popular in business, they were generally too expensive for home use or for school typing classes.

Because of the uniform spacing in conventional typewriters, the space between words was often too large, and the period at the end of a sentence was detached from the last word in the sentence `like this .` Instead of **like this.**

Therefore, kids were taught to insert two spaces between sentences (i.e., two spaces after a period) to make it easier to identify the beginning of a new sentence.

`Compare old-style period.  Next sentence.`
Compare new-style period. Next sentence.

`A single space after a period typed with`
`an old typewriter could make it hard to`
`spot where a sentence ended. And where blah`

`The extra space made it easier to find the`
`end of a sentence.  And the beginning of the`
`next one.`

With modern computers and word processing software, each letter and punctuation mark get the appropriate width and adjacent space. Periods hug the words they are attached to. There is no need to allow extra space between sentences, and a document will look weird if you do. **This** sentence has too much space before it. **This** sentence was done properly.

If you learned to type on an old machine, or if you pasted in some text that has the old-style double spaces, you can use Word's **find and replace** feature to bring it up to 21st century standards. In the **Home** tab, click on **Replace** on the far right. When the window opens, type two spaces in the **Find what** space and type one space in the **Replace with** space. Then click on **Replace All**, for an automatic conversion or **Find**

Next to view possible changes one-at-a-time and approve or reject them individually.

The next holdover from ancient typewriters and even recent typewriters, is the accidental use of **straight apostrophes and quote marks** rather than the more professional curly *typographers' marks*. This commonly happens when an old word processing document or part of a web page is copied and pasted into a modern Word document.

Because of their *limited character set*, emails and web pages, like old typewriters, make double-duty of some punctuation marks.

❙ The same straight symbol was used for feet, an apostrophe and a single quotation mark (also "quote mark" or "quote").

❜ Replace it with a curly apostrophe.

◆Watch out for apostrophes that Word causes to curl the wrong way, common with **contractions** that substitute an apostrophe for the missing beginning of the word or number. The problem is common with 'em (them), 'tis (it is), 'twas (it was) and years like '09 (2009). To eliminate this error, just type a second apostrophe after the first one (it should curl the right way), and then delete the first one.

Don't let ❝ em do it in ❝ 12. **(wrong)**

Let ❜ em do it in ❜ 13. **(right)**

◆The tip of the curl should face toward the piece of the word or number that was removed to make the contraction.

 The same straight "ditto" symbol was used for inches

and a double quote  .

" Replace it with curly quotes, which are different

before and after the quotation " .

◆In the USA, the final quote goes before the period. In the U.K., the period goes first. I think the British system is more logical—most of the time.

◆Using curly apostrophes and quote marks can get you in trouble if you are referring to feet and inches, or minutes and seconds. Instead of the curlies used for quotations, you should use straight slanted marks known as *prime* and *double prime*.

 is wrong (for five feet, nine inches).

 is right.

◆You can find the prime and double prime by clicking on the **Insert** tab and then **Symbol** at the right end of the ribbon bar, and **More Symbols**. If you can't find the primes in the typeface you've been using, try a similar face. If your document is filled with the wrong marks, you can use the **Find and Replace** feature to track them down and fix them.

Another holdover from ancient high school typing is the use of <u>underlines</u> instead of **bold** or *italic* type for emphasis. With modern software and the huge variety of fonts, there is generally no need to use underlines for emphasis. When you underline a word, the line will cross through the descenders of lowercase letters g, j, p, q, and y, making an <u>ugly</u> word.

If you do choose to use an underline, you can sometimes avoid the <u>ugly</u> problem by choosing a word with no descenders (not always an option, and you can't alter a web address). You can also underline part of a word. It doesn't work well with <u>ugly</u>, but it's interesting with <u>beau</u>ty and <u>J</u>eep. The effect can be dramatic or confusing. Use this technique sparingly. It can be nice for logos.

I use <u>underlines</u> in my writing in a few cases:

1. Sometimes an italic word just looks weak. That's why I underlined <u>Real</u> in one book's title. I would not underline <u>regal</u> or <u>royal</u>. <u>You may be able to insert a horizontal rule</u> below a word without crashing into descenders, but it's tough to position the rule properly without creating extra spacing between lines.

2. When I want to call particular attention to the actual ("physical") word above the line, not just a concept.

3. Sometimes when I want to print a web address such as **www.BookMakingBlog.blogspot.com**. I also switch from the normal serif body text to a sans serif bold font.

4. *If a section of text is set in italics, and there's a word or phrase within it that normally would be in italics, don't put it in roman instead. <u>Underline</u> it to make it distinctive. A little bit of roman type in an italic block might not get noticed.* (Did you notice the roman "in" in the second line?)

5. **Sometimes *Italics look strange* next to roman text** because of the distorted spacing between the italics and roman letters caused by the slanted italics.

◆A self-published author has an *extra burden* to produce a quality product, because a bad self-pubbed book reflects badly on other self-published authors. Ironically, one of the ugliest and worst-written books I've ever seen tries to give advice to self-published authors. It was apparently never edited.

◆The limitations of the Internet create the need for typographic compromises. Web pages show lots of underlines that smash through descenders, and as people get used to typographic compromises online, those compromises may become more acceptable in print. You should still maintain high standards.

➔➔➔◆Don't just dump words onto pages. Carefully examine EACH line so you can improve its appearance by changing words, spacing and hyphenation. Read this paragraph again.

◆Just because a block of text—or an entire book—is set flush-left/ragged-right, does not mean that words should not be hyphenated. Ragged does not have to mean jagged, or gap-toothed. The right edge of your text should be relatively even, with no lines much shorter than the others (except for the last line of a paragraph). You'll need either hyphens or rewriting or both to make it right.

It's not just a matter of esthetics. Wide variations in line width are disconcerting to the reader. They slow down reading and hinder comprehension.

◆Avoid hyphenation that leaves a one-letter syllable by itself, as in "e-ven," "a-bout," "a-void," "o'-clock," "o-ver," "earl-y," and "sex-y." Substitute or shift some words to solve the problem.

Are you a lowly amateur or a near-professional?

◆ Don't use bold or heavy fonts in small sizes.

    ◆Oversized half-inch indents are a holdover from 1960s-era typing classes, when kids were instructed to indent five spaces. They're OK in a letter, but generally look bad in a book.

◆Beginning designers and cheapskates often use **undersize margins** to squeeze more words on a page, so fewer pages will be needed and a book can be printed for less money.

Just as the appearance of a picture is improved by having a *matte* within its frame, your text needs adequate white space, too. Small margins make a book look lousy, and hard to read. One good **rule of thumb** is that if you hold your book in your hands, your thumbs should fit in the margins, and not cover up words or pictures. (You put your thumb on the fingerprint—didn't you?)

One of the worst examples of too-tiny margins is *Become a Published Author*, a promotional book from Infinity Publishers. The book has useful information about book preparation but it is a major failure in one important area. It says it answers the question, "Can you send me a sample of a book that you have published?" It's a very poor example that may not win over many potential customers.

In addition to the tiny margins, it has misaligned text across spreads, and other problems. The company does not print in the common 6×9-inch format, and also has some dishonest criticism of competitors.

◆Minimize gimmicks ON THE same page.

◆Don't use lots of text boxes having thick or ornate borders, rounded corners, dark tints or strange shapes.

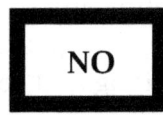

NO   NO   NO   NO

◆**Don't use LOTS of fonts, or decorative fonts which may be HARD TO READ.**

◆One way to add a lot of class to your book is to use *hanging punctuation*, where bullets, commas, periods, quote marks, etc. are placed beyond the normal margins in justified text. It's a lot of work, and may look funny with a long hanging em dash—

If you read this book, you'll have no excuses for publishing an ugly book

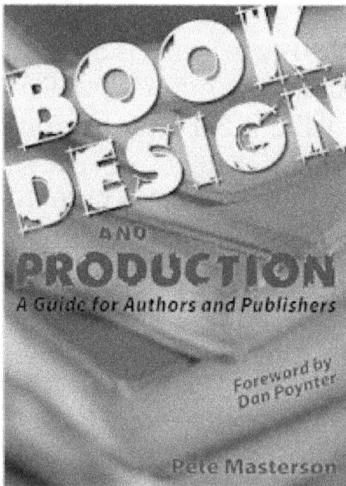

Pete Masterson's ***Book Design and Production*** is ideal for self-published authors of all types.

It will help you understand the principles of good cover and interior design, and the book production process. It will help you to analyze your book to find what you or your publisher has done wrong. You'll learn how to spot and correct the mistakes that might mark you as an amateur and cripple your sales—regardless of the validity of what you've written.

There are also extensive sections on publishing software, the publishing sequence, selecting and dealing with printers and hiring a designer. There's a large and well-picked list of online and printed resources for writers.

The glossary is almost an encyclopedia. It's nearly 100 pages long and could be a book by itself. You'll learn a lot.

Lightning Source
createspace

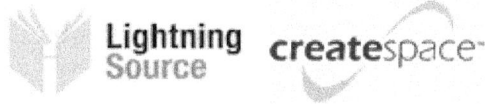

LIGHTNING SOURCE VS. CREATESPACE

The next two chapters deal with Lightning Source ("LS") and CreateSpace ("CS")—the two companies that provide most printing and distribution services for independent self-publishing authors.

- Both companies provide good quality and will make your books available through the major online and terrestrial booksellers.
- Neither company can guarantee that your book will be stocked and displayed in terrestrial bookstores.
- ➜CS is easier to use than LS, and is particularly appropriate for self-publishing newbies, and authors who intend to publish few books.
- Historically, CS was less expensive for printing than LS, but you could make more money per book if LS printed and distributed your books. As I was finishing this book, there were reports that Amazon was delaying shipments of books printed by LS and favoring books from CS. I have not personally experienced this. It's important that you keep up with changes posted by authors at such websites as **http://finance.groups.yahoo.com/group/pod_publishers/**
- CS does not print hardcover books, but LS does. This may change.
- LS offers both glossy and matte-finish paperbacks and hardcovers. CS prints glossy paperbacks only. This may change.
- LS prints books in the USA and in other countries. CS prints in the USA, only.

- CS does better color pages. This may change.
- CS provides "booklike" templates which you can modify for your own book. LS provides nearly blank templates, which merely show where your artwork should be inserted.
- CS can have books on sale on Amazon.com less than an hour after you approve a proof. LS usually takes a few days.
- CS books are automatically set up for "Search Inside This Book" and "Look Inside" on Amazon.com.

The following chart shows approximate numbers for a 300-page, 6×9-inch, $15.95-list, paperback sold at Amazon.com in mid-2011.

	LS	CS
Initial Cost	$75	$0 or $39
Annual cost	$12	$0
Cost to print one book	$5.40	$4.45 or $7.50
Cost for proof	Up to $115*	$10-$20
What you earn when a book is sold	$7.36	$5.12

NOTES: ①Prices and company policies may be different now. ②LS charges $30 to print and ship (for next-day delivery, after printing) a proof of a paperback book, and $35 for a hardcover. There is also a charge of $40 to change an interior file and $40 to change a cover file. ③ Book size and selling price affect earnings. On a 100-page, $9.95 book, you'll earn $3.82 from CS (with the Pro Plan). With LS, you'll earn $5.76. ④If you sell a dozen books, the greater earnings from LS won't change your life. If you sell 1,000 books, the earnings difference is significant. ⑤With CS you can save money on proofs by specifying "slow" shipping. LS ships only for next-business-day delivery. If you expect to need many generations of proofs, start with Create-Space for the proofs, and then switch to Lightning for distribution. ⑥LS charges a little more per page ($.002) to print books for you than for booksellers' orders. ⑦LS takes longer to print hardcovers than paperbacks.

CHAPTER 53
Working with Lightning Source

Lightning Source ("LS" or "LSI") is not a publisher. It's a printer. Because of its close link to book wholesaler Ingram Book Group, it's also your doorway and pathway to the world's booksellers—both online and on-earth.

Lightning serves traditional giant publishers, and self-publishing companies, but it will also work with independent self-publishers. It has good service, fast service, and competitive prices. Lightning is set up to work with publishers, not writers, and Lightning *won't* hold your hand. If you have your own publishing company, even if you are the only employee, Lightning will work with you; but it's vital that you know what you are doing or you will waste time and money.

Lightning stores the digital files for about 500,000 books and, on a typical day, it adds 500 titles. Lightning prints about 50,000 books per day from 27,000 orders—so the average order is for fewer than two books. They are truly printing on demand.

They can print an 800-page book in less than a minute. Most books are shipped out within 24 hours after the company receives an order—just as if the books were on a warehouse shelf. That's impressive, but there is something that may be even more impressive.

Lightning Source is a big part of a huge and diversified, private company which you've probably never heard of.

Ingram Industries includes Ingram Marine Group (with about 4,000 barges, tugs, and other boats); Ingram Digital Group (distributor of e-books and audio books); Ingram Insurance Group (individual and small group health insurance); and Ingram Book Group. Ingram Micro, a major distributor of computer equipment and software, was spun off in 1996.

Ingram Book Group's history goes back to a school textbook warehouse founded in Nashville in 1935, and acquired by Ingram in 1964. By 1970, Ingram's operations had expanded to supply books to bookstores and libraries, and it gradually grew to become the nation's largest book wholesaler, supplying almost every bookseller as well as many libraries and schools.

In 2009, the corporation announced the formation of Ingram Content Group, to combine Ingram Book Group, Ingram Digital, and Lightning Source— the subject of this chapter and the company you should be most interested in.

Lightning Source's close ties with Ingram Book Group and Ingram Digital make it easy for a self-publishing author to arrange for books in almost any form to reach almost any reader.

Well, it's at least *relatively* easy. As a wholesaler, Ingram does not market or promote books to stores, websites, or libraries. It supplies them after receiving an order. The publisher and author—and they both may be you—have to build the demand so Ingram will receive and fill orders.

As sister companies (or brother companies) Ingram Book Group and Lightning Source work together, with apparently none of the sibling rivalry that messes up human relationships.

Ingram sells every title that Lightning prints (and a great many titles printed by others). Some of the Lightning books are actually on the Ingram warehouse shelves. The others are so quickly available because of POD that Ingram considers them to be in stock for immediate shipping—which usually means the next business day.

The Ingram/Lightning combination means that any self-publisher who uses Lightning to print can supply books to Amazon, Barnes & Noble, and hundreds or thousands of other booksellers around the world by doing nothing other than approving a proof after receiving it from Lightning.

I generally submit revisions to Lightning on Tuesday, receive a proof on Thursday, approve it on Friday, and see the book on sale on Amazon.com on Saturday. Lightning automatically transmits information about your book and a cover photo to Amazon and other online booksellers.

When Amazon or one of its competitors receives an order for your book, it is drop-shipped directly to the reader. Generally, Amazon makes its money without ever seeing or touching your book. Amazon does stock some of the popular books that Lightning prints so Amazon can quickly ship those books along with other titles that it stocks.

In addition to its family connection with Ingram Book Group, Lightning also supplies other wholesalers including Baker & Taylor (the major wholesaler serving American libraries and schools) and NACSCORP (the wholesale division of the National Association of College Stores). Barnes & Noble gets books from Ingram/Lightning, for both store and website sales.

Lightning has overseas branches with similar connections to book wholesalers and their bookseller customers. If you are in the U.S., you decide if you want your books to be available in other countries through Lightning. The last time I counted, my books were on sale in 21 nations. Some were on Amazon's websites in Japan, Germany and elsewhere. Others were being sold by non-Amazon dealers in other countries such as India and Israel.

Lightning Source uses acid-free, book-grade, opaque paper stock. Books are printed on either a 55# cream ("crème") or

50# white paper. Paperback covers are printed on a bright white 90# cover stock. You can also get hardback books with or without jackets. If you want something really fancy, you can even get a cloth cover with gold stamping.

Books can be submitted as electronic files or as paper pages, to be scanned and digitized.

Lightning's print quality is usually quite good. They say they conduct ten quality control checks on each book before it is shipped. I have seen a few books where the spine text was tilted and a photograph had a strange green-yellow tint, but this is not common.

When Lightning receives an order and ships your book, they'll pay you the wholesale price (minus the cost of printing) about three months later. The cost of shipping is included in the printing cost, $5.40 for a 300-page, 6×9-inch paperback.

If you want to buy books to sell or give away, or to send out for reviews, you can get a discount of from 5% to 25%, starting at 50 books. You *do* pay shipping on these orders.

If you need a lot of books, Lightning also prints offset, starting at 750 copies for hardback and 1,500 for paperback.

About three "business days" after you've submitted either a new book file or a revision to Lightning, they will send you a proof for next-day delivery via UPS. The proof price is $30 for paperback books and $35 for hard covers (PLUS a fee to modify files: $40 for the cover and $40 for the interior pages).

If you want two proofs, even to be sent at the same time to the same address, you pay double (UNFAIR!). You may have trouble if you want Saturday delivery. Several times when I agreed to pay a surcharge for Saturday, I was told that UPS did not deliver to my area on Saturday—which was not true—and I received the proof on Monday.

Sometimes the proof does not accurately represent what Lightning will manufacture for others. I don't know how this happens, but with my first book I wasted a lot of time adjusting the contrast on photos based on the proof, only to find that books supplied to Amazon looked just fine.

It's easy to establish yourself as a Lightning customer. You don't need to submit any character references or a financial statement. You merely fill in a few blanks and make some simple choices online.

Go to **www.Lightningsource.com**. Click on the "New Client" tab and then click on "Open New Account" from the dropdown menu and click on "proceed to our New Account Page." That's where you choose a login name and password, and enter information about your company. It's VERY IMPORTANT that you have a business name if you want to be taken seriously in the publishing business. Remember: Lightning wants to work with publishers, not authors. Fill in the blanks or make selections from the dropdown menus. For "Primary book category," select "Trade Publisher." When you're through, click on "Submit."

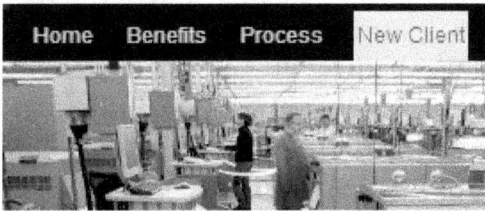

Assuming you filled out the registration form properly, within a day or so you should be notified that you've been approved, and you'll be given the names of your contacts within Lightning, and other information.

Lightning charges an annual $12 "Digital Catalog Fee" to keep your book in the system, make its information available to distributors and booksellers, handle price changes, etc.

How to upload files for your book:

1. Click on **Login** from the top of the Lightning screen, enter your Login Name and Password, and click on **Login**.
2. Put your cursor on **My Library** and then click on *Setup a New Title*.
3. The "New Title Setup" screen will appear. Under "Print-On-Demand Setup Options," click on **Title for Full Distribution Services - (includes Wholesale US/UK/EU Distribution and Publisher Direct Distribution)** and then click on **Continue**.
4. The "Title General Information" screen should now appear. It should already show your business name and imprint (probably the same as your business name, unless you registered several imprints). Type in a "Pub. Ref. Number" to help you keep track of your books. It can be almost anything that makes sense to you. Type in the ISBN and title, and then select the language from the dropdown menu.

Click on **Find Subjects** and you'll see a screen that will help you find appropriate entries. Type something such as "architecture" or "agriculture" and click on **Search**. The next screen will show you a list of possible classifications. Scroll down and select the best one. You'll then go back to the "Title General Information" screen and you should see your selection in the "Subject 1" window. Click on the second **Find subjects** and pick another suitable classification. Then do it a third time. You don't really have to pick more than one classification, but you may sell more books if you can find multiple matchups.

Title General Information

Publisher: Silver Sands Books

Publisher Number: 603

? Imprint: Silver Sands Books ▼

? Pub. Ref. Number: Test 1

? ISBN: 1234567891234   Autofill Title Metadata

? Title: Prehistoric Architecture

? Language: English ▼

Subjects:

Subject 1: Architecture : General   Find subjects

Subject 2: Architecture : History - General   Find subjects

Subject 3: Architecture : History - Ancient & Cla   Find subjects

Contributors:

	✓ Last Name	First	Middle	✓ Role
1:	Flintstone	Fred	L	Author
2:	Rubble	Barney		Editor
3:	Slagheap	Samuel	J	Illustrator

Subject Lookup

Type a portion of the subject code or description that you are looking for and click on "Search".

Subject: agriculture   Search

Select	Subject Code	Description
☐	JNF051020	Juvenile Nonfiction : Technology - Agriculture
☐	SOC055000	Social Science : Agriculture & Food
☐	TEC003000	Technology & Engineering : Agriculture - General
☐	TEC003010	Technology & Engineering : Agriculture - Tropical Agriculture
☐	TEC003020	Technology & Engineering : Agriculture - Animal Husbandry

5. Fill in the names of up to three people involved in the project and select their roles from the dropdown menus. Make sure that people you list are willing to have their names associated with the book, because their names will be included in the book description at online booksellers worldwide. Carina, my cover artist, accumulated nearly 1,000 Google links from working on my books. It's an easy way to become famous.

6. When you're finished with the page, click on **Save**. If you've made any errors, such as entering an invalid ISBN, the next screen will tell you to fix them.

7. Lightning Source requires that your book files be uploaded as Postscript files processed with Acrobat Distiller. The procedure is covered in Chapter 47.

8. The screenshot below shows where you specify which files you will be supplying (i.e., cover and/or interior) and what form they are in (e.g., Internet upload, CD).

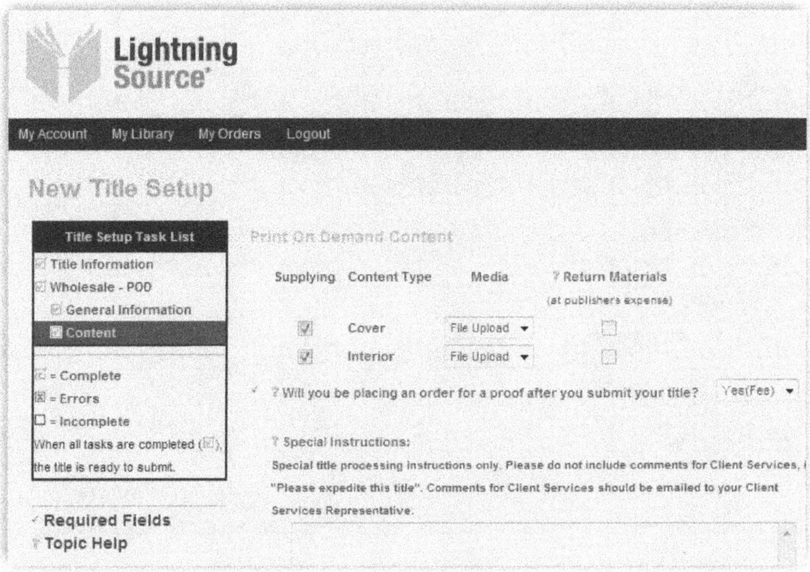

9. The next screenshot shows where you agree to pay the fees for the files which will become your book. Click on "I Agree."

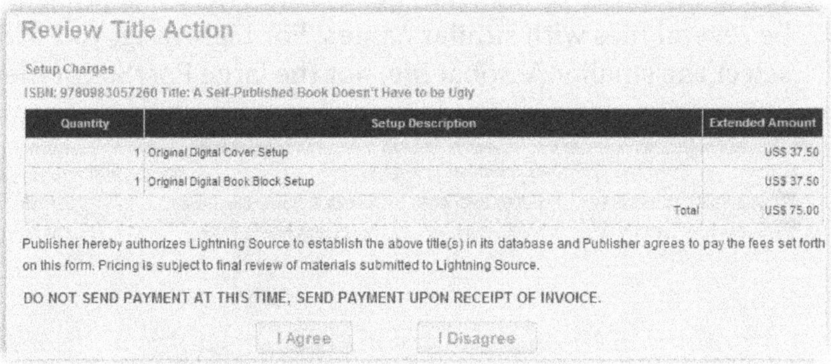

10. Then you will specify which file you will be uploading and select it from your computer (unless you are mailing a file).

Content Upload

Welcome to Lightning Source Content Upload

How to upload your files to Lightning Source

ISBN: 9780983057260

Title: A Self-Published Book Doesn't Have to be Ugly

Format: Print On Demand Book

☐ Uploading Cover

☐ Uploading Interior

Content Upload for Print On Demand Book Interior

ISBN: 9780983057260

Title: A Self-Published Book Doesn't Have to be Ugly

Your file(s) will not be uploaded to Lightning Source until you see the 'Thank You' page after completing step 2 of 2.

Step 1 of 2: Use the Browse button to select files to upload for the Interior, then click Upload File to begin the upload:

Please click Browse to select a file.

[Browse]   [Upload File]

11. Locate the new file in the folder on your computer when you are ready to upload it to Lightning. There will probably be several files with similar names. For Lightning, you will select the smaller Acrobat file, not the large PostScript file.

Name	Date modified	Type	Size
📄 book-1.30-testPDF-1	7/5/2009 8:31 AM	Adobe Acrobat Document	4,826 KB
📄 book-1.30-testPDF-1	7/5/2009 8:04 AM	PostScript File	118,279 KB

After you upload your files you can periodically go online to check your book's proofing progress. Log in to Lightning Source and click on **My Library**, then **Title Information and Links**, then **Start Search**. The screen shot below shows the production progress of one of my books.

Title Status Details

Publisher:	Silver Sands Books
Publisher No.:	6039917
Publisher Reference No.:	VAN-1
LS Title ID No.:	CSS621050
ISBN:	978-0-9816617-7-3
Title:	Get the Most out of a Self-Publishing Company. Make a better deal. Make a better book.
Author:	Marcus, Michael N.

Title Setup Status History

Title Submitted, Awaiting Materials	07/20/2010 10:38:22
COVER Accepted	08/27/2010 12:39:46
Title in Premedia	09/14/2010 15:03:57
Publisher Accepted Proof	09/16/2010 17:04:19
Available for Printing/Download	09/16/2010 17:04:51
Available for Distribution	09/26/2010 17:48:21

If Lightning Source prints multiple books for you, you can see the status for all of them.

ISBN/SKU	Binding	Title	Contributor	Submit Date	Status
9780981661773	Perfect	Get the Most out	Marcus, Michael N.	7/20/2010	Title in Revision
9780981661759	Perfect	Stories I'd Tell M	Marcus, Michael N	9/22/2009	Title On Hold
9780981661742	Perfect	Become a Real S	Marcus, Michael N	7/21/2009	Available for Printing/Download
9780981661735	Perfect	the AbleComm G	Marcus, Michael N.	1/21/2009	Available for Printing/Download
9780981661711	Perfect	Phone Systems	marcus, michael n	1/7/2009	Available for Printing/Download
9780981661704	Perfect	I Only Flunk My E	Marcus, Michael N	11/4/2008	Available for Printing/Download

Some tips for using Lightning Source

◆Lightning's standard processing may result in poor printing of photographs, with loss of details and blotchy dark areas. For the best possible results, use high-resolution 300 DPI photographs saved as TIF files.

◆Minimize post-publication revisions. After you send a revision to Lightning, Amazon may mark your book as unavailable if Amazon has no copies in stock. You may be saved by other booksellers who offer your book on Amazon. They'll accept orders even if they really can't get the book. If you must revise, try to do it during relatively slow sales times (which you will have to judge for yourself). If you sell with Amazon Advantage, your own inventory can be available even when Amazon can't get books from Lightning. Be very careful because you don't want to get stuck with a big pile of the old version when Amazon starts offering the new version.

◆Your book covers may not look as good as they could if you don't use Lightning's template and Adobe Acrobat and Distiller. Lighting will email a custom template to you at no extra charge once you have finalized your book size and page count.

◆*Ingram Advance* is a monthly catalog that is distributed to booksellers and libraries worldwide. Titles can be included only once, when they are first released through Lightning Source. The catalog includes a short paragraph about the book title, its price, and a black & white cover image. A publisher may request that a title be in *Ingram Advance* only at the time a title is submitted to Lightning for initial set-up. Titles submitted to *Ingram Advance* will not appear until 3-4 months after the title has been approved for printing and the listing will be invoiced separately after publication.

CHAPTER 54
Working with CreateSpace

As discussed previously, Amazon's CreateSpace is a "split-personality" publishing services provider. It can provide complete publishing and distribution services—or just printing.

If you form your own publishing company, and have books printed and distributed by CreateSpace, you should *not* use the "free" standard program. The $39 "Pro" program can provide *much* more profit per book. It also allows you to participate in the "Expanded Distribution Channel," which offers you the potential to distribute your book to a larger audience through more outlets including bookstores, libraries, academic institutions, wholesalers and distributors.

Why use CreateSpace to print your books?

1. The website is very user-friendly, geared to help beginners, with an easy step-by-step process. It's easy to know what you've done so far, and what has to be done.
2. You can get started for very little money: zero or $39.
3. You pay about $5 plus shipping for a proof of a revision of your book, as opposed to $70 if Lightning Source does your printing.

4. You can upload your book interior as a simple PDF. Lightning Source requires extra steps to produce and upload a Postscript file.

5. CreateSpace has free cover templates. They will not give you a great cover, like a professional designer can achieve; but if used properly, you can have a "good enough" cover. Take advantage of the choices in colors and typefaces.

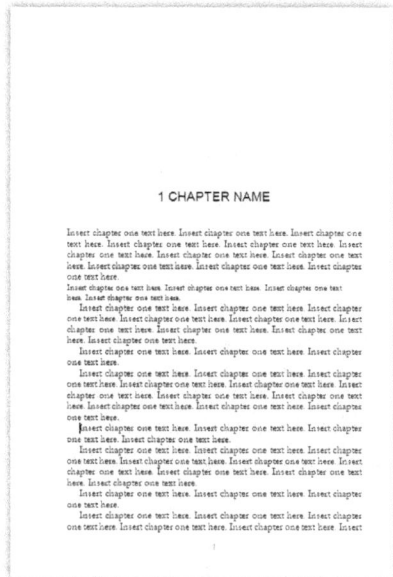

6. CreateSpace provides downloadable page templates to use with MS Word, but they're not really necessary.

7. CreateSpace can provide a free ISBN.

8. The price to buy books is low.

9. Very fast availability on Amazon.com.

10. CreateSpace may give you generous credits and freebies to make up for mistakes or delays.

11. Online community to help you, at **https://www.createspace.com/en/community**

Disadvantages of CreateSpace

1. Your customizing options when using the cover templates are very limited. You may have to work hard to produce an attractive cover, and it will still not be as good as a professional designer could achieve.

2. Standard shipping takes longer than with Lightning Source, and tracking numbers are not provided.

3. It's hard to contact a human being. Email responses may come from frustrating robots which don't understand your comment or question (or from human beings with limited experience using the English language).

4. There is more chance that the plastic laminate on a book cover will start peeling off, than if your book is printed by Lightning Source.

5. CreateSpace does not print hardcover books. This could change.

6. You'll make less money per book sold on booksellers' websites.

7. If CreateSpace provides the ISBN, CreateSpace—not you—will be identified as the publisher. If you want to switch to another printer, you'll need to get another ISBN. There can be confusion if the "same" book is available with two ISBNs.

8. CreateSpace is paranoid about potential copyright violation, and demanded that I show proof that I had permission to use every photograph in a book. I've never encountered this with other printers, and it delayed publication. Another time, CreateSpace did not question my photos, but rejected a book simply because it mentioned the name of corporate parent Amazon.com. I complained publicly and got a quick apology. Appar-

ently, the robot censor was hyperactive and needed to be recalibrated.

9. CreateSpace's robots will point out lots of potential problems with an interior file—many of which are not really problems. Responding to each one can waste lots of time.

10. Even though CreateSpace may use Lightning Source to print books in its Expanded Distribution service, it has different requirements. CreateSpace rejected an interior bleed on two pages that were identical to bleeds that were acceptable to Lightning Source.

How to get started:

1. At **www.CreateSpace.com**, click on ① **Publish**, and then ② **Books on Demand**.

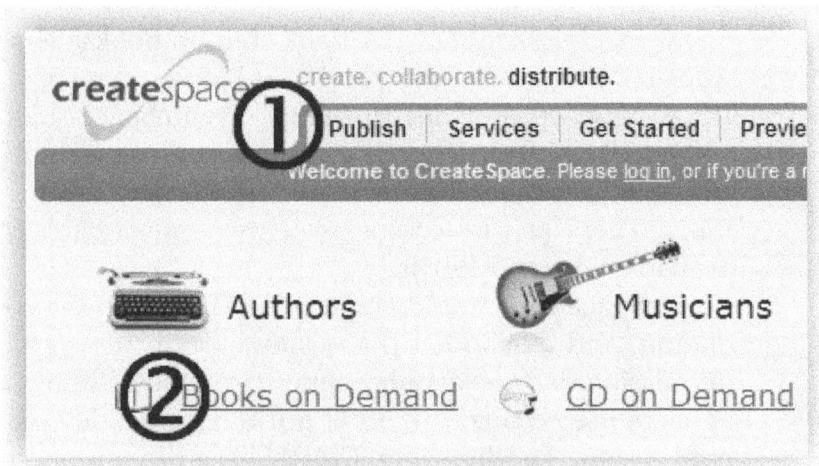

2. Click on **Create a Book**.

3. Click on **Sign up now** to create a new account, enter the requested information, and then click on **Create My Account.**

4. Read the long, boring and obtuse membership agreement and check the box to indicate that you agree, and then click on **Continue.**

1. Amendment; Notice of Changes.
We reserve the right to change the terms and conditions contained in this Agreement, other Service-specific term or guidelines governing the Services, including without limitation, any of the information posted on the Products the Content G... ...es, Submission Guidelines (as defined below), Pricing pages, Site Terms and Privacy Notice pa discretion. ... ...es to the Site, including Service-specific terms and conditions, or policies and guidelines refer effe... ...sting of such revisions on the Site and without notice to you. We will, however, post a notice of on... ...at least thirty (30) days after the changes are effective. You are responsible for regularly reviewing of... ...es. Changes to referenced policies and guidelines or any other information in any Products, Help, or

☑ I agree to all terms and conditions of this Membership Agreement and agree to comply with them at all times.

○ I do not agree to these terms.

Continue

5. Next you have to decide and specify whether you want to do most of the work yourself, or have it done for you. If you want to do it yourself, click on **Set Up Your Book Now**.

💡 **Welcome to CreateSpace!** Your new member account has been created.

Do-It-Yourself

Able to create the interior pages of your book as a PDF? Start our **free** ... ...ided publishing process today.

You can use o... ...er Creator to design your cover o... ...ad your own PDF.

Set Up Your Book Now

Set up a CD, DVD, or other product...

Call in the Pros!

Not sure about creating your own PDF book files? Want to learn more about our editing, book design, or marketing services before you get started?

Discuss your options with one of our knowledgeable publishing consultants.

Talk to a Consultant

Spoken with a consultant and ready to move forward? Continue to your Member Dashboard

Community
Network and get answers from other authors and industry professionals.
Join the conversation!

Resources
Find expert advice in our growing library of articles, tutorials, and more.
Get in the know!

Account Video Tour
Walk through your new account with this video guide.
Watch it now!

Continue to your Member Dashboard

6. On the next page, you start the book project. You give the book a title (which can be changed later), specify that it's a paperback, and (at least for your first book) choose the **Guided** setup process and click on **Get Started**.

7. Next you enter specific information about your book, including title and the names of people associated with it. This information can be changed later. You either **Save** the information and go mow the lawn, shovel the snow or take a nap, or **Save & Continue** working on the book.

8. The next page deals with the physical properties of your book. You don't have to specify the page count. When you upload your interior files, the CreateSpace computer will count the pages.

9. Next you specify how you will provide the ISBN (see chapter 34). ①If you *don't* want to establish your own publishing company brand and are not likely to use another company to print this book in the future, choose the first option. ②Use the second option if you plan to establish your own publishing company with an ISBN assigned by CreateSpace, unless you want your books to be available to libraries and colleges. ③I can't think of any reason to use the third option. ④The fourth option is right if you have already obtained an ISBN which you want to use.

ISBN   ◄ Back   Next ►

What to do on this page: An ISBN is required to publish and distribute a book. Compare ISBN options and find the one that's right for you.

* You can skip this section if you haven't decided which ISBN option to use, but you'll need to complete this page before you can publish your book. Return to your Project Homepage

Choose an ISBN option for your book:

⌐ Free CreateSpace-Assigned ISBN
We can assign an ISBN to your book at no charge.

Only $10

⌐ Custom ISBN
Set your own imprint to be listed as the publisher.

Only $99

⌐ Custom Universal ISBN
Set a custom imprint while keeping your distribution and publishing options open.

⌐ Provide Your Own ISBN
If you have an ISBN that you purchased from Bowker® or through your local ISBN agency, you can use it to publish your book through CreateSpace. You must also enter the imprint name associated with the ISBN.

10. Then you either tell CreateSpace that you want to pay for interior design, or upload your own PDF file for your book's pages. If you are providing the file, you select it from your computer and upload it to CreateSpace.

11. Next, you build a cover with CreateSpace's free Cover Creator software, request a professional (paid-for) design, or upload you own cover file.

Here's an example of a cover closely based on a Cover Creator template, where I supplied the artwork and text, and specified color and typefaces:

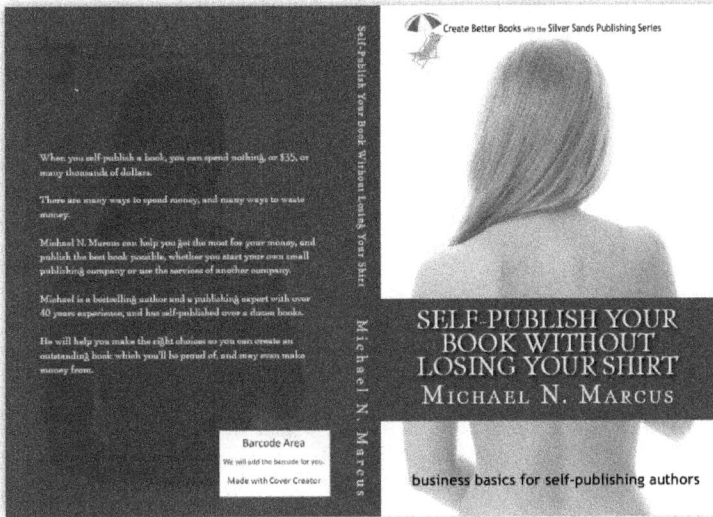

Next is an example of a cover made with Cover Creator, but where I applied my own designs for the front and back.

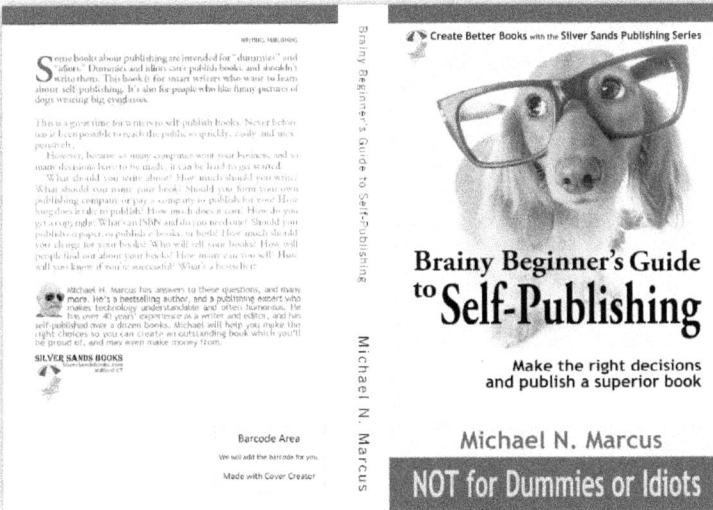

And, finally, here is a complete cover design produced by a professional artist, Carina Ruotolo.

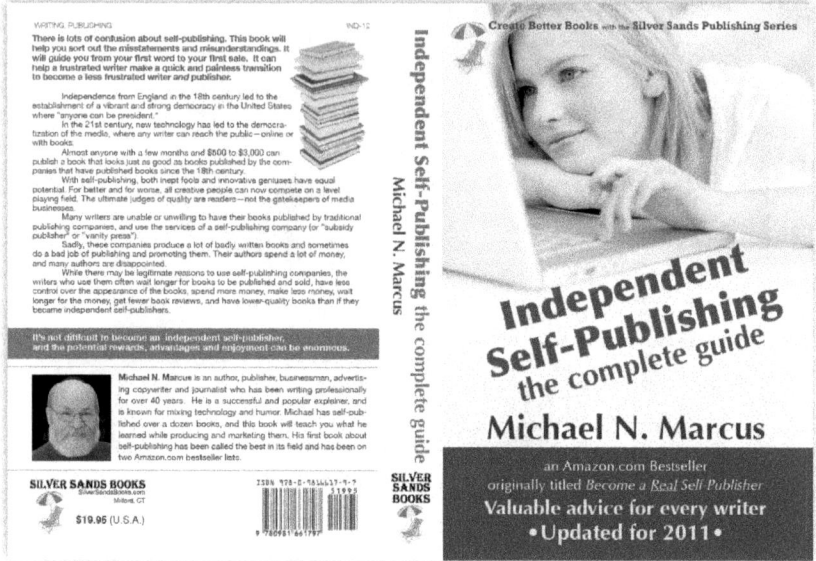

12. After you've uploaded your files, the screen will tell you that the files will be checked and that you'll be notified if you have to make changes.

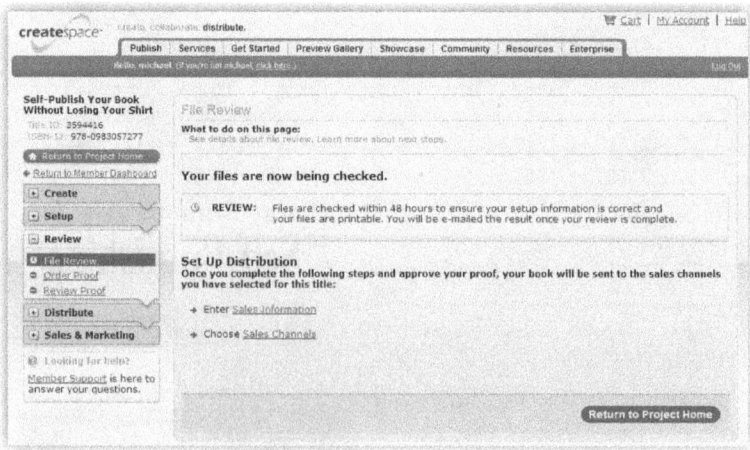

13. If your files are approved, you'll get an email like this one:

> **Files for Book..., #3594416 require your attention**
>
> The interior and cover files for Self-Publish Your Book..., #3594416 have been reviewed and are printable in their current state.
>
> If you wish to proceed with the publishing process using the current files, your next step is to order your book's proof copy. To do so, log in to your CreateSpace member account, click on the 'Order a Copy' link corresponding to your book and follow the on-screen instructions. Please note you will need to click 'Confirm Order' for us to receive your order.
>
> The cover file meets our submission requirements; it is not necessary for you to make any revisions to this file or upload it again.
>
> The Interior file meets our submission requirements; it is not necessary for you to make any revisions to this file or upload it again.

14. On the other hand, you may get an email pointing out errors that *must* be corrected, or errors that *may* be corrected, such as this: "Additionally, we have noted the concerns listed below. You may choose to move forward with the below issues as-is; however, we wanted to bring them to your attention. The interior file contains images that range from 74 to 250 DPI, which may appear blurry and pixelated in print. For optimal printing, we recommend all images be at least 300 DPI. Examples of Pages with low-resolution images include but are not limited to: PDF page 3, 6, 9."

15. Then you make any needed repairs and order one or more proofs. If you think the proof will be good enough so that it will not embarrass you, you can order additional copies which you can circulate to obtain book blurbs and suggestions for improvement.

1. Shopping Cart Incomplete	2. Shipping 1 of 2 complete	3. Billing Incomplete	4. Review Incomplete

Shopping Cart

Owner Orders

Quantity	Item	Unit Price	Total Price
1	Self-Publish Your Book Without Losing Your Shirt By Michael N. Marcus Title ID: 3594416	$4.42	$4.42
		Subtotal	**$4.42**

16. When you receive a proof, study it very carefully, and then either submit a corrected file and order another proof, or approve the book for sale. It's extremely unusual for a first proof (or a second proof) to be error-free. Take your time, and have at least one other person read it, too. Errors can be on the cover, too. I once left out a letter in the name of my publishing company in a tiny logo.

17. Be sure to fill in the information about your book's price and the sales channels. NOTE: You can make much more money with books sold directly by CreateSpace, but unless you send potential purchasers to the CreateSpace site, you won't sell many books there.

Sales Channels   ◄ Back   Next ►

What to do on this page: Set the list price for your title and select the sales channels for your book. Your list price must be set at or above the minimum price threshold for any sales channels you wish to enable. Note that fees due for a given sale vary by sales channel.

List Price * $ 17.95   [Save]
What's this?
                      Minimum price threshold for this title is **$7.09**
                      What's this?

💡 **Not sure what to do?**
→ Use our royalty calculator to see what you could earn at any list price.

Expand Your Reach
Distribute your work to the widest possible audience. Choose your Sales Channels now.

CreateSpace eStore   ✓ Pending [Edit]
Earning **$8.69** per sale

Amazon.com   ✓ Pending [Edit]
Earning **$5.10** per sale

Expanded Distribution Channel   ✓ Enrolled (1 of 3)
Earning **$1.51** per sale

CreateSpace Direct   [Select]
What's this?

Libraries & Academic Institutions   [Select]
What's this?

⚠ WARNING: Your book must have a CreateSpace-assigned ISBN.

Bookstores & Online Retailers   ✓ Enabled
What's this?   Disable

Changes to your title, including list price and listing information, can take up to 6 weeks to appear through selected sales outlets.

Another book that caused me to redo a book

Robin Williams   Robin Williams

This page is about two books inhabiting one body. And, although the author is "Robin Williams," it's a woman with decades of design experience, not the man who played Mork from Ork and Mrs. Doubtfire.

The book combines a new edition of the female Robin's *The Non-Designer's Design Book* (in color for the first time) and *The Non-Designer's Type Book*. Robin defines and demonstrates the principles that govern good design and type. You'll learn what looks best—or worst—and why.

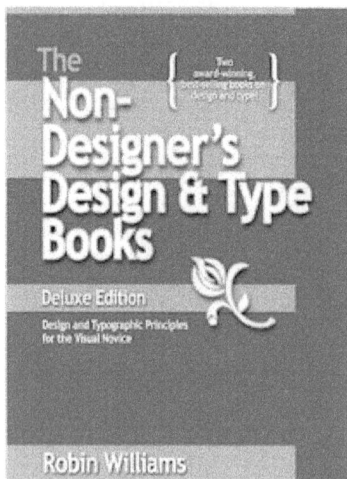

Robin's dual-book-pack has help for *anyone* who has to design a print project, whether it's a book, a poster or a business card. Her informative and wise lessons are for experts as well as for beginners. I learned a lot—and some of what I learned influenced the book you are now reading. One important lesson: "Listen to your eyes." If something looks wrong, it *is* wrong.

CHAPTER 55
Publishing terminology

This is a selective list. I avoided common terms like "design" and tried to include the most useful terms. I included obscure terms that may not be very useful, but are interesting or fun, like "fleuron," "dingbat," "kern," "OOP," "hickey," "lede," "pilcrow" and "virgule." More: www.cmykgraphix.com/?Page=glossary

Acid-free paper: Paper made without chemicals that cause paper to deteriorate. It costs more and lasts longer. This book is made from acid-free paper. Inexpensive mass-market paperbacks are not expected to be around for long and generally don't use acid-free paper.

Advance Reader (or **Readers** or **Reader's** or **Reading** or **Review**) **Copy:** A book from a Not-Ready-For-Prime-Time, limited print run, distributed for book reviews and publicity, usually about three to six months before publication of the final version of the book. Also called an "**ARC**."

Air: Graphics industry slang for the white spaces where there is no text or illustration. "Harry, the margins on this page design are too small. It needs more air."

Appendix: A section at the end of a chapter, or, more commonly, in the back matter of a book, that contains additional material, such as statistical tables which would not conveniently fit in the main part of the book

Artwork (art): Visual material, such as drawings, pictures and photographs used to explain, clarify or decorate a book. Sometimes called a "**graphic element**" or a "**graphic.**"

Author's Alteration (AA): A change made to a book after it was assumed to be ready for printing, at the request of the author. Publishers usually charge for AAs.

Back matter (end matter): Material, such as appendixes (or appendices), notes, references, author's biography, bibliography, glossary and index—placed after the chapters of a book.

Back-of-the-room sales: Book sales made at table, usually in the back of or just outside an auditorium, at an event such as a conference or convention where the author is speaking.

Binding: The process, such as stitching or gluing, used to attach the pages of a book to its cover.

Bleed: When a photograph or illustration bleeds, it extends beyond the normal edge of a page or cover. When the paper is trimmed, the picture extends to the actual edge of the book, with no white space surrounding it.

Blurb: A brief quote from a reader, often someone famous, which is used to promote a book. Blurbs are often printed on book covers or on the first page.

Bodoni Bold: Evil son of Hagar the Horrible—and a cool name for a typeface. I learned about it in print shop in eighth grade.

Body copy: The main section of a book, between the front matter and the back matter. In an ad, it's words below the headline.

Boldface: Letters, words, phrases or sentences printed in **heavier and darker print** for emphasis.

Book block: A digital file containing the entire book except for the covers.

Bookland: A fictitious country created to reserve an EAN (originally *European Article Number*) Country Code for books, regardless of their country of origin. Country codes for Bookland are 978 and 979. Bookland is located north of Lower

Slobovia, south of Grand Fenwick, east of Chelm and west of Oz. It's not far from Atlantis.

Breaker head (subhead): A distinct-looking word or phrase that runs between paragraphs, usually to introduce a section. It's often in large, bold type.

Bricks-and-mortar retailer: A physical store, as opposed to an online business. Some companies, such as Barnes & Noble, are both. Some people use the singular "brick-and-mortar." Since buildings use multiple bricks, I use the plural form.

Bulk: The thickness of paper in pages-per-inch ("PPI"), or the thickness of a book without its cover.

Casewrap: A hardcover book binding without a dust jacket.

Cataloging in Publication (CIP): Detailed book data on the copyright page of a book, and used in library catalogs

Character set: The complete set of letters, punctuation, etc. in a particular font.

Chick lit: Not to be confused with Chiclets candy-coated gum, it's chick literature—the print equivalent of chick flicks. The books are often romantic and written for women in their 20s and 30s. There are sub-genres for teen, matron, Latina, Christian and Asian chicks.

Clip art: Drawings and photographs that have few or no restrictions on use. Years ago, the artwork was printed on sheets of glossy paper and literally "clipped" apart and pasted into page layouts. Today, most clip art is digital.

Coated paper (coated stock): Smooth paper with a coating of clay or other substances to reproduce photographs better than the uncoated paper in this book. When used in books, coated paper generally has a glossy surface. When used for printing photos, it can have glossy, matte or other finishes.

Column inch: Newspaper jargon for how much space is used for an article. A typical column is a bit less than two inches wide and contains about 30 words—so five column inches can contain about 150 words. The number of column inches used for an article is an indicator of its importance.

Compressed: An extremely narrow typeface, narrower than condensed. Compressed faces are often used in movie posters. This is Bodoni MT Poster compressed.

Condensed: A typeface that is narrower than normal, but wider than compressed. This is Bodoni MT Condensed.

Consignment: A business method common in book publishing that allows dealers to return unsold products to the manufacturers (i.e., the publishers).

Co-op (co-operative) advertising: A plan where two businesses share the cost of advertising. Typically, a manufacturer (which could be a publisher) pays a percentage (usually 50%) of the cost of advertising products made by the manufacturer and sold by a dealer. Generally there are restrictions on media selection and ad content and limits to the expenditure.

Copy: Words written for or appearing in a book, article, ad, etc.

Copyeditor (CE, copy editor): This is the editor who concentrates on form, rather than on content. She (usually not he) corrects grammar, spelling, punctuation and inconsistencies.

Copyright: The government-backed rights to copy, publish or modify a creative work, such as a book, photo or website.

Co-venture: A business entity where expenses and responsibilities are shared by several people or business.

Crop marks: Small lines on a page design or cover design to indicate where it will be trimmed after printing. Nothing important should be placed outside the crop marks.

Crowdfunding (crowdfinancing): A method of raising money for a project, such as book publishing, by appealing to large numbers of people for small donations. It's often done through social media such as blogging and Facebook. Sometimes donors make outright gifts to support a project they believe in. Sometimes, there is an expectation of repayment, perhaps with interest. Sometimes, the donors are listed as sponsors of the project.

Cut line: newspaper jargon for the caption under a photograph or illustration. Before they published photographs, newspapers used engravings, which were often called "cuts."

Developmental editor: An editor, usually employed by a large publisher, who deals with the overall organization of a book rather than the fine-tuning done by a copyeditor. A developmental editor may suggest changes in a book's sequence and deletion or addition of material, and may even write some additional material as a ghostwriter.

Dingbat: Printers' slang for small, icon-like drawings of hearts, snowflakes and other shapes and items (◈ ⌘ ♦ ✈ ✍) which can be used to dress up a document. Also, what Archie Bunker frequently called wife Edith on *All in the Family*.

Discount: A percentage taken off the retail price of a book that is retained by a distributor, wholesaler and retailer. Also, a reduction from list price which saves money for shoppers.

Display type: Type used for book titles, chapter titles, subheads, etc. that is larger than the type used for the text.

Distributor: A "middleman" company that buys books from a publisher and sells them to a retailer. Unlike a wholesaler, a distributor usually has a sales force that calls on booksellers. A wholesaler usually just fills orders.

Domain name: A web address, also known as a URL (Uniform Resource Locator).

DPI (Dots per Inch): A measurement that represents the resolution ("sharpness") of a printer or scanner.

DRM (Digital Rights Management): the modification of a digital file, such as a book, song or movie, to prevent it from being copied in violation of its copyright.

E-book (electronic book): A book formatted and distributed as a data file rather than printed on paper. Various e-book formats are used with dedicated "readers," cellphones and PCs.

Edition: A particular version of a particular book. First editions are sometimes valuable.

End matter: See "Back matter."

Endnote: See "Footnote."

Endorsement: See "Blurb."

E-tailer: An online retailer.

Figure: Typographers' jargon for a number or numeral.

Flack: A derogatory term for a public relations (PR) person.

Fleuron: A flower-like decoration used to enhance a book or to divide sections.

Flong: One of my favorite words! A flong was originally a dry, papier-mâché mold made from type text which could be curved to fit the cylinder of a rotary press. Later flongs were wet, and made of plastic or rubber.

Flush-left/ragged-right: An informal typographic design in which the lines of text are aligned against the left margin but "run wild" on the right, as opposed to "justified" type. Flush-left is nearly universal for websites and is widely used in advertisements and periodicals. It is less common in books. See "justified" and next entry.

Flush-right/ragged-left: The opposite of above. It's seldom used for long text, but may be a good choice for headlines and short sections of text that have to appear distinctive.

Folio: A page number. Also a leaflet, a page size, a typeface and various other meanings. A **drop folio** is a page number in the **footer** at the bottom of the page, like this page. A folio is also a feature on some luggage such as a "pilot's case." A **blind folio** is a page number that is counted, but not printed.

Font: A specific typeface (e.g., Verdana) in a specific style (e.g., **bold**) and a specific size (e.g., 11 points).

Footer: Words or numbers below the main text on a page

Footnote: A reference or explanatory detail printed at the bottom of a page. Footnotes can be hard to keep in the right place as a book evolves, so "endnotes" either at the end of a chapter or at the end of the book may be easier to handle. If there are lots of notes, I recommend putting them at the end

THIS IS A FOOTER

of each chapter to avoid forcing readers to scan through many pages of notes at the end of a book.

Foreword: An introduction to a book, written by someone other than the author; part of the front matter.

Formatting: At least three meanings: ①the process of "laying out" text and illustrations to convert a manuscript into a finished book page design; ②modification of letters, numbers, or punctuation to make them **bold**, *italic*, etc.; ③conversion of one type of data file into another, such as a Word file into a PDF (Portable Document Format).

Frontispiece: Seldom found in modern books, it's an illustration, often an engraving, facing a book's title page.

Front matter: The information that goes on the pages between the front cover and the main text of a book. It usually includes a title page, a copyright page, a table of contents, a dedication and various introductions.

Fulfillment house: A company that provides some or all of the order-handling work for a publisher, such as warehousing, packing, shipping and record-keeping.

Galley proof (galley, galleys): Galley proofs get their name from hand-set type. Years ago, a typesetter would prepare a book page by arranging pieces of type into a metal tray called a *galley*. The galleys for a book would be used to print a small number of copies for editing and proofreading, and some would be provided to reviewers and booksellers. After the author and editors marked up the galleys, the typesetter would make corrections and books would be printed and shipped. Today, it's more common for publishers to provide reviewers with **ARC**s rather than galleys.

Genre: A book's general category, such as chick lit, crime, sci-fi, historical fiction, fantasy, how-to, porn, business.

Gerund: A part of speech frequently used, but seldom thought about after third grade. It's a noun made from a verb, like "thinking," "eating" and "writing."

Ghostwriter: A writer paid by a publisher or by another writer to write or co-write a book. Some ghostwriters are unnamed in the book. Some are listed: "with Peter J. Ghostly."

Graf: Journalists' timesaving slang for "paragraph."

Graphic (graphic element, graphic image): Something on a page other than text or space—such as a photo or chart.

Grayscale: A graphic image with no color—just black, white and shades of gray, possibly converted from color.

Gutter: The vertical white space centered between the blocks of text and illustrations on two facing pages. In DaBronx, it's pronounced "guttuh," and is a synonym for "roadway," as in "Don't play in the guttuh—you could get hit by a cah."

Halftone: A method to prepare a photograph or other graphic image for printing by converting it into thousands of little dots of various sizes. If the dots are small enough, the printed image appears to be continuous, like a real photograph.

Hand selling: A personal book recommendation in a store, convention, trade show, book fair, etc.

Hanging indent (hanging indentation): A page design technique in which the first line of a paragraph is flush left and the following lines are indented, as on this page.

Hardcover book: A book with a cover made of cloth, leather, foil or other flexible material glued to rigid cardboard. Hardcovers are more durable and may look better than paperbacks.

Header (page header, running head): Words or numbers above the main text on a page, often in a distinctive typeface. Headers often include book title, author's name, chapter name and/or number, page number.

Hickey (bull's eye, fish eye): A spot or imperfection on a printed paper caused by dirt.

Independent publisher (indie): A small publishing company that is not a subsidiary of a larger publishing or media company. It may be a self-publishing author who also publishes books for others.

Initial caps: A Typesetting Style Where The First Letter Of Each Word Is Capitalized (set in "uppercase").

International Standard Book Number (ISBN): A unique, 13-digit number that identifies a version of a book. Until 2007, ISBNs had ten digits.

ISPITA: Industrial Strength Pain In The Ass (much worse than a mere PITA), common in publishing.

Justified: A typography design in which lines of text reach all of the way to the left and right margins of a page or a column. The first and last lines of a paragraph may be shorter than the others.

Kern: That's the way some people born in Brooklyn pronounce "coin." In typography, "to kern" means to adjust the spacing between two adjacent letters. It can also mean to squish two letters together so they overlap to avoid awkward white spaces. **WA** is one common use of kerning, and the two letters fit together unusually well. A kern is also a part of one letter that reaches into another letter's personal space—like the curled "hood" on this **f**.

Keyword: An important word or phrase that is typed into an online search engine to find relevant web pages. Websites and blogs can be "optimized" for keyword searches.

Layout: The overall design of a page, book, magazine, ad, sign or other graphic project. A "rough layout" is a quick preliminary sketch of the design. The preferred verb form is "lay out."

LCCN: Library of Congress Control Number used to identify books. The LCCN is frequently printed on the copyright page of a book, and used by many libraries.

Leading: Extra space added between lines of type. It rhymes with "bedding," and gets its name from thin strips of lead that were inserted between lines of type when type was set by hand. With modern typesetting, a designer can specify, for example, 11 point type with 13 point leading. This means that two points of extra space would be added between lines.

Lede: The first sentence or two in a news story, with the most important information. It's pronounced "leed", but spelled "lede" to avoid confusion with another typographic term, "lead," which rhymes with "bread."

Letter Spacing: Changing the spacing between characters in a block of text, like a headline—in contrast to **kerning** which deals with the spacing around individual characters. NOTE: letter spacing sometimes is used to mean kerning.

Ligature: Several letters joined together to improve appearance and save a little space.

Compare **fi** and **ffl** ligatures to **fi** and **ffl**

Line art: A graphic image made of solid lines, usually against a white background, common in cartoons and charts in modern publishing. Before photography and halftone printing, line art was the standard format for printed illustrations.

Line editor: Often the same as a **copyeditor**, but sometimes a line editor will make modifications, not just corrections.

Literary agent: A person who tries to interest a publisher in an author's work, and who usually is involved in contract negotiation and sale of subsidiary rights. If a deal is made, the agent gets a percentage of the author's income. Sometimes, an author can make a deal with a publisher without an agent, but this is uncommon with larger publishers.

Manuscript: Text and graphic elements of a book prepared by the author and usually submitted to an agent, editor or publisher. It can be either on paper or in a digital file.

Mass-market paperback: A small, less-expensive version of a hardcover book which is usually printed after the hardcover version has been on sale for about a year. Often not as nice as a **trade paperback** because of rough paper, small margins and poor photographic reproduction.

Media kit: See press kit.

Media release: See press release.

News release: See press release.

Offset printing: The common method used for printing large quantities of books, magazines, newspapers and brochures. Ink is spread onto metal plates with etched images of the pages, then transferred to an intermediary surface such as a rubber "blanket," and finally applied to paper by pressing the paper against the intermediary surface.

Out of print (OOP): A book that is no longer being printed but may still be for sale. *Alley Oop* was a comic strip, created in 1932 by V. T. Hamlin. He wrote and drew the strip through four decades. The stories combined adventure, fantasy and humor, and were often satires of American suburban life like the later *Flintstones* cartoon series. Alley Oop, the strip's title character, wore fur shorts, lived in Moo and rode a dinosaur named Dinny. (Houghton Mifflin would've removed this. When you self-publish, you can print *whatever* you want.)

Overrun: An extra quantity of books printed beyond the requested quantity. Printers often print additional copies of a book to make up for possible defective copies. If the extra copies are not needed to make up the required total, the customer is usually required to pay for an overrun of up to 10%.

Over the transom: See "slush pile."

Page proofs: Printed typeset pages that look like the interior of a book, but without the covers. They may not be trimmed to the size of the final book pages.

Parchment: The skin of a sheep or goat prepared for use as a material for writing or printing. Paper can also be made to look like real parchment. It's often translucent.

Pay-per-click advertising (PPC): An advertising payment system in which the advertiser pays the operator of a website, particularly a search engine, every time someone clicks on an ad that could lead to another website and will perhaps buy something, support a cause, etc.

P-book: The opposite of an e-book, it's Printed on Paper.

PDF (Portable Document Format): A digital document file format, developed by Adobe Systems, which allows a document to be accurately reproduced on computers using different operating systems.

Perfect-bound: The binding method used for most paperback books, including this one. Pages are glued to the spine.

Permission: Agreement from a copyright holder to permit another person or entity to use copyrighted material.

Pied type: Back in the days when type was set by hand, if a careless or lazy typesetter did not sort out the pieces of type after a print job, but just dumped them, the type was "pied."

Pilcrow: Symbol indicating where a new paragraph should begin. ¶

PITA: Pain In The Ass (not limited to publishing).

Prepress: Preparation of a manuscript for printing. POD printing requires minimal prepress.

Press kit (media kit): A package of promotional material sent to writers and editors and intended to announce and gain publicity for a new book. There are now online press kits as well as paper-based kits.

Press release (news release, media release, publicity release, PR release): It's an announcement distributed to the news media with the hope of receiving publicity for a new book or other product, person or event.

Print-On-Demand (POD): Manufacturing books in small quantities—even one—as orders are received.

Print-ready: The digital data files (usually in PDF format) that have been checked and are ready to be printed.

Proofreading: Reading of typeset pages to find errors. Years ago, proofreaders would compare a typeset page against the author's final edited manuscript. With self-publishing, the author may produce the equivalent of typeset pages, so proofreading is an intense reading before printing, with no comparison to a previous generation of text.

Publication date: The official date on which a book is allowed to be sold. It is often fictional and arbitrary because many books are sold before their "pub date."

Publicist: Formerly call a "press agent," it's a person who tries to generate media coverage for a book or an author by contacting the media. The publicist may also produce and distribute publicity materials and assist an author with personal appearances and other promotional activities.

Remainders: Books that are discounted to low prices, often one dollar, because they are outdated, damaged, selling poorly or excess inventory. A book may be "remaindered."

Returns: Books sent back from a bookstore to a publisher for a refund or credit because they did not sell.

Royalty: Payment to an author after books are sold, usually a percentage of sales in the 5 to 50% range. There's often a sliding scale for which higher rates are paid when sales reach certain thresholds. The rate may be applied to either the cover price or a publisher's net receipts. Pay attention.

Rule: In typography, it's a line used for separation or decoration, such as this one: ━━━━━━━━━━━ Rules are not called "lines" except for a "hairline rule," which is ½-pt high.

Running head: see "Header."

Sans serif (gothic): A typeface style like **Arial**—simple, with no serifs or other decorative effects. Sans serif faces are commonly used for chapter names and subheads in books.

Self-publishing: A writer's becoming the publisher of her or his own books, or using a self-publishing company.

Sell-sheet: A one-page flier, describing and promoting a new book, aimed at booksellers, distributors and the media.

Serif: A thin line attached to the top or bottom of letters, or other decorative effects such as the "flag" attached to the top of the lowercase "h," which may make text easier to read. Serif faces are generally used in books, but not on websites.

Short discount: A smaller-than-usual discount from the cover price of a book, common with POD books sold online. A short discount is typically 20%, compared to the standard discount of 50% or more with traditional sellers.

Sic: Latin word for "thus." It's used to indicate that the preceding error or unusual wording or punctuation was in the source, and not copied incorrectly. The word should be italicized and within square brackets like this: [*sic*]. "Sic transit gloria mundi" has nothing to do with ailing trains or buses. Look it up.

Signature: A large sheet of paper, holding multiple book pages and printed on both sides. A signature is folded and cut to become a group of pages. Years ago, printers *signed* their names to indicate that pages were OK.

Slush pile: Unsolicited manuscripts received by an agent or a publisher and often piled up on a desk, a shelf or the floor, awaiting evaluation or disposal. These are also described as **"over the transom"** manuscripts. The phrase refers to the horizontal bar above a door and below a hinged window provided for ventilation in an office without air conditioning. Writers allegedly tossed their manuscripts over the transom of a publisher's office and hoped for the best.

Small caps: SMALL CAPITAL (UPPERCASE) LETTERS ABOUT THE SAME HEIGHT AS LOWERCASE LETTERS. They're good for abbreviations and acronyms like FBI, A.M. and RADAR.

Small press: A small publishing company that produces a relatively small number of titles each year, often in niche subjects or for specialized audiences.

Spine: The narrow section of a book that connects the front and back covers and shows the title and the author's name.

Stet: Latin for "let it stand"—an editor's or proofreader's indication to cancel a previous change.

Style book: A book, produced by a publishing authority such as the *Associated Press* or the *New York Times,* which dictates standards for spelling, punctuation, etc.

Style sheet: A set of rules assembled by an editor, designer, publisher or writer which dictates the standards for spelling, punctuation, listings, spacing, fonts, abbreviation, etc.

Subhead (sub-headline): See "breaker head"

Substrate: Material that is printed on, such as paper or cloth.

Subtitle: Words below the title of a book which explain or amplify the title. A title should "work" without its subtitle. Subtitles are important for online searching.

Subsidiary rights: Rights sold by a book publisher for reuse of a book's contents in other forms, such as magazine excerpts, movie scripts or books in other languages.

Subsidy publishing: An uncommon publishing arrangement in which the publisher and author share the cost of publishing.

Supported self-publishing: Yet another term for a system where an author pays to produce books.

Swash: An extra bit of decoration added to a printed letter, often an extended or exaggerated serif on the first letter in a paragraph.

Swoosh: the Nike symbol designed by student Carolyn Davidson for $35. She later received a diamond ring and Nike stock.

TIFF (Tagged Image File Format): One of several formats for compressing graphic images to make smaller digital files. The images in this book are TIFFs. Websites generally use JPGs or GIFs. TIFF file names end in .tif.

Thin space: Narrower than a regular space. Used between the dots in an **ellipsis**: …, not ... (very subtle difference) or . . .

Title: In addition to the name of a book, it's book-biz jargon for a specific variety of book—but not an individual physical book. "Wow! Did you hear that PassKey Publications is putting out 50 titles this year? That's nearly twice as many as last year."

Title page: The recto (right-hand) page at the beginning of a book that shows the book's title, subtitle, author's name, publisher and perhaps other information.

TK: Shorthand for "To Come," a notation made on a layout to show that an element (such as a photograph or chart) will be provided later and space should be reserved for it.

> photo
> TK

Tracking: Adjusting the spaces between letters in one or more words. Tracking and **kerning** are types of **letter spacing**, but letter spacing usually means tracking.

Trade paperback: A book like the one you are reading now, with a cardboard cover, bigger pages and better grade of paper than used for mass-market paperbacks.

Trade publishing: Traditional book publishing where a publisher pays an advance and perhaps royalties on books sold.

Trim size: The final width and height of a book page and covers after the book is bound and trimmed. This book is trimmed to be six by nine inches—a common size.

True Type: A type font standard, originally developed by Apple in the 1980s to compete with Adobe's PostScript fonts. Microsoft soon added TrueType fonts to Windows, most notably the ubiquitous **Times New Roman** and **Arial**.

Typeface: A distinct family of type, such as Andy, **Rockwell,** ALGERIAN, Verdana, Elephant or Franklin Gothic.

Typesetting: Formatting a document on a computer to produce page layouts suitable for printing. In the past, actual pieces of type were arranged to form words and pages.

Typo: Short for **typographical error**, an error on a typed or printed page, sign, web page, etc. caused by equipment or finger failure—not by lack of knowledge.

Underrun: Book printing that results in fewer books than ordered due to damage (*spoilage*) during printing. An underrun of up to 10% is considered acceptable.

University press: A publishing business owned by a college or university. Most of its books are written by professors who teach or do research at the institution.

Unsolicited manuscript: A manuscript sent to a publisher that did not request it in advance. Most large publishers do not accept unsolicited manuscripts.

URL (Uniform Resource Locator): A web address.

Vanity press (vanity publisher): A publisher paid by authors to publish their books. The term has negative connotations.

Virgule: A forward slash (/). It's also the French word for "comma." (Merci beaucoup, Mademoiselle Sheila.)

Virtual Book Tour (VBT): An online simulation of a physical book tour, where an author would travel to be interviewed and sign books. In a virtual version, an author "visits" websites and blogs to be interviewed and to answer questions, and may write something special or post a book excerpt.

Wholesaler: A "middleman" company which buys books from a publisher and sells them to a retailer. Unlike a distributor, a wholesaler usually just fills orders and does not have an active sales force.

Long-winded

Nigel Tomm may hold the record for the world's longest book title. It has 670 words. The full title is:

"Selected Works of Nigel Tomm (2006/2007) (Shakespeare's Sonnets Remixed 2006 / Shakespeare's Hamlet Remixed 2007 / Shakespeare's Romeo and Juliet Remixed 2007 / Including Previously Unpublished Elvis Presley's Love Me Tender Remix 2007) Nigel Tomm is The Winner of The Anonymous Writers Club Award 2006 for The Best Anonymous Writer / Deconstructed Poetry Award 2006 for Innovations and Teamwork in Poetry / Decadence Prize 2007 for The Lifestyle / Flashy Rococo Coco Award 2006 for Flashy Thoughts / Baby Boomers Award 2006 for The Best Marketing / Anonymous Artists Prize 2007 for The Best Anonymous Artist / Life Academy Award 2006 for Ignorance of Some Aspects of Life / Graphomania Award 2007 for Writing / Formal English Institute Award 2006 for English Grammar Improvements / House of Original Remixes Award 2006 for Creativity / WordKillers Award 2006 for Killing Some Words Sometimes in Some Books / iStyle Award 2006 for Being Unnamed Style Icon / Librarians Under Sixty Award 2007 for Staying Young / Comedy Association Award 2007 for The Best Drama / Happy Dramatists Award 2006 for The Realest Reality Show / New Forms Award 2006 for Rediscovering Something Old / Best of The Best Award 2007 for Being The Best of The Bests / Alaska Lifetime Achievement Prize 2006 for Bringing The Sun to Canada / Flaming Unisex Award 2007 for Coming to Flaming Unisex Awards / Random Books Award 2006 for Random Words Which Sometimes Sell / Happy Housekeepers Award 2007 for Being an Example to Follow / Wild Foresters Award 2006 for Saving Trees from Book Lovers / Writing Bodybuilders Award 2007 for Keeping Nice Forms / Life Coaching Without Words Award 2006 for Bringing New Life to Some Words / Writing for Writing Foundation Award 2007 for Rewriting Some Writings / Speaking Parr" **Whew!**

Index

Index

Index

Index

Index

Index

Index

Index

About the author

Michael N. Marcus has been a journalist, author, publisher, advertising copywriter, publicist, photographer, band manager, amateur attorney, golf ball diver, recording engineer, and is founder and president of AbleComm, Inc. ("The Telecom Department Store").

His writing career started when he published a newspaper in elementary school, and since then he has been an editor at *Rolling Stone* and has written for many other magazines and newspapers. Michael has provided the words for over one hundred websites and blogs. He specializes in making technology understandable, and often humorous.

Born in New York in 1946, Michael's a proud member of the first cohort of the Baby Boom.

At the urging of a misguided guidance counselor, he went to Lehigh University to become an electrical engineer and was quickly disappointed to learn that engineering was mostly math—and slide rules were not nearly as much fun as soldering irons.

Michael was one of the few literate people in his engineer-filled freshman dormitory and made money by editing term papers for classmates. He got into big trouble when he was caught running wire from his dorm room to a friend's room two floors below, and when an inspector found a payphone in his suitcase.

Later, his college apartment had an elaborate and illegal multi-line phone system, a phone booth with a toilet in it, and an invisible phone activated by two handclaps.

Michael lives in Connecticut with his wife Marilyn, Hunter the Golden Retriever, and a lot of stuff—including both indoor and outdoor telephone booths, a "Lily Tomlin" switchboard, lots of books, CDs and DVDs, and many black boxes with flashing lights. Marilyn is very tolerant.

More about Michael: www.MichaelMarc.us

Photo and illustration credits

Graphic images are licensed, produced by the author, public domain, publicity photos, used with permission, or believed to qualify as "fair use" under U.S. copyright law and do not compete with the copyright holder. If you are the owner of any copyrighted image and want it removed from future editions of this book, or if you find an error in the credits, please contact the publisher.

•Cave art by Terry Katz •Morgan photo from Images of American Political History •Franklin postage stamp from U.S. Postal Service •Blood pressure meter photo from Rob Byron •Chihuahua photo from Eric Isselée •Brando photo from Library of Congress, Prints & Photographs Division, Carl Van Vechten Collection •Brooklyn Bridge photo from KSM DigiPhoto •Bargain books photo by author •Team photo from Andres Rodriguez •Ghost graphic from Michael Wrede •Genova photo from LisaGenova.com •Barnum portrait from The Barnum Museum •Lamborghini photo from Automobili Lamborghini •Keds sneaker photo from Zazzle •Ransom note type from Cristina Cazen •Sanka photo from Kraft Foods •Roman coin photo from Claudio Divizia •Thumb drive photo from Sandisk •UPS photo from Minuteman •Poe portrait from U.S. Postal Service •Grandma photo from Mateusz Zagorski •Police cars photo from Dirk Paessler •Telephone photo from Panasonic •Thinking man photo from Amir Kaljikovic •Thinking woman photo from Sergey Tumanov •Woman driver photo from Kristian Sekulic •Author-as-kid photo from H.Tarr •Clinton photo from WhiteHouse.gov •Old typewriter photo from Stephen Coburn ZDM •Fingerprint from MarFot •Kids with five hands photo by author •Binding photos from Lulu •SUV photo from Goce Risteski •Kindle photos from Amazon •Recycle bin photo from David Smith •iPhone and iPad photos courtesy of Apple •Sony Reader photo from Sony •Nook photo from B&N •Espresso photo by author •Mouse photo from Microsoft •Chiclets photo from Cadbury Schweppes •Fleuron graphic by Roman Dekan •Coin photo from U. S. Mint •Swash from Linotype Corp. •Radio Flyer photo from Radio Flyer •California Job Case illustration from A.D. Farmer •Black woman portrait by Karen Struthers •Astor painting by Jacob H. Lazarus •Author portrait by Victoria Scoppetto

The California Job Case stores pieces of type when they are not being used for printing. It was a vital part of teenage males' education in 1959, and maybe in 1859.

LAST WORDS

When I was in the eighth grade at Sheridan Junior High School in New Haven in 1959-60, I was forced to take a "print shop" course taught by Bruce Brown. It seemed utterly inappropriate for our college-oriented class to learn about *em quads*, *ligatures* and the *California Job Case*.

In college in Pennsylvania, seven years later, I voluntarily took a course in "advertising art production" so I could sit near a girl I liked. Douglas Dawson taught us about *roughs*, *thumbnails* and *comps*.

Much to my surprise, in both courses I unintentionally absorbed a lot that turned out to be very useful years later when I worked in advertising, website design and especially in book publishing.

All knowledge has value, but the value may not be immediately apparent. So, pay attention.

MNM

NOTE: Some books shown on the following pages may not be available yet. Some cover designs may change.

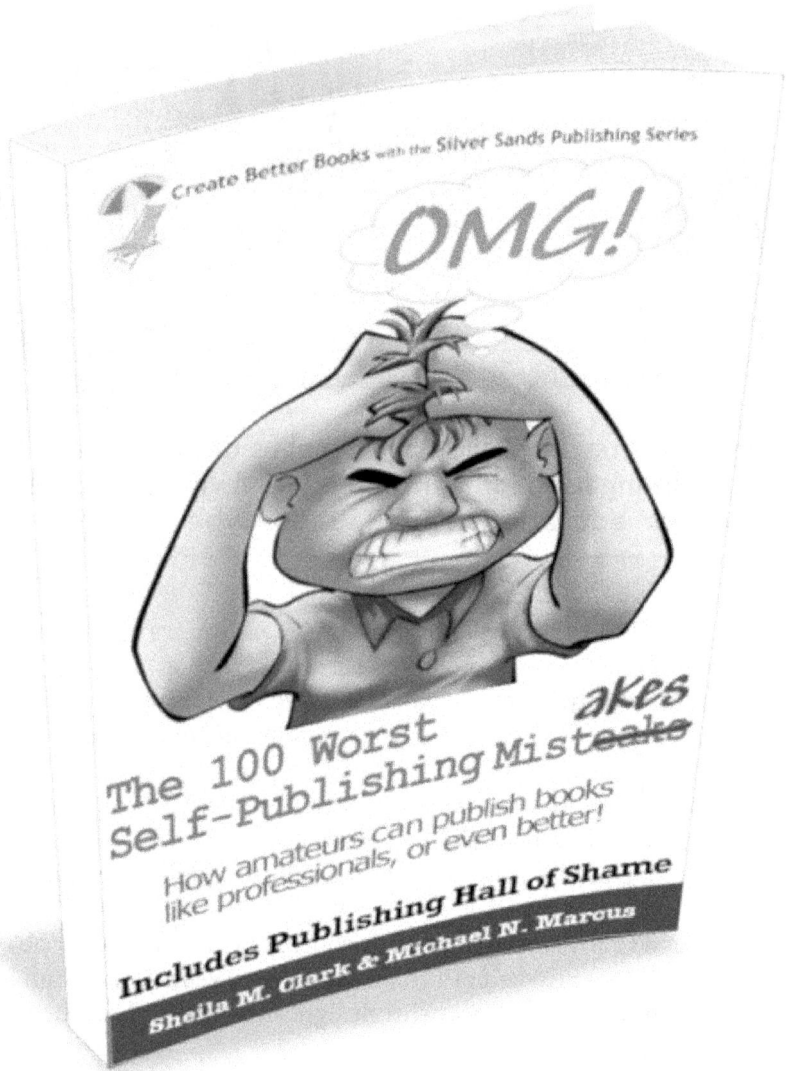

Learn what not to do and why you shouldn't do it. At Amazon, Barnes & Noble and other booksellers.

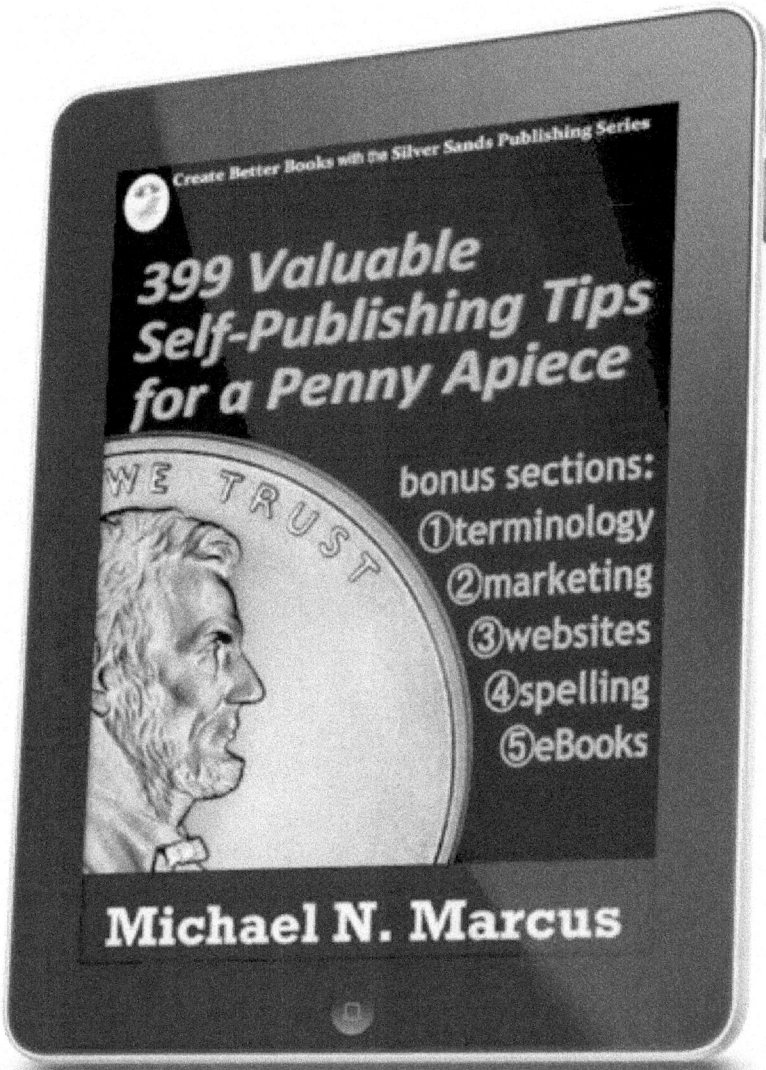

399 Valuable Self-Publishing Tips for a Penny Apiece

bonus sections:
①terminology
②marketing
③websites
④spelling
⑤eBooks

Michael N. Marcus

Available as an e-book only—in multiple formats—this is a collection of important advice which is worth *much* more than $3.99

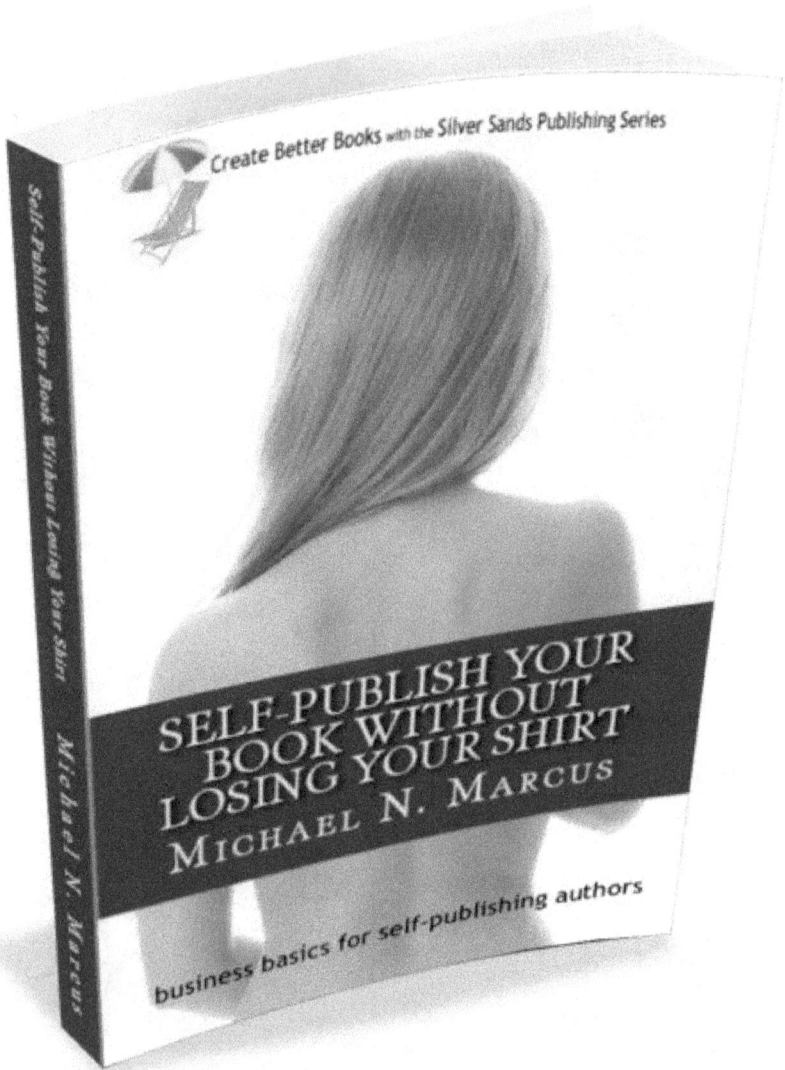

If you are an author who spends money for publishing and promotion, you are not just an artist. You are running a business. This book will help you do it the right way. At Amazon, Barnes & Noble and other booksellers.

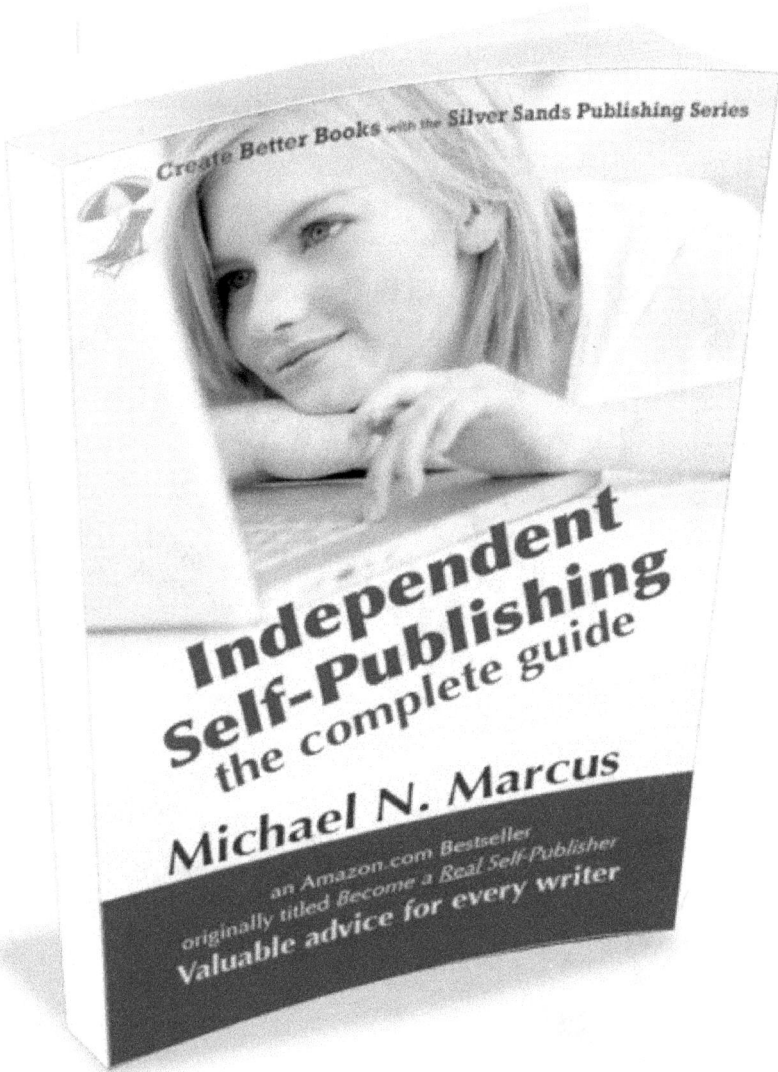

Create Better Books with the Silver Sands Publishing Series

Independent
Self-Publishing
the complete guide

Michael N. Marcus

an Amazon.com Bestseller
originally titled *Become a Real Self-Publisher*
Valuable advice for every writer

An update of the book *this* book is based on, for writers who want to be the boss and maybe make more money. At Amazon, Barnes & Noble and other booksellers.

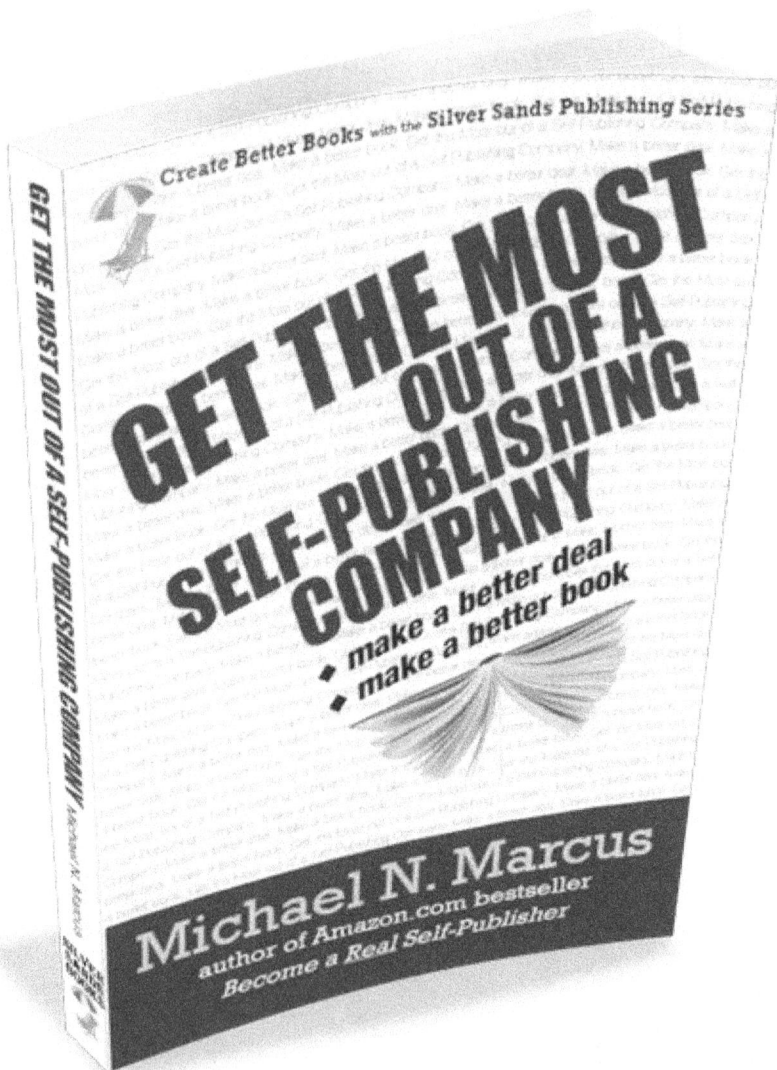

The authoritative book for authors who use a self-publishing company. At Amazon, Barnes & Noble and other booksellers.

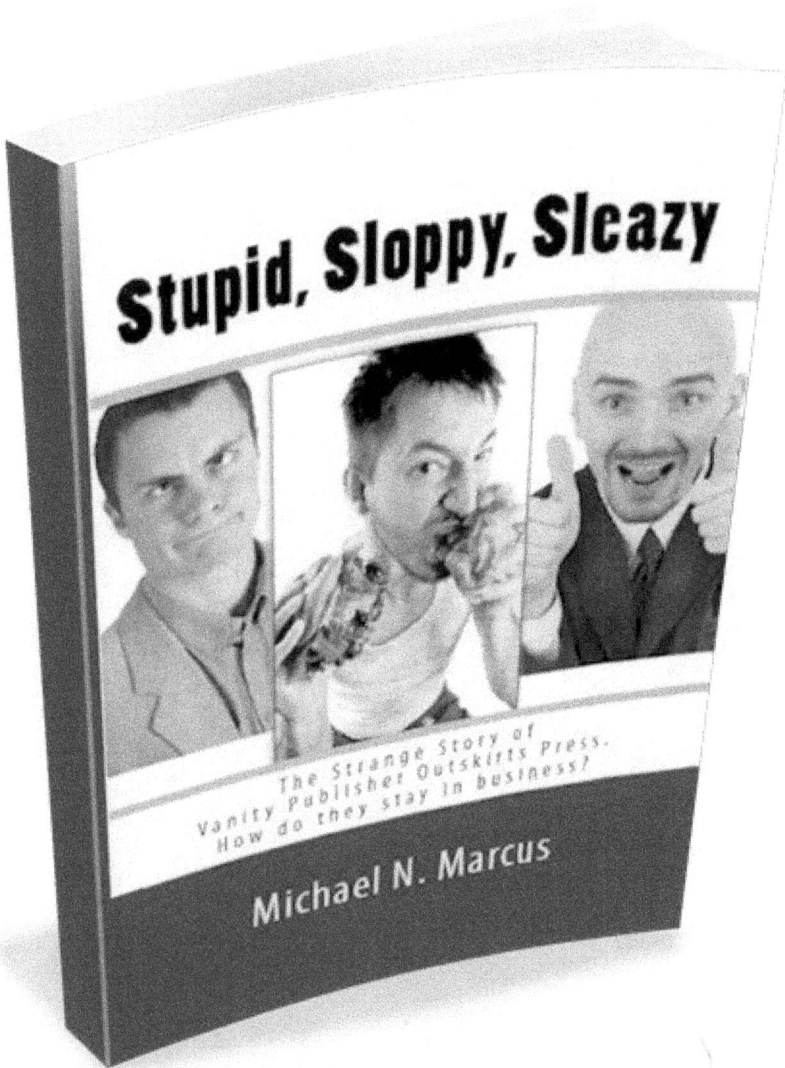

Stupid, Sloppy, Sleazy

The Strange Story of
Vanity Publisher Outskirts Press.
How do they stay in business?

Michael N. Marcus

For any writer considering publishing through Outskirts Press. Revealing, infuriating... and funny. At Amazon, Barnes & Noble and other booksellers.

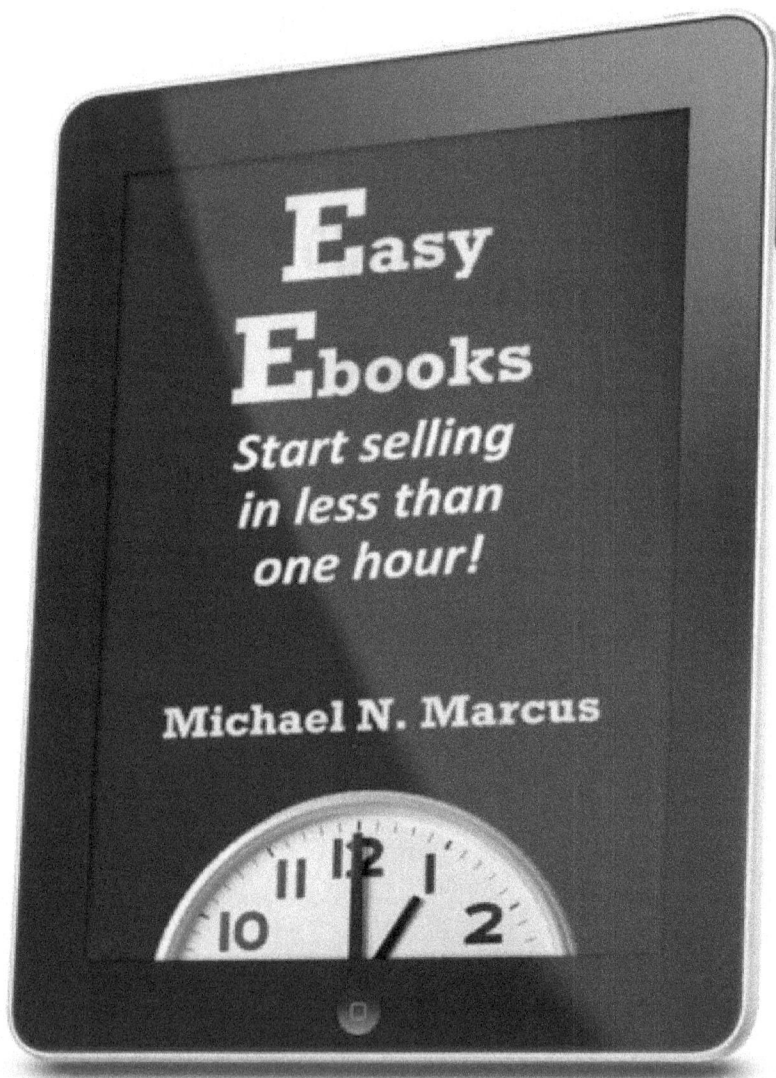

Easy Ebooks

Start selling in less than one hour!

Michael N. Marcus

This book, published both electronically and on paper, will show you how to produce and promote a high-quality e-book. You can start selling e-books in less than one hour after a p-book is completed.

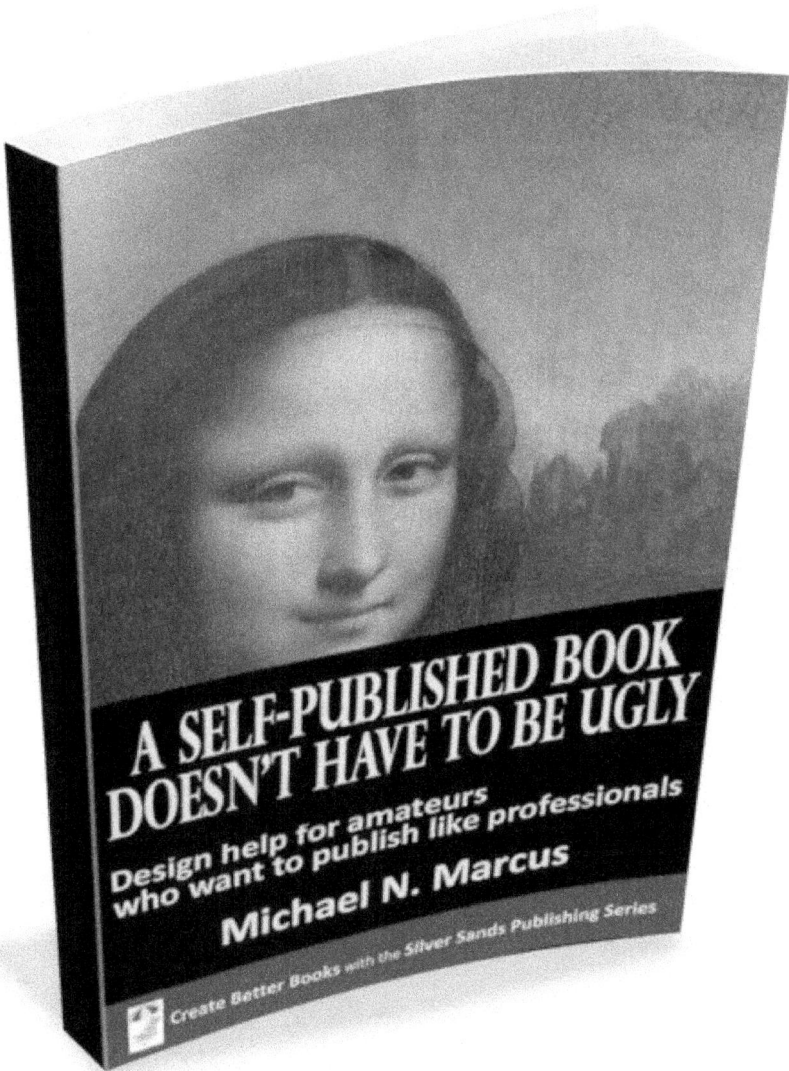

A SELF-PUBLISHED BOOK DOESN'T HAVE TO BE UGLY

Design help for amateurs who want to publish like professionals

Michael N. Marcus

Create Better Books with the Silver Sands Publishing Series

Most self-published books look much worse than books from the major publishers. It doesn't have to be that way. This book will help you to avoid making awful mistakes. At Amazon, Barnes & Noble and other booksellers.

Create Better Books with the Silver Sands Publishing Series

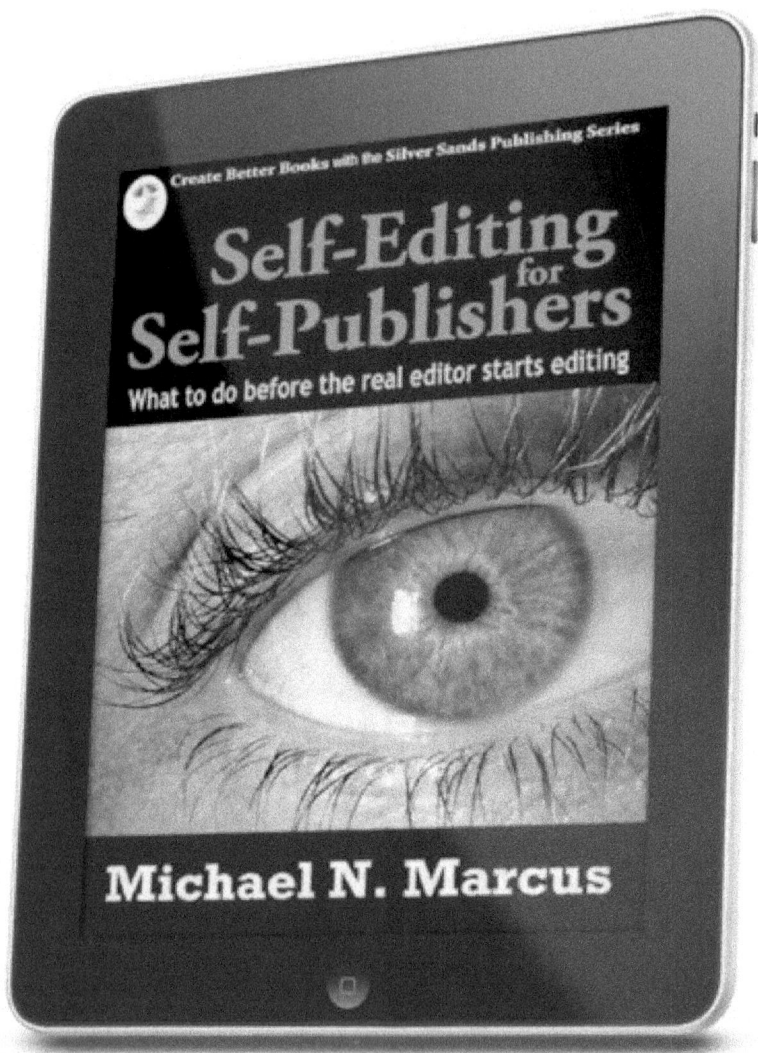

Self-Editing for Self-Publishers

What to do before the real editor starts editing

Michael N. Marcus

No writer should be her only editor, but she has to be *one* of the editors. The more you self-edit, before the pro gets started, the better the book will be. You might even save money. Multiple e-book formats.

Just for fun ☺

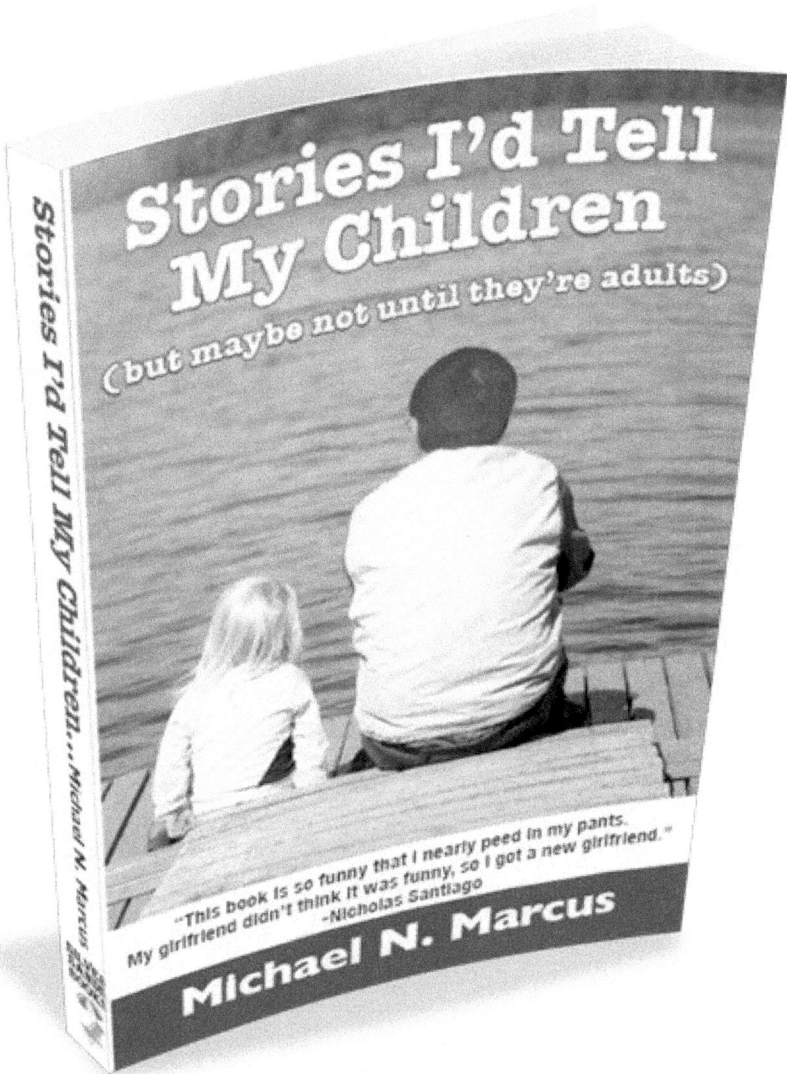

Extremely funny, often raunchy, and sometimes poignant. Guaranteed to be at least 80% true. At Amazon, Barnes & Noble and other booksellers as a paperback, hardcover, and in multiple e-book formats.